ENTERING THE MORAL MIDDLE GROUND

Many social and political groups consider each other as enemies rather than opponents with whom one can openly disagree. By introducing the concept of a moral middle ground, this book aims to overcome the perceived separation between good and bad, highlighting the possibility that human actions are permissible, understandable, and even valuable. To elucidate the nature of the moral middle ground and its psychological potentials, the author uses his theoretical framework, Dialogical Self Theory (DST). On the basis of these ideas, he portrays a variety of phenomena, including healthy selfishness, black humor, white lies, hypocrisy, and the worldviews of some historical figures. He then demonstrates how the moral middle ground contributes to the development of a human and ecological identity. As a result, students and researchers in various disciplines, including psychology, literary studies, moral philosophy, political science, history, sociology, theology, and cultural anthropology, will benefit from this book.

HUBERT J. M. HERMANS is Emeritus Professor at Radboud University. He is internationally recognized as the founder of Dialogical Self Theory (DST). He is also the Honorary President of the International Society for Dialogical Science, and he was decorated as Knight in the Order of the Netherlands Lion for exceptional scientific achievements.

T0384787

CAMBRIDGE SERIES ON POSSIBILITY STUDIES

Edited by Vlad Glaveanu

Possibility Studies are an emerging, interdisciplinary field of study with a long past but a short history. The theme of human possibility is as old as our reflections about human nature and our place in the world. For centuries, answers to questions related to how we discover and explore possibilities have been offered by philosophers, theologians, and natural scientists. From the nineteenth and twentieth centuries onwards, these interrogations came to be placed mostly at the intersection between the humanities, social science, and the arts. Nowadays, calls to take into account themes such as the future, hope, anticipation, creativity, and imagination, among others, are frequent across psychology, sociology, anthropology, and connected disciplines. A paradigm shift is under way in all these fields, built on the background of the multiple emergencies we are faced with, from climate crises to the challenge of "post-truth," and accentuated by the impossibilities brought about by the COVID-19 pandemic.

The Cambridge Series on Possibility Studies welcomes books that aim to expand our theoretical and practical understanding of how individuals and collectives become aware of and explore new possibilities in the realms of the psychological, material, technological, social, cultural, and political. Its volumes showcase and advance current thinking on agency, creativity, innovation, imagination, improvisation, serendipity, wonder, hope, utopias and dystopias, anticipation and futures studies, counterfactual thinking, and all other phenomena that focus on our engagement with what is possible (and impossible) in our existence. The series is particularly open to inter- and trans-disciplinary contributions with high potential for cross-fertilization and, with it, for the development of new theories, methodologies, and practices that can help us study and cultivate human possibility.

A full list of titles in the series can be found at: www.cambridge.org/csps

ENTERING THE MORAL MIDDLE GROUND

MIDDLE GROUND

Who Is Afraid of the Grey Wolf?

HUBERT J. M. HERMANS

Radboud University

CAMBRIDGE
UNIVERSITY PRESS

CAMBRIDGE
UNIVERSITY PRESS

Shaftesbury Road, Cambridge CB2 8EA, United Kingdom

One Liberty Plaza, 20th Floor, New York, NY 10006, USA

477 Williamstown Road, Port Melbourne, VIC 3207, Australia

314–321, 3rd Floor, Plot 3, Splendor Forum, Jasola District Centre, New Delhi – 110025, India

103 Penang Road, #05-06/07, Visioncrest Commercial, Singapore 238467

Cambridge University Press is part of Cambridge University Press & Assessment, a department of the University of Cambridge.

We share the University's mission to contribute to society through the pursuit of education, learning and research at the highest international levels of excellence.

www.cambridge.org
Information on this title: www.cambridge.org/9781009432009

DOI: 10.1017/9781009432016

First published 2024

A catalogue record for this publication is available from the British Library

Library of Congress Cataloging-in-Publication Data
NAMES: Hermans, H. J. M., author.
TITLE: Entering the moral middle ground : who is afraid of the grey wolf? / Hubert J.M. Hermans, Radboud University.
DESCRIPTION: Cambridge, United Kingdom ; New York, NY : Cambridge University Press, 2024. | SERIES: CSPS Cambridge series on possibility studies | Includes bibliographical references and index.
IDENTIFIERS: LCCN 2023031197 (print) | LCCN 2023031198 (ebook) | ISBN 9781009432009 (hardback) | ISBN 9781009431996 (paperback) | ISBN 9781009432016 (epub)
SUBJECTS: LCSH: Social ethics. | Polarization (Social sciences) | Group identity.
CLASSIFICATION: LCC HM665 .H437 2024 (print) | LCC HM665 (ebook) | DDC 303.3/72–dc23/eng/20230824
LC record available at https://lccn.loc.gov/2023031197
LC ebook record available at https://lccn.loc.gov/2023031198

ISBN 978-1-009-43200-9 Hardback
ISBN 978-1-009-43199-6 Paperback

To my beloved great-grandson, Damián,
whose birth reminds me that giving and receiving is a
most basic form of dialogue and a precious gift to be
cared for across generations.

Contents

Figures

Tables

Preface

On a memorable fall afternoon, my younger brother, Matthew, and I were together in his garden. Sitting side by side, we looked at the sun slowly sinking below the horizon. After some moments of silence, he said: "The Grim Reaper came already around the corner." I answered: "Can't we throw a stick between his legs, so that he falls flat on his face and his pace is slowed down a bit?" Matthew smiled broadly, a sign that he liked the remark.

A few months before, Matthew had been diagnosed with pancreatic cancer, and he knew that he would die. Yet, he continued to ride his horses, play tennis, take care of his farm, and have fun with friends. When someone, worried about his health, asked him: "Matt, how are you?" he answered, annoyed: "Please, don't ask me this, you draw my attention to my illness!" He wanted, as much as possible, to spend his days actively and optimistically and not worry too much about the sword of Damocles that was hanging over his head.

Some weeks before his death, he sent me a short video that showed an old man lying on a bed in an ambulance. A nurse dressed in a white uniform was behind the steering wheel. The destination of the ride was apparently unknown to the man. After some time, he turned his head to the nurse and asked: "Where are we going?" The nurse replied indifferently: "To the cemetery." In a hoarse voice, the man protested: "But I'm not dead yet!" The nurse replied imperturbably: "We are not there yet."

Apparently, Matt did not like to talk, in a serious way, about his disease and his upcoming death but preferred to keep it light and tell jokes that made us smile and laugh together. He found a way of addressing the topic of death indirectly, as doing otherwise would feel "too heavy" for him and would make him sad. Instead, laughing together allowed him to address the fate of his death in a way that was bearable to him, and, at the same time, it created a strong sense of intimacy and close contact between us. I had the strong impression that talking about his death with humor gave him a sense of vitality that helped him to go on, with courage, through this final and difficult period of his life.

The conversations with Matt instigated my interest in what is known as "black humor," which treats sinister subjects like death, disease, deformity, being disabled, or warfare with bitter amusement and presents tragic, distressing, or morbid topics in comic terms.[1] I realized that this kind of humor has two sides. It is morally questionable to make jokes about events that touch a person's most personal sensitivities and vulnerabilities because we have learned to assume an attitude of respect for death and dying. At the same time, joking together feels morally acceptable as it provides social support, expresses concern, and stimulates bonding. Apparently, black humor is a kind of behavior in which good and bad come closely together to form a combination that, depending on the moment and context, has the potential of having a vitalizing influence on participants who share the experience.

Black humor is just one of the many topics I want to address in this book as examples of phenomena that occur on the moral middle ground, the area between good and bad: healthy selfishness, Machiavellianism, transgressive art, and many others. I mention black humor only as the first experience that instigated my interest in the topic and motivated me to explore its scale, variety, and energizing impact. I discovered that on this ground moral good and bad form a combination that has its own uniqueness and has, moreover, the potential of contributing to the vitality of self and society.

During the preparation of this book, I discussed the topic with some friends and colleagues. I noticed that many of them were hesitant to bring moral good and bad together and to allow that they can function, in specific situations, as "allies." Many of my conversation partners preferred to keep them separate and wanted to know whether a particular behavior was morally good *or* bad. I got the feeling that, in their view, good and bad functioned like two magnets that repel each other. I noticed an irresistible tendency on their part to respond with a "thumbs up" or a "thumbs down," with nothing in between. I wondered where this hesitation comes from, and I posed this question to some of my conversation partners.

Some of them thought the distinction and separation of moral good and bad to be deeply entrenched in our education and upbringing. From childhood onward, we have learned to be rewarded for "good" behavior and to be punished for "bad" actions. From an early age, we are classified

---

[1] Willinger et al. (2017).

as a "good girl" or "good boy" or, as vice versa, as a "bad girl" or "bad boy." If we would persist in clinging to unacceptable behavior, we would be at risk of losing the love and affection of our parents and educators, and this would make us feel unsafe or hurt. The most we could do would be to "test the limits," but we should not cross any red lines.

Looking at the topic from a broader perspective, I realized that good and bad are deeply associated with the opposition between the clarity of the day and the danger of the night. From the beginning of life, we have come to fear the night as the realm of evil, where light is absent and where we feel unsafe. It is the playing field of thieves, monsters, and witches and a landscape where the law disappears.[2] In Tolkien's work, the orcs are a brutish, aggressive, ugly, and malevolent race of monsters who hate the sunlight. In J. K. Rowling's Harry Potter book series, Lord Voldemort, or alternatively the "Dark Lord," is feared as the most powerful and dangerous dark wizard of all time.

I realized that the separation between good and bad, and its deep connection with light and darkness, was already exposed in the book of Genesis: "And God saw that the light was good. And God separated the light from the darkness."[3] So, good was associated with light and bad with darkness. These associations received explicit form in the tradition of Manichaeanism as founded by the Persian prophet Mani (c. 216–274 CE), who believed that the cosmos is involved in a permanent struggle between a good, spiritual world of light and an evil, material world of darkness. This dualistic theology of good versus bad had, via the church father Augustine, a far-reaching influence on the moral groundworks of Christianity.[4]

Initially impressed by the experience and effect of black humor, I became fascinated by phenomena where, in contradiction to moral dualism, good and bad come closely together and form hybrid combinations. Studying a variety of sources in the literatures of the social sciences and philosophy, I decided to explore, in biographies and social research, a variety of phenomena under the label "moral middle ground." I made it my task in this book to discuss phenomena and processes on this fundament and demonstrate their vital possibilities. In the area in between good and bad there are potentials for self and society that would be lost in any form of moral dualism or toxic polarization where good and bad are thought to be mutually exclusive.

---

[2] Gerlach (2022).   [3] Genesis 1.4 (English standard version).   [4] van Oort (2020).

Acknowledgments

This was the most difficult book for me to write in my whole career. Sometimes I had the feeling that it was "loaded with dynamite" as it evoked heated debate with my readers who were willing to provide their critical comments during discussion of the book proposal and, later, the writing of the book. One of them jokingly said: "What is left for you to write, now you have brought God and the Devil together?" Given the explosive nature of the text, I'm extra grateful to my friends and colleagues who discussed its content with me – their comments often occupied my mind until late at night. They were masters of bringing me into a state of inner questioning, doubt, and struggle, sometimes liberating eureka moments.

My first thanks go to Anti Bax, who, as my personal editor, carefully and in a creative way inspected all my texts and gave numerous suggestions that enriched the content and structure of the book. Rens van Loon and Peter Zomer read all chapters of the book and gave their critical and highly useful comments that significantly improved the text. Some other colleagues and friends read selected parts of the text and were willing to give their valuable suggestions: Agnieszka Konopka, Reineke Lengelle, Toon van Meijl, Tim Magee, Cees van der Staak, Durk Stelwagen, and Frans Wijsen. I'm deeply grateful for their commitment and critical remarks that significantly widened my horizons during the struggles and inspirations of the writing process.

I'm also indebted to four very helpful anonymous reviewers, who provided me with many valuable literature suggestions, and to Vlad Glaveanu, who, as the series editor, functioned as my perfect guide through the submission stage of my book proposal.

Introduction

There are precious few at ease

With moral ambiguities

So we act as though they don't exist

L. Frank Baum[1]

Even evil must not be a triumphant or degrading enemy,

but a power collaborating in the whole.

Paul Klee[2]

This book proposes a nondualistic conception of moral good and bad. There exists an area where human behavior can be evaluated, depending on circumstances, as permissible, understandable, excusable, or even valuable. I propose to call this in-between area the "moral middle ground." In addition to what is usually defined as morally good or bad, behavior on this middle ground cannot simply be judged in terms of mutually exclusive opposites. The existence of this ground opposes the idea that there are only two polar categories: good and bad, and therefore it objects to the dualistic conception: "good is not bad and bad is not good." In contrast to this narrow view, I propose that on the moral middle ground "good" and "bad" can form productive coalitions that have the potential of delivering vitalizing contributions to self and society. In this book, I want to argue that there is not always and necessarily a "battle between good and bad" because there are moments and situations in which they go well together and fertilize each other.

This work can be read as a plea for the development of *moral multiplicity*, referring to the idea that various manifestations of moral good *and* bad exist not only in the other or in the outgroup, but also in one's own self and one's ingroup. Recognition of this multiplicity works as a counterforce to any

---

[1] Baum (1900).　　[2] Quoted by Jung (1964, p. 270).

I

premature definition of one's self or ingroup as morally unified. Moral multiplicity serves as an antidote to seeing individuals, social categories, or groups as either good or bad and serves as a counterforce to processes of toxic polarization[3] between individuals, groups, or nations. Moral dualism entails the risk of hypocrisy resulting from the misconception that moral bad is attributed to the other individual or to the outgroup only.

Moral multiplicity not only allows us to distinguish good and bad within individuals and within social groups, it also creates space for the *possibility* that, in some situations, good and bad coexist and function as "allies." My main focus in this book is to explore situations where good and bad form combinations that are valuable to both self and society. I'm fully aware that a distinction between moral good and bad is necessary in any well-organized society because individuals have to rely on each other regarding what is allowed and what is not allowed. My central thesis, however, is that an excessively sharp distinction between them doesn't leave room for the existence of a moral middle ground and its potential fertility for self and society.

The book starts from two basic premises. First, moral good and bad are ways of *positioning* oneself toward the world, and as such they are part of a relationship with the world. And in different relationships, different conceptions of good and bad may emerge. What is considered good in one situation may be seen as bad in another. Second, the various ways people position themselves toward the world are not good or bad in themselves, they are not things in themselves, they are not inherent aspects of reality, but they are *judged* as morally good or bad. At most we can say: In this or that social, cultural, or historical context, behaviors of individuals or social groups are judged as being good or bad. These starting points provide the demarcation of good and bad with a *flexibility* that may lead to moral uncertainty, confusion, and even shock, but also to moral constructions where good and bad are brought together in ways that are productive to self and society.

Good and Bad as Coalition

I want to demonstrate that the coalition of moral good and bad on the moral middle ground has its own unique quality that differs from what a society or community usually considers to be right *or* wrong. With this purpose in mind, a range of phenomena on this middle ground will be discussed where good and bad can generate productive or even creative

---

[3] Coleman (2021).

coalitions: *healthy selfishness* in which altruistic and selfish tendencies go together; so-called *Machiavellians*, adolescents who in their interactions with others use a combination of coercive and prosocial strategies, are evaluated as socially skilled, are liked by their peers, and are well-adjusted; the case of *Oskar Schindler*, whose morally problematic qualities were precisely the ones that put him in a position to save thousands of Jews from Hitler's genocide; *black humor* as expressed in sinister or misanthropic jokes by people who, surprisingly, put a low rather than high value on aggression; the existence of *grey hackers* who combine elements of white (good) and black (bad) hacking in their efforts to create transparency in society; the existence of a parent as a *morally bad other-in-the-self* that leads finally to accepting and acknowledging the other as an internalized problematic part of oneself; and forms of *transgressive art*, like Leon Ferrari's work "Western and Christian Civilization," a replica of a North American bomber jet hurtling downward with a wooden figure of the crucified Christ on its fuselage, or Chris Ofili's "The Holy Virgin Mary," in which elephant dung is placed on her right breast. These works, which may be experienced as offensive by adherents to a certain religion at first sight, may have a deeper moral messages and become acceptable and educational after a "second thought" (Chapter 4).

The argument behind this selection refers to the problematic aspect of any view that treats moral good and bad as mere opposites, as mutually exclusive, or as expressions of moral dualism. *If bad is rejected as entirely undesirable and as intrinsically conflicting with good, then, as a result of this rejection, the vitalizing energy of bad as part of a coalition with good would be lost.* The notions of vitality and vitalizing energy are used in the sense of zest, enthusiasm, and strength.[4]

The word "ground" in the concept of the moral middle ground refers, metaphorically, to the natural basis from which *life*, including the energy of the combination of good and bad, emerges and to which it returns. At the same time, the "ground" metaphor refers to the potential *fertility* of the combination of moral good and bad. I prefer it to the usual term "grey areas" because what emerges from this ground is, due to its rich multiplicity, more multicolored than grey. Moreover, the term "ground" creates room for the process of *positioning* as a spatial concept that is central in this book (Figure I.1).[5]

---

[4] Peterson and Seligman (2004).
[5] For the relevance of the concept of positioning in the social sciences see Davies and Harré (1990), and for its role in Dialogical Self Theory see Raggatt (2012).

'AKELA' THE LONE WOLF

Figure I.1   Akela, also called "Big Wolf," a fictional character in Rudyard Kipling's stories *The Jungle Book* (1894) and *The Second Jungle Book* (1895). He is the leader of a pack of Indian wolves and presides over the pack's council meetings. When at such a meeting the pack adopts the lost child Mowgli, Akela becomes one of Mowgli's mentors. The wolf is portrayed as large, strong, and grey, and he cooperates with the child. I take the grey wolf, as the subtitle of this book, as representing a field of tension between environmental protection and the perception of the wolf as bad.
Source: Transcendental Graphics/Getty Images.

The Flexibility of Definitions of Good and Bad

In this book, I follow a dialectical method in order to demonstrate what the middle ground is but also *what it is not*. With the definitional *flexibility* of good and bad in mind, I decided to devote an extensive discussion to two moral views that have left their marks in human history and that *differ* essentially from the moral middle ground. One is the view that fully *embraces* bad as valuable in itself. The focus is on worldviews that, in strong opposition to the morality of the established institutions of their time, elevate bad to the level of goodness and even holiness so that no space is left for the existence of a middle ground. As prominent examples of such revolutionary philosophies, I analyze the works of authors who proposed a radical reversal of bad into good, not removing, sublimating, or changing bad, but adoring it just because it is bad and holds value in itself. In his autobiographical work *The Thief's Journal*,[6] the French novelist Jean Genet appropriates Christian concepts to pursue alternative forms of "sainthood" celebrating theft and betrayal as "virtues." Similarly, in his novel *The 120 Days of Sodom*,[7] the revolutionary writer Marquis de Sade worships crime as "the soul of lust" and observes that "[i]t is not the object of debauchery that excites us, but rather the idea of evil."[8] A more recent instance of reversal of good and bad is *The Satanic Bible*,[9] the codification of the Church of Satan, a religious organization dedicated to Satanism established in San Francisco in 1966 by Anton Szandor LaVey, who served as the Church's High Priest until his death in 1997. He perceived Christianity as a lie that promotes self-denigration and herd behavior and stimulates hypocrisy. The conclusion of the analysis of these works – *The Thief's Journal*, *The 120 Days of Sodom*, and *The Satanic Bible* – is that they advocate the combination of lust and violation of moral norms as a liberating act of protest against the dictates of the official religious institutions, which are accused of hypocrisy and suppressing the vitality of the self (Chapter 2).

A very different expression of the flexibility of good and bad, also essentially different from the moral middle ground, is *rejecting* bad entirely, by radically removing it from one's self and from one's own social group and putting it exclusively in the shoes of the other. Elaborating on this theme, I analyze the worldviews of two political figures who, despite their apparent differences, nonetheless show a remarkable similarity on a deeper positional level: Nazi leader Adolf Hitler's autobiographical and political manifesto *Mein Kampf* (*My Struggle*)[10] and Vladimir Putin's worldviews as expressed before and after his invasion of Ukraine on February 24, 2022. One of Hitler's biographers, Paul Ham,[11] has made an insightful remark that is, in my view, also applicable to Putin. It is all too easy and lazy, this biographer writes, to brand Hitler as a monster, a psychotic killer, the incarnation of evil, and then walk away as if we have understood his personal influence as the main cause of World War II. The unsettling truth is that Hitler, like Putin in our current time, personified the attitudes of significant parts of the population and still does so in many parts of the world. So, more important than to conclude prematurely what kind of

---

[6] Genet (2004).   [7] Marquis de Sade (1785/1966).   [8] Quoted by de Beauvoir (1966, p. 44).
[9] LaVey (1969).   [10] Hitler (1939).   [11] Ham (2014).

people Hitler and Putin are, it is more productive to pose the question of how did they *become* that way, followed by the question: What can we *learn* from that? Precisely for this reason, I have dwelled, as a psychologist, on the consequences of these views for the identity construction of their followers (Chapter 3).

An additional reason for including these figures and their stories in this book is because life-historical methods and narrative analyses allow for a deep and rich description of people's moral conceptions as emerging from their social milieux and historical times. Such narratives also reveal the ways in which personal experiences play significant roles in shaping the morality of individuals and communities, for good or for bad.[12]

The structure of the book can be summarized in one sentence: On the moral middle ground bad is neither embraced as good (Chapter 2), nor separated from good (Chapter 3), but interwoven with good in a vital coalition (Chapters 4–6).

What Can We Learn from Moral Psychology?

Motivated by the question of what we can learn from the views presented in the previous section, I started to study recent developments in the thriving field of moral psychology.[13] I decided to include some of these developments in this book because they show us which moral processes occur in the selves of people in their everyday lives. Moreover, they demonstrate what can be our response to our own moral transgressions. Discussion of research in this field leads to the formulation (at the end of each chapter) of a series of practical implications.

For example, as a response to the problem of moral hypocrisy (Chapter 2), explorations in the field of moral psychology show that *self-awareness* manipulations have been found to reduce discrepancies between one's own behavior and relevant personal standards. Moreover, empirical studies have demonstrated that *perspective taking* is found to be a profitable way of reducing hypocrisy. Imagining oneself in the other's position significantly increases moral action.

As a correcting response to the worldviews of Hitler and Putin, or any other leader who puts the morally rejectable in the other group only, I strongly recommend, in the line of recent research in moral psychology, the development of *moral multiplicity* as a counterforce to any premature definition of the self or ingroup as morally unified. Both Hitler and Putin developed a worldview aimed at realizing a purification of their empire by

---

[12] Zigon (2009).   [13] See Ellemers et al. (2019) for a review of studies in moral psychology.

setting up a powerful propaganda machinery. The consequence was that Hitler became engaged in a project of killing a whole group of people – the Jews – that he defined as polluting the purity of the Aryan race. Likewise, Putin's goal is to clean the population of Ukraine that he sees as polluted by a process of "Nazification" and moral degeneration under the influence of Western sexual liberties, gender liberties, and same-sex marriage. As both dictators placed the moral bad purely at the outside, in enemies or dissidents, they rejected any moral multiplicity, a process that resulted in moral dualism with sharp boundaries between good and bad.

By analyzing the worldviews of Hitler and Putin, I find four common features that I qualify as the "dead ends" of identity construction: *purification, dehumanization, internal unification/external division*, and *enemy image construction*. They seem to offer a promising future but actually lead to aggression, violence, and even genocide. Along these lines I will argue that many utopic visions (e.g. communism, Nazism, the existence of heaven versus hell in Christianity, teachings of holiness that preach death to unbelievers in some Islamic traditions) often start with ideals of pure goodness but, finally, may result in discrimination, extermination, or genocide. That leads to the conclusion that bad is not simply the opposite of good but, instead, that moral bad is *potentially present* in moral good from the onset. See Figure I.2 for an example of the irreconcilable conflict between heaven and hell as a form of moral dualism.

Investigating the moral implications of the four dead ends, I place them in the context of recent developments in the psychology of morality. I will pay special attention to Albert Bandura's[14] dynamic model of self-sanction because it gives a clear insight in what happens in the self when good people do bad things. I will also elaborate on a highly dynamic model proposed by Stephen Reicher and colleagues that shows how a process that starts with ingroup unification can ultimately result in outgroup annihilation. This led them to conclude that "the way we define ourselves may often be more relevant to genocide than the way we define others."[15] In our thinking of racism, discrimination, and hate, they argue, our gaze is so firmly focused on our perception of the outgroup, and on negative outgroup perceptions in particular, that we almost totally ignore the fact that our definition of ingroup virtue is a first step toward outgroup destruction. Therefore, the researchers conclude that it is "important for psychologists and anti-racists to redirect their gaze and understand the centrality of *self-understandings* to the treatment of others."[16]

---

[14] Bandura (1990).   [15] Reicher et al. (2008, p. 1338).   [16] Ibid., emphasis added.

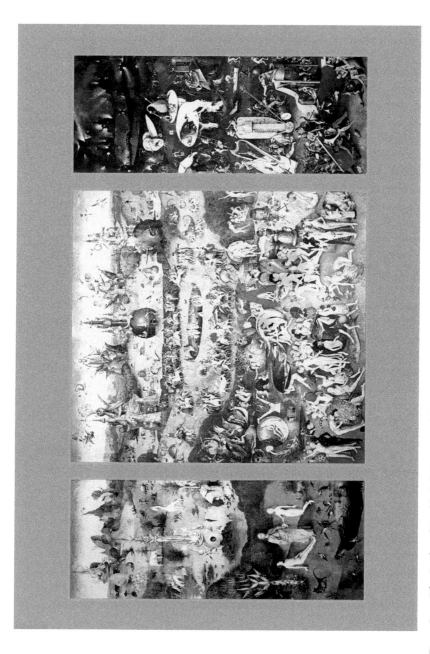

Figure 1.2   *The Garden of Earthly Delights*, triptych by Hieronymus Bosch (c. 1450–1516). The left panel portrays Eden and the right panel refers to the Last Judgment. The middle panel depicts the fleshly lusts spread over the earth. I take this garden as symbolizing the irreconcilable conflict between good (Eden) and bad (condemnation).

Source: Buyenlarge/Getty Images.

Dialogical Self Theory as a Bridging Conceptual Framework

Conceptually, the book is based on Dialogical Self Theory (DST),[17] which defines the self as a *dynamic multiplicity of relatively autonomous I-positions in the society of mind.* This nuclear definition of the dialogical self will appear in different parts of the book as it allows us to establish a diversity of relationships with other concepts and theories. DST is developed as a bridging theory[18] that aims to search for productive connections with other developments in the social sciences and beyond.

I-positions function as ways of placing oneself and orienting oneself toward the other and oneself (e.g. I as caring for my children, I as strongly opposed to injustice, I as dreaming about a better future). Moral good and bad are ways of positioning oneself toward the world, and as such they are *subjective* configurations of a relationship with the world. The theory allows these processes to be studied both at the individual level (as I-positions) and at the collective level (as we-positions). Positions are considered to be morally good if they are *judged* by one's social group, society, or culture as beneficial to the physical or psychological well-being of others and oneself (e.g. I support my family members). They are considered to be morally bad when they are judged as damaging the physical or psychological well-being of others and oneself (e.g. I benefit myself at the expense of others).

In stark contrast to dualistic evaluations of good and bad, conceived of as different in their essences, this book starts from the assumption that they are dynamically related in the sense that we can move from one I-position to another one and back and that positions can change over the course of time. Just as individuals or groups can cooperate in society at large, positions in the self also can cooperate in adaptive or maladaptive coalitions. At the moral middle ground, the "meeting" and cooperation of good and bad have the potential of generating hybrid I-positions (e.g. I as grey hacker) or we-positions (e.g. we as violating the law in the service of a sustainable environment) that contribute to the vitalization (increasing zest, vigor, force) of self and society. The middle ground is assumed to be fertile soil for the emergence of coalitions of positions that work as a buffer against sharp good versus bad dichotomies.

I-positions can express themselves with a *voice* so that their needs and purposes can be exchanged with the positions of other people and with other positions in the self. DST assumes that, as part of dialogical

---

[17] Hermans and Gieser (2012); Hermans and Hermans-Konopka (2010); Lehmann and Valsiner (2017).
[18] Hermans and Gieser (2012).

relationships, the tensions, discrepancies, and conflicts amongst positions can be discussed, compared, and shared. The moral middle ground is a space par excellence where dialogues between moral positions have a chance to develop. This aligns with developments in moral psychology where there has been, in the past decades, much debate over the relative merits of deliberative and intuitionist models.[19] Researchers in this field have proposed dual-process models of moral judgment in which emotionally driven gut feelings take primacy but can be overridden by effortful reasoning, leading to more deliberative moral judgments.[20] Such deliberations fit very well with the conception of dialogue between emotion and reason as voiced positions in the self as stipulated by DST[21] (see Chapter 5). Moreover, the principle of dialogue allows discussion, criticism, and correction of alternative or opposing moral judgments and, as such, escapes the problem of "anything goes."

More specifically, the moral middle ground can be defined as a space in the self or between different selves where moral positions, judged as good or bad, come together in coalitions. Sometimes these coalitions feel "natural" (e.g. healthy selfishness) and don't need much dialogical processing. When a tension among these positions is experienced (e.g. I'm helpful but this also feels egoistic), they can be reflected upon and compared in internal and external dialogical relationships. This may result in agreement, disagreement, conflict, or reconciliation of good and bad positions as a basis for decision-making. Moral positioning is a highly dynamic process that is personally, socially, and culturally contingent and may change over time. The middle ground is conceived as an open space where positions are not fixed and static. Positions that are usually considered to be exclusively good or bad can enter the middle ground and become included as parts of good and bad coalitions and stimulate internal or external dialogues. Even when dialogues evoke disagreement and are sometimes experienced as "difficult" or "unpleasant," they have the potential of energizing internal or external processing of moral issues. After all, where there is friction, there is energy. On the moral middle ground this energy stimulates, at the edge of confusion, moral dialogues and controversies (Chapter 6).

The Moral Middle Ground as Part of a Multilevel Identity Concept

Taking into account the dominance of individual and social (group) identity levels in the area of moral psychology, I explore the relationship

---

[19] For a review, see Ellemers et al. (2019).   [20] Feinberg (2012).   [21] Hermans (2018).

between moral positions and identity at different levels of inclusiveness: individual, group, human, and ecological. Keeping this in mind, I critically discuss John Stuart Mill's[22] utilitarian thesis of good as the greatest happiness for the greatest number of people, as it seems difficult to have the same feelings for people who are "far away" as we have for our intimate and familiar ones. I also discuss arguments that many of our moral rules, such as not betraying our friends or abandoning our children, are shaped by natural selection to optimize our capacity to live in groups.[23] For sure, evolutionary models of morality have the advantage that they help us understand that our moral codes emerge from our evolutionary ancestry and have a significant impact on individual and social norms. However, I argue that we need, particularly in our present era of conflicting issues such as climate change and pandemics, a more encompassing morality that includes not only the promotion of well-being of individuals and social groups, but also of all humanity and our natural environment, including animals and plants. Stimulated by this consideration, I present a model for the development of multiple identities at four levels of inclusiveness: individual (I as an individual being), group (I as a group member), human (I as a human being), and ecological (I as a part of nature). In this model, the different identities are linked by mutual dialogical relationships that enable the individual to compare, weigh, and evaluate the moral implications of different and multiple identities, thereby taking into account their contradictory nature. In order to explore the moral middle ground in this model, I explore different forms of selfishness and group favoritism that can be combined with concerns for the future of humanity and care for nature and the earth, thereby using the energy of bad as contributing to human welfare and ecological sustainability. The presented multiple-identity model aligns with developments in moral psychology[24] such as the finding that the most optimal condition for reducing dehumanization (see Chapter 3) is the combination of multiple categorization (i.e. placing somebody in more than one social position) and concern for a human identity. This will lead to a definition of *conscience* that encompasses the concerns regarding the different levels of identity (Chapter 6).

Contradictions in the Self and How to Deal with Them

More than ever, we live today in a permanent state of tension and contradiction, dragged back and forth by continuous, often nerve-racking

---

[22] Mill (2015).   [23] Churchland (2019).   [24] Albarello and Rubini (2012).

fluctuations between clarity and confusion, certainty and uncertainty, wisdom and ignorance. We are faced with increasing international tensions in an interdependent world where a hero admired in one country is spurned as a terrorist in another community; a world in which we would like to live peacefully together but where many people are systematically indoctrinated by a powerful propaganda machinery that fosters the construction of enemy images; a world where we try to protect our privacy in a situation where digital giants create products, such as social media, that we cannot avoid; a world where we have to deal with self-learning algorithms and artificially intelligent chatbots such as ChatGPT that, in certain tasks, surpass our own intelligence and knowledge; a world where we cherish the freedom of our democracy but where we see the rise of autocratic leaders who have gained significant popularity even in our own countries; a world where we have learned to function as autonomous individuals but have to face the reality of being a tiny particle in an infinite universe; and a world where we have learned that we are free individuals but scientific advances show that we are to a significant degree determined by our genes.

Faced with these and other contradictions, empirical research[25] has indicated that we as Westerners are less equipped to deal with contradictions than East Asians are. Therefore, I will explore why it is difficult for the Western self to deal with contradictions that are generally experienced as threats to our self-esteem. After a comparison of Eastern and Western conceptions of the self, I will continue to explore, inspired by the work of Carl Jung, the meaning of shadow positions as undesired or rejected parts of the self. When positions are defined as morally bad, they are experienced as counter to positive self-esteem and, as a result, are banished to the domain of shadow positions. I will try to answer the question of how tolerance of contradictions and dealing with them can contribute to the enlargement of the dialogical space in the self, where a wider range of possible trajectories can be explored.

The Moral Middle Ground and "the Possible" as a Field of Inquiry

This book fits within the concept of "the possible" as an emergent field of psychology and related disciplines. As psychologist Vlad Glaveanu[26] has argued, the possible grows out of a social perspective grounded in notions of difference, position, perspective, reflexivity, and dialogue. The notion of

---

[25] Boucher et al. (2009); Spencer-Rodgers et al. (2010).   [26] Glaveanu (2018).

dialogue between a multiplicity of positions is central not only in DST but also in the field of the possible: "[W]hat creative actions do is open up, exploit and expand the possible for both self and others. In other words, multiple perspectives, growing out of difference and enhanced by dialogue, are the basis of the possible in all its forms of expression (possible worlds, possible selves, possible pasts and futures, among others)."[27]

SUMMARIES OF CHAPTERS

INTRODUCTION

In this Introduction, I present an integrative overview of the different chapters of the book, with the concept of moral middle ground as its core. The main purpose of this book is to analyze the relationship between good and bad through the lens of DST, with the worldviews of historically influential figures as "food for thought" and with connections to the psychology of morality resulting in practical implications for education.

CHAPTER 1:   DIALOGICAL SELF THEORY AND THE PROCESS OF POSITIONING

This chapter provides the theoretical basis of the book. The main tenets of DST and its historical context are briefly presented. As preparation for the next chapters, special attention is given to radical changes in the relative dominance of I-positions or we-positions that are defined as good or bad in particular social or cultural contexts. These changes are explained via the notion of transpositioning, which refers to processes that convey energy from one position to another one and vice versa. For theoretical purposes, I focus on William James's[28] description of "falling out of love" as a reversal of love into hate and on Mikhail Bakhtin's[29] description of carnivalistic life in terms of "life turned inside out" and the "reverse side of the world."

CHAPTER 2:   EMBRACING BAD AS GOOD VIA INTERNALIZATION

This chapter provides an in-depth analysis of some philosophies and worldviews that, in strong opposition to the morality of the established institutions of their time, elevate bad to the level of goodness and even holiness so that no space is left for the existence of a moral middle ground. As prominent examples of such revolutionary philosophies, I analyze the works of some authors who proposed a radical reversal of bad into good, not removing, sublimating, or changing bad per se, but adoring it just *because* it is bad and holds value in itself. In his autobiographical work *The Thief's Journal*,[30] the French novelist Jean Genet appropriates Christian concepts to pursue alternative forms of "sainthood" and to celebrate theft and betrayal as

---

[27] Ibid. (p. 527).   [28] James (1890).   [29] Bakhtin (1984).   [30] Genet (2004).

"virtues." Similarly, in his novel *The 120 Days of Sodom*,[31] Marquis de Sade worships crime as "the soul of lust" and embraces the idea of evil. The topic of dehumanization, widely discussed in moral psychology, is present in Genet's work and even more radically in de Sade's oeuvre. Another example of the reversal of bad into good is *The Satanic Bible*, the codification of the Church of Satan, a religious organization dedicated to Satanism established by Anton Szandor LaVey, who served as the Church's High Priest. He perceived Christianity as a lie that promotes self-denigration and herd behavior and stimulates hypocrisy. I analyze these works – *The Thief's Journal*, *The 120 Days of Sodom*, and *The Satanic Bible* – from the perspective of moral psychology and through the lens of DST. The conclusion is that these works advocate a coalition between lust and religion as a liberating act of anti-positioning against the dictates of the official religious institutions, which are accused of being full of hypocrisy and of suppressing the vitality of the self. Among the practical implications for dealing with hypocrisy I discuss stimulating self-awareness of the discrepancies between one's behavior and relevant personal standards and stimulating imagination of how it is to stand in someone else's shoes.

CHAPTER 3:   REJECTING BAD VIA EXTERNALIZATION

Whereas the focus in Chapter 2 is on *embracing* bad as good, this chapter goes to the opposite extreme: *rejecting* bad entirely and radically removing it from one's self and from one's own social group. Elaborating on this theme, I analyze the worldviews of two political figures who, despite apparent differences in personality and time frame, nonetheless show remarkable similarities on a deeper positional level: Nazi leader Adolf Hitler's autobiographical and political manifesto *Mein Kampf* (*My Struggle*) (1925/ 1939) and Putin's worldview as expressed before and after his invasion of Ukraine on February 24, 2022.

An analysis of the worldviews of Hitler and Putin leads, from a moral point of view, to four basic commonalities that I call "the four dead ends" because they are particularly problematic, even destructive, in a globalized world where we are interdependent as never before: (1) purification, (2) dehumanization, (3) the combination of internal unity and external division, and (4) enemy image construction. In order to learn some lessons from the stories of Hitler and Putin, I formulate some moral guidelines at the end of the chapter: recognizing the moral multiplicity of the self as a counterforce to any premature definition of the self as morally unified; avoiding the identification of people on the basis of *one* category only; broadening one's moral circle beyond one's favorite ingroup; the stimulation of intergroup contact; and promoting a superordinate identity as a way to emphasize the similarities and shared interests of different subgroups.

---

[31] Marquis de Sade (1785/1966).

CHAPTER 4:   THE VITALITY OF THE MORAL MIDDLE GROUND

In this chapter, I argue that there exists, between what is usually evaluated as specifically good or bad, a moral middle ground where bad is neither embraced (Chapter 2) nor rejected (Chapter 3) but recognized in its dynamic interplay and coexistence with good. In the tradition of dualistic thinking, good and bad are typically expressed as a coin with good on the one side *or* bad on the other, or as a thumbs-up or thumbs-down. But where is the "open hand" where they can meet? Stimulated by this thought, I explore in this chapter the middle ground between good and bad, referring to a diversity of phenomena in which they meet and generate productive or even creative combinations: *healthy selfishness*, operating in the middle ground between altruism and selfishness; so-called *Machiavellians*, adolescents who, in their interactions with others, use a combination of coercive and prosocial strategies; *moral exemplars*, who combine social power with conscience; the case of *Oskar Schindler*, whose morally problematic qualities were precisely the ones that put him in a position to save thousands of Jews from Hitler's genocide; *black humor* as expressed in sinister or misanthropic jokes by people who, surprisingly, put a low rather than high value on aggression; *grey hackers*, different from white and black hackers, who transgress rules in the service of transparency; and *transgressive art*, which aims to violate morals and sensibilities yet expresses a moral message. All these phenomena are analyzed as coalitions of I-positions with their own unique qualities that have the potential of contributing to the vitality of self and society.

A significant practical implication and educational guideline following from this chapter is to encourage my readers to think more dynamically than usual concerning moral issues. For example, a five-step model is outlined that shows how purposes that initially appear to be morally good (e.g. unification of the ingroup) can have immoral consequences (e.g. annihilation of the outgroup) in a later stage of development. This means that unification as moral good is a *potential* road to moral bad. A potentially good purpose might have a possible bad outcome. Awareness of this process can be enhanced when students learn to include this potentially bad position (unity *can* become bad) in the middle ground, so that good and bad can be explored in their dynamic relationship. At the end of this chapter, I contemplate on the existence of "grey areas" in the abortion debate and the #MeToo debate.

CHAPTER 5:   CONTRADICTION AS INTRINSIC TO THE MULTIPLICITY OF THE SELF

The multiplicity of identity is full of contradictions, particularly when different identity positions have divergent wishes, goals, or interests. In this chapter, I want to show that contradictions, although hard to process, have an honored place in intellectual history, as exemplified by scientific discoveries in physics and biology. Contradictions are also present in the self, as vividly demonstrated by the philosopher Montaigne's prolific self-investigation.

The relevance of complexity in the self is symbolically expressed by Linville's[32] recommendation: Don't put all of your eggs in the same basket. A central part of this chapter is devoted to the differences between Western and Eastern conceptions of the self and to the finding that East Asians view the world as being in a constant state of flux and are more tolerant of contradictions. The Japanese folkloristic figure of *yokai* is presented as an example representing a coalition of good and bad in one and the same character. At the societal level, the avoidance or rejection of contradiction is demonstrated by utopian ideals that embrace one ultimate end-position, with the denial of the fundamentally contradictive nature of human beings and their moral multiplicity. In order to explore the fundamental role of contradictions in the self, I turn to the work of the psychoanalyst Carl Jung, who introduced the shadow as one of his main archetypes. In one of his last publications,[33] he argued that it is possible to take a position in the middle of good and bad, from where one can see "light" and "shadow" simultaneously, a view that is comparable to the moral middle ground in DST. This leads to a sketch of the main differences between Jung's concept of shadow and the notion of shadow positions in the dialogical self. The process of generative dialogue will be proposed as a way to deal with contradictions between and within selves. I end this chapter with some practical implications: the fostering of self-empathy, the value of stimulating tolerance of uncertainty and the impact of "high-quality listening" on softening the boundaries of the self so that it becomes more open to bringing good and bad together on the moral middle ground.

CHAPTER 6:   MULTILEVEL IDENTITY AND THE MORAL MIDDLE GROUND: TOWARD
A HUMAN AND ECOLOGICAL IDENTITY

The whole book culminates in this chapter. I explore the relationship between moral positions and identity at different levels of inclusiveness: individual, group, human, and ecological. With this purpose in mind, I critically discuss John Stuart Mill's utilitarian thesis of good as the greatest happiness for the greatest number of people, as it seems difficult to have the same feelings for people who are located "far away" as we have for our intimate ones or people experienced as similar. I also discuss the view that many of our moral rules, such as not betraying our friends or abandoning our children, are shaped by natural selection to optimize our capacity to live in groups. However, I argue that we need, particularly in our present era of climate change and pandemics, a more encompassing morality that includes not only the promotion of the well-being of individuals and social groups, but also of all humanity and the natural ecosystem. Stimulated by this consideration, I present a model for the development of multiple identities at four levels of inclusiveness: individual (I as an individual being), group (I as a group member), human (I as a human being), and ecological (I as a part of nature). In this model, the different

---

[32] Linville (1985).   [33] Jung (1960).

identities are linked by mutual dialogical relationships that enable the self to compare, weigh, and evaluate the moral implications of different and multiple identities, thereby taking their contradictory nature into account. In order to explore the moral middle ground in this model, the question is posed as to whether there exist forms of selfishness and group favoritism that can be combined with concerns for the future of humanity and care for nature and the earth, thereby using the energy of bad to contribute to good. In that context, I compare the lives and works of two philanthropic icons, Jane Addams and Andrew Carnegie, the former being located outside the moral middle ground and the latter one acting on this ground. In the case of Carnegie, I argue that his selfishness and moral engagement were not simply juxtaposed as two different sides of his personality. Rather, he could do his beneficial work not despite but *due to* his selfishness. This all culminates in a definition of conscience in which our human and ecological identities are included.

Some practical implications are presented: acknowledging that one has more than just one identity and that different identities each have their unique character; creating dialogical relationships among them, with special emphasis on the emotion–reason dialogue; placing people in multiple categories instead of one category only; identification with moral icons; and a rule of thumb for the inclusion of an action on the moral middle ground.

The Central Thesis of the Book in a Nutshell

The book is summarized schematically in Figure I.3. The moral middle ground is a specific area between the domains of what is evaluated as good or bad by a particular social group, community, or culture. The *diverging* lines that are moving to different sides go in the direction of good *or* bad. The middle lines are *converging* and form a triangle, demonstrating that on the moral middle ground good *and* bad have the potential of creating vitalizing coalitions. Near each of the diverging lines a name is placed, representing a dominance of good or bad in the behavior of a particular individual. Near the converging lines, two individuals, Oskar Schindler and Andrew Carnegie, are placed, whose behavior is supposed to be on the moral middle ground. The other individuals are extensively discussed (Adolf Hitler, Vladimir Putin, Marquis de Sade, Jean Genet, Jane Addams) or briefly mentioned (Martin Luther King, Mahatma Gandhi). Note that the lines don't refer to the development of these individuals during their lives but to the moral evaluation of their orientations in our contemporary Western society.

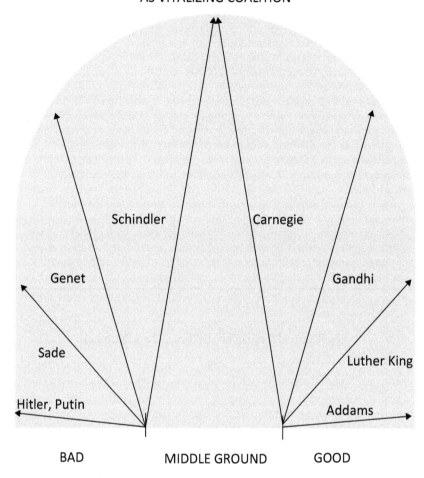

GOOD AND BAD
AS VITALIZING COALITION

Schindler   Carnegie

Genet   Gandhi

Sade   Luther King

Hitler, Putin   Addams

BAD   MIDDLE GROUND   GOOD

Figure I.3   On the moral middle ground the energy converges as a coalition of good
and bad.
Source: The author.

To Avoid Some Misunderstandings

To avoid misunderstandings, I want to emphasize that the middle ground
is different from the well-known Aristotelian "golden mean" or "golden
middle way," which refers to the desirable middle (good) between two
extremes (bad). In contrast, the moral middle ground as proposed in this

book is not about good in the middle but about the *combination* of good and bad in the middle. Furthermore, it should be noted that the moral middle ground is not simply covered by the traditional notion of moral dilemmas. Certainly some moral dilemmas have their place on the moral middle ground, such as the evaluation of transgressive art (Chapter 4), but it also encompasses other phenomena (e.g. adaptive Machiavellianism or healthy selfishness) that don't necessarily evoke dilemmas. Also, the concept of the "lesser evil"[34] is different from the concept of the moral middle ground. The lesser evil refers to the principle that, when faced with two immoral options, the least immoral one should be preferred (e.g. vote for the crook, not the fascist). This principle is about the choice among two forms of evil, neither of which necessarily figures as good. Instead, the moral middle ground brings together bad with good.

Finally, I frequently refer to "good" and "bad" throughout the whole book. These short descriptors are not used to reify the moral processes that they represent. It should be reminded that, from the perspective of the proposed theory, good and bad are understood as subjective and contextualized ways of positioning toward oneself and the world.

How to Read This Book?

The chapters of the book can be read independently from each other. To check the definition of a particular concept of the theory, you can peruse the Glossary at the end of the book. For readers who want to know more about DST, Chapter 1 gives a summary of its historical background, its central thesis, and its main concepts.

I have written this book as a combination of biographical descriptions of influential historical figures, empirical research in the field of moral psychology, and, at the end of each chapter, a series of practical implications of the presented ideas. If you want to know more about typical examples of phenomena representing the moral middle ground and feel the urge to delve deeper into this concept, go to Chapter 4. If you prefer to understand the commonalities between the worldviews of Hitler and Putin, with a focus on the dead ends of identity construction, read Chapter 3. If you are interested in the reversal of moral bad into good, represented by figures like Jean Genet, Marquis de Sade, or Anton LaVey, then Chapter 2 gives elaborate examples and quotations. If you

[34] Ignatieff (2004).

are particularly interested in contradictions and how to deal with them in dialogical ways, read Chapter 5. Personally, I consider Chapter 6 as the most complex one and, at the same time, the most innovative one because it brings together a proposal for a multilevel identity model and central ideas about the contribution of the moral middle ground to a multilevel identity. Moreover, that chapter deals with the indispensable role that dialogue plays in the linkages among the different levels, and it proposes a new view on conscience. If you want to focus on practical implications and educational guidelines, you can find them at the end of each chapter. It is possible to first read the practical implications then go to the corresponding concepts as explained in the chapter or as defined in the Glossary. I devote Chapter 1 to presenting some fundamental concepts of DST, and in the next chapters I dwell on the relationship between this theory and the psychology of morality.

Readership

The readership of this book is broad as it addresses a moral topic of general significance. It is primarily written for academic specialists in psychology, sociology, cultural anthropology, literary studies, history, theology, philosophy, and ethics. It addresses all those who are interested in the deeper connections between moral issues, dialogue, and the multiplicity of identity.

I also would recommend the book to advanced and graduate students in the mentioned disciplines. I think that students may profit, in the early stages of their education, from the insights into the flexibility or rigidity of moral positioning and the concept of moral multiplicity, particularly in a world that is often divided into identity camps and subjected to processes of toxic polarization. The awareness is growing that many people develop moral convictions that trigger powerful psychological processes that also influence political attitudes and actions, resulting in the "moralization of politics."[35] Moral convictions are significant driving forces of identity-based moral beliefs that can easily lead to hostility. Such convictions increasingly characterize segments of the electorate in many countries of the world, often in extremely polarizing ways.

The book is also useful for practitioners and educational specialists who are faced with the question of which moral opinions or convictions are

[35] Garrett (2016).

better or worse than other ones and what can be done to foster moral awareness. Therefore, I have, at the end of each chapter, included a section on "practical implications," based on the literature in the field of moral psychology and rich with both theoretical considerations and research findings. Given the strong emphasis on identity building, which is often associated with rigid ingroup–outgroup boundaries, considerable attention is devoted to broadening one's moral circle, also described as the circle of moral regard (Chapters 3 and 6).

Similarities to and Differences from Some Previous Works

For the reader, it may be useful to know about some of my own and my colleagues' works that have both similarities to and differences from the present book. In *Society in the Self: A Theory of Identity in Democracy*,[36] I have broadened the theory from I-positions to we-positions and, correspondingly, from self to society. As such, it can be considered as a precursor to the current book. The subsequent books *Inner Democracy: Empowering the Mind against a Polarizing Society*[37] and *Citizenship Education and the Personalization of Democracy*[38] are applications of DST to democracy and create links between psychology, political science, and educational practice.

My recent book *Liberation in the Face of Uncertainty: A New Development of Dialogical Self Theory*[39] is an exploration on the interface between psychology and philosophy, whereas the present book is written on the interface between psychology, biography, and moral psychology. With climate change and the coronavirus pandemic serving as wake-up calls, the *Liberation* book focuses on the experience of uncertainty, the disenchantment of the world, the pursuit of happiness, and the cultural limitations of the Western self-ideal. The book also critically discusses this ideal by comparing it with applications of DST in different cultures: African, Japanese, Chinese, and indigenous American.

The earlier work *Dialogical Self Theory: Positioning and Counter-Positioning in a Globalizing Society*[40] provides a general introduction to the theory, and the *Handbook of Dialogical Self Theory*[41] includes theoretical, methodological, and practical contributions by colleagues from different parts of the world.

---

[36] Hermans (2018).   [37] Hermans (2020).   [38] Hermans and Bartels (2021).
[39] Hermans (2022).   [40] Hermans and Hermans-Konopka (2010).
[41] Hermans and Gieser (eds.) (2012).

   Applications of the theory in the field of education are outlined in the book *The Dialogical Self Theory in Education: A Multicultural Perspective*[42] and in the work *The Identity of Education Professionals: Positioning, Training, and Innovation.*[43] Applications to the field of psychotherapy are provided in the *Handbook of Dialogical Self Theory and Psychotherapy: Bridging Psychotherapeutic and Cultural Traditions.*[44] Applications to the area of developmental psychology are brought together in the book *Dialogic Formations: Investigations into the Origins and Development of the Dialogical Self.*[45] A diversity of new methods for practical applications are provided in the book *Assessing and Stimulating a Dialogical Self in Groups, Teams, Cultures, and Organizations.*[46]

---

[42] Meijers and Hermans (eds.) (2018).   [43] Monereo (ed.) (2022).
[44] Konopka et al. (eds.) (2019).   [45] Bertau et al. (eds.) (2012).   [46] Hermans (ed.) (2016).

CHAPTER I

Dialogical Self Theory and the Process of Positioning

Dialogical Self Theory (DST) is extensively presented in previous publications.[1] For readers not familiar with the subject, I will summarize the theory, its historical influences, and some of its tenets that are relevant to the theme of this book. Then, I focus on the *transfer of energy* within the self that reflects the highly dynamic process of positioning that is central to the whole book. This is exemplified by the phenomenon "falling out of love," which illustrates how the energy of one I-position (I as loving) is transferred to another one (I as hating), leading to a reversal of the relative dominance of the two positions in the self-system. Then I will show how dominance reversal also occurs in the ritual of carnival, where the serious order of hierarchically organized life gives way to the laughter, mockery, and freedom of disorganized life. Both phenomena, falling out of love and carnival, demonstrate the *flexibility* of the process of positioning and repositioning. As a preparation for the following chapters, I will argue that carnival goes one important step further than falling out of love. While the phenomenon of falling out of love represents a sudden dominance reversal from love to hate without any existence of a moral middle ground, the carnival festival creates room for a moral middle ground by creating space for the combination of obscenity and social cohesion or the coalition of insult and playfulness. Finally, I will present and analyze, in a preliminary way, several events in everyday life in which moral good and bad form coalitions in which they work together on a moral middle ground.

Summary of Dialogical Self Theory

DST combines two basic concepts, self and dialogue, in the composite notion of the dialogical self. Traditionally, the self refers to processes that take place "internally," *within* the self, whereas dialogue is considered to

---

[1] Hermans (2018); Hermans and Hermans-Konopka (2010).

happen "externally" – that is, *between* the self and the other. By bringing the two concepts together into the dialogical self, the in-between realm is interiorized into the within realm and, reversibly, the within is externalized into the in-between. Therefore, the self is not an entity within the skin, defined as having an existence separate from the social and natural environment, but is considered as an active participant. The self becomes a "mini-society" or, to borrow a term from Minsky,[2] a "society of mind." Society at large is not simply "surrounding" the self, defined as a purely external determinant. Instead, society is composed of a diversity of selves involved in communication with each other, with the immediate implication that the society is confirmed, changed, or innovated by its participants. This means that changes and developments in the self automatically imply changes and developments in the society at large and vice versa. In other words, self and society are mutually inclusive, and they are interwoven in a process of transforming each other.

In essence, the dialogical self can be conceived of as a *dynamic multiplicity of relatively autonomous I-positions in the micro-society of the self.* As a verb, "positioning" refers to the process of receiving, finding, and taking one's place in a field of relationships. It is the process of placing oneself and being placed by others in a field of connections. In this view, the I emerges from its intrinsic contact with the environment and is bound to the process of positioning in time and space. In the course of time, some forms of positioning are more frequently used than other ones, and they create "traces" in the self so that habitual patterns are formed. In this way, the embodied I is able to move from one position to another in accordance with changes in situation and time. During processes of positioning, counter-positioning, and repositioning, the I fluctuates among different and even opposed positions, and, like in the society at large, these positions are involved in relationships of relative dominance and social power. Positions can be expressed verbally and nonverbally so that dialogical relationships can develop, both with other positions in the self and with positions taken up by other individuals. The voices behave like interacting characters in a story or movie, involved in processes of question and answer, agreement and disagreement, conflict and struggle, negotiation and integration. Each of them has a narrative to tell about their own experiences from their own perspective, and these narratives can be constructed and reconstructed in contact with other individuals, social groups, and the natural environment.[3]

[2] Minsky (1986).   [3] Lengelle (2021a; 2021b); Neimeyer (2006).

What Is an I-Position?

An I-position is a spatiotemporal act in the context of other I-positions in the self. It is the sediment of processes of positioning, counter-positioning (space), and repositioning (time). As a spatiotemporal act, positioning means placing and replacing oneself vis-à-vis somebody or something else and, at the same time, toward oneself in the metaphorical space of the self. As a relational process, it represents a stance toward the other, either physically or virtually, and addresses the other and oneself via verbal or nonverbal orientations and communications. I can be harsh toward a person I dislike, but when I think about this encounter when I'm alone I can become critical of myself as I consider my behavior toward this person as inappropriate and plan to position myself toward the other in a different way when we meet next time. Positioning and repositioning oneself to another person or group have immediate repercussions for the organization and reorganization of the inner cosmos of the self, and therefore both processes are dynamically interwoven with each other.

A useful distinction can be made between social positions and personal I-positions. Social positions (e.g., I as a mother, I as a colleague) are subject to societal expectations and norms. Personal positions receive their con-figuration from the particular ways in which individual people organize their own lives (e.g., I as a lover of music, I as a dreamer). Many positions, however, are simply outside the conscious horizon of the self, and the person might not or cannot be aware of their existence. As implicit positions, however, they may enter the self-space at some moment in time depending on changes in the situation that take place in the self or between self and other. For example, someone may be entirely unaware of the existence of shadow positions in oneself: I-positions that are warded off, rejected, or suppressed as if not belonging to oneself (e.g., I as envious, I as vengeful, I as hating someone; see Chapter 5 for more on the shadow position concept). Depending on the nature of dialogical processing and the development of those positions over time, they can become accepted and acknowledged as "owned" by the self.[4]

Other-in-the-Self

The self is not limited to processes that happen "within the skin." Other people, animals, nature, and even physical objects can become part of the

---

[4] Stiles (2019).

extended self. Typically, they are felt as "mine," such as my friend, my child, my dog, my house, my neighborhood, the nature of which I'm a part. The external I-position or the other-in-the-self does not imply that the other as part of the extended self is an exact copy of the actual other's perspective. Already Cooley[5] was aware of this when he introduced the "looking glass self," which does not reflect how others *actually* see us but rather how we *believe* others see us. Research[6] shows that people's self-perceptions are substantially in accordance with the way they perceive themselves as being viewed by others. However, there is no consistent similarity between people's self-perceptions and how they are *actually* viewed by others. I can believe that the other likes me while this is actually not the case. DST assumes that *external* I-positions are, at least in a great deal of cases, constructions produced by the needs, aspirations, and anxieties of *internal* I-positions (e.g., when I'm distrustful, I position the other as dangerous). However, when external I-positions would become *purely* subjective constructions, they would ultimately result in a confusing mixture of phantasy and reality or even in delusions. Therefore, the self, including its external I-positions, needs contact with the actual other in order to maintain or develop a minimally realistic image of the other as part of the extended self. According to DST, this contact is realized via the processes of positioning, repositioning, and dialogue (see Chapter 5).

Self and society are closely interconnected, leading to the conception of the self as a "society of mind." This society is populated by internal positions and external positions (perceived, remembered, or imagined others) that, in their mutual dynamic relationships, construct and reconstruct each other in reciprocal ways. External positions construct and reconstruct internal positions and vice versa. In fact, external positions are constructions of the other as part of the extended self, and they *mediate* between internal positions and the actual others as "objective" realities in the outside world. Dialogues within the self and with actual others are significant ways to confirm, correct, or further develop the construction of others as external positions in the self. External positions are located in a field of tension between the necessity of maintaining contact with the outside reality and the tendency to structure the images of the other in the self on the basis of the needs and concerns of internal positions. Internal dialogues within the self and external dialogues with actual others need each other in order to achieve cross-fertilization of the mini-society of the

---

[5] Cooley (1902).   [6] Shrauger and Schoeneman (1979).

self and the society at large. (For other central concepts in DST and their definitions, see the Glossary.)

Historical Influences: William James and Mikhail Bakhtin

DST is not an isolated development in the social sciences. It emerged at the interface of two traditions: American Pragmatism and Russian Dialogism. As a theory about the self, it goes back to James's[7] classic formulations on the self. As a dialogical theory, it elaborates on the fruitful insights into dialogical processes in Bakhtin's work.[8] Although some of the insights of these authors were crucial in the initial publications of DST, I want to go beyond these authors by proposing a view on judgments of moral good and bad that is based on the consideration that, in the present era, we are experiencing significant historical changes in our human and ecological awareness (see Chapter 6).

James's Extended Self

For an understanding of the dialogical self and the central notion of the I-position in particular, it makes sense to start with a basic distinction, introduced by William James (Figure 1.1), between the "I" and the "me," considered as a classic one in the psychology of the self.[9] The I is equated with the self-as-knower or the self-as-subject, whereas the me is equated with the self-as-known or the self-as-object. As such, the self is able, as knower, to reflect on itself as known. This distinction is relevant to understanding the capacity of an I-position to become aware of itself: I can become aware of a position in a particular situation due to self-reflection and imagination.

In his further elaborations of the self-as-known, James made an additional distinction, also highly relevant to DST, between "me" (I myself) and "mine" (that which belongs to me). He was well aware of the gradual transition between me and mine as an extension of the self to the external world. This was well expressed in a frequently cited quotation in which he made clear that the self-as-known is composed of all that the person can call their own, "not only his body and his psychic powers, but his clothes and his house, his wife and children, his ancestors and friends, his reputation and works, his lands and horses, and yacht and bank-account."[10] As this quotation suggests, people and things in the

---

[7] James (1890).   [8] Bakhtin (1984).   [9] Rosenberg (1979).   [10] James (1890, p. 291).

Figure 1.1   William James (1842–1910).
Source: Bettmann/Getty Images.

environment belong to the self as far as they are felt as "mine." An important implication is that not only "my body" but also "my mother" and even "my enemy" (the bad guy) are part of the self as extensions into the environment. The extended self contrasts sharply with the Cartesian self, which is based on a dualistic conception not only between body and mind, but also between self and other. Through his gradual transition between self and nonself, James paved the way for later developments in psychology, including DST, in which negotiations with the other-in-the-self, in close connection with the actual other, are part of an extended, multivoiced dialogical process.[11] James's proposal of the extended self allows the inclusion of a great variety of I-positions as belonging to the mine: my funny friend, my always-competitive colleague, my despised enemy.

Bakhtin's Polyphonic Novel

External I-positions become "voiced characters" in Bakhtin's (Figure 1.2) metaphor of the "polyphonic novel," which assumes the existence of a multiplicity of voices involved in dialogue with each other. He proposed this metaphor after extensive reading of Dostoyevsky's literary productions, which led him to conclude that in these works there is not one single author at work – Dostoyevsky himself – but several authors or thinkers, such as Myshkin, Raskolnikov, Ivan Karamazov, and the Grand Inquisitor. In these novels, the characters figure as the authors of their own ideologies and not as the products of Dostoyevsky's finalizing artistic vision. The characters are not obedient slaves in the service of an omniscient author-thinker elevated above his characters but appear as independent thinkers, each with their own ideology and view of the world. Instead of a unified objective world organized from above, there is a plurality of consciousnesses with a diversity of life views. This is similar to a polyphonic musical work, like a canon or fugue, where a multiplicity of voices accompany and oppose one another in dialogical ways. Along these lines, Dostoyevsky creates a surprising diversity of perspectives, portraying characters as conversing with the devil (Ivan Karamazov and the devil), with their alter egos (Ivan Karamazov and Smerdyakov), with the superior part of themselves (The Double), and even with caricatures of themselves (Raskolnikov and Svidrigailov). In this construction, dialogical relationships allow the author to differentiate the inner worlds of one and the same individual in the form of an interpersonal relationship instead of unifying them in a Cartesian ego. By transforming an "inner" thought of a particular character into an utterance, dialogical relations can be developed between this utterance and the utterances of imagined others. This dialogical construction makes it possible to contract temporally dispersed events into spatial oppositions

[11] See Hermans (2018) for an overview. For the other-in-the-self, see also Aron et al. (2005).

Figure 1.2   Mikhail Bakhtin (1895–1975).
Source: The History Collection/Alamy Stock Photo.

that are simultaneously present in an act of juxtaposition, thereby creating, in DST terms, a "landscape of the self." In this landscape, characters function like I-positions that receive a voice so that they can become involved in dialogical communications.

A recent development in DST[12] is the distinction between *I-positions* as individual ways of placing oneself in relation to the world and to ourselves and *we-positions* as ways of placing ourselves, as participants of social groups, communities, and cultures, in relation to the world and ourselves. This distinction is relevant as our individual I-positions are, to a large extent, *organized* by we-positions that are even present before we are born. In the following, I will illustrate the dynamic nature of I-positioning by presenting the phenomenon of "falling out of love" and the dynamic quality of we-positioning by referring to the collective ritual of carnival. In the latter case, the notion of moral middle ground will show up.

[12] Hermans (2022).

Individual Dominance Reversal: James's Exposé on Falling Out of Love

The phenomenon of dominance reversal[13] that I want to discuss in detail in this section was one of the intriguing topics discussed by William James in his Gifford Lectures on natural theology, which he delivered at the University of Edinburgh, Scotland, in the period 1901–1902. His book *Varieties of Religious Experience: A Study in Human Nature*,[14] which was based on these lectures, can be read as a psychological study of religious conversions and mystical experiences. One of his most prominent examples was the well-known conversion of the biblical figure of Paul, described in the New Testament, who was on his way from Jerusalem to Damascus with a mandate to seek out and arrest followers of Jesus. His journey was interrupted when he saw a blinding light and heard a voice speaking that gave him a divine, revelatory message of a miraculous nature that was powerful enough to transform him into an ardent follower of Christ. James also refers to less startling conversions, such as the case of a homeless drunkard who used to pawn or sell everything he owned so that he could buy alcohol. Walking in desperation along the river and sitting there for a while, he felt a "mighty presence" that he later interpreted as the presence of Christ. From that moment, this person felt the power in himself to control his destructive habit. James also describes a young man who started to pray according to the ritual he had practiced from childhood. He was then addressed by his brother, who said: "Do you still keep up that thing?" No more was said. However, after that day, the man never prayed again. As James explains, the words of the brother were like the "light push of a finger against a leaning wall already about to tumble by its own weight."[15]

The phenomenon "falling out of love," the opposite of the more familiar falling in love, serves as a proper example of dominance reversal of I-positions and the transmission of energy in the self. Let's listen to James's report of a man who was desperately in love with a woman who functioned as another I-position in his tormented self. James presents this case as an instance of a latent process of unconscious preparation preceding the sudden awakening of a sharp insight that irrevocably enters conscious awareness:

---

[13] A case study on dominance reversal was extensively presented and discussed by Hermans and Kempen (1993, pp. 80–88).
[14] James (1902/2002).   [15] Ibid. (p. 141).

> For two years of this time I went through a very bad experience, which almost drove me mad. I had fallen violently in love with a girl who, young as she was, had a spirit of coquetry like a cat. As I look back on her now, I hate her, and wonder how I could ever have fallen so low as to be worked upon to such an extent by her attractions. Nevertheless, I fell into a regular fever, could think of nothing else; whenever I was alone, I pictured her attractions, and spent most of the time when I should have been working, in recalling our previous interviews, and imagining future conversations. She was very pretty, good humored, and jolly to the last degree, and intensely pleased with my admiration. Would give me no decided answer yes or no, and the queer thing about it was that whilst pursuing her for her hand, I secretly knew all along that she was unfit to be a wife for me, and that she never would say yes. Although for a year we took our meals at the same boarding-house, so that I saw her continually and familiarly, our closer relations had to be largely on the sly, and this fact, together with my jealousy of another one of her male admirers, and my own conscience despising me for my uncontrollable weakness, made me so nervous and sleepless that I really thought I should become insane. I understand well those young men murdering their sweet hearts, which appear so often in the papers. Nevertheless I did love her passionately, and in some ways she did deserve it.[16]

In this case we see a clear example of admiration and uncontrollable attraction, but it is not pure love, as the man suffers, at the same time, from self-accusation, expressed in his lament "my own conscience despising me for my uncontrollable weakness." Apparently, this positioning was, during that phase, not strong enough to change his behavior and his emotional attachment to his girlfriend. However, in what follows, we see a moment of radical change, even a reversal:

> The queer thing was the sudden and unexpected way in which it all stopped. I was going to my work after breakfast one morning, thinking as usual of her and of my misery, when, just as if some outside power laid hold of me, I found myself turning round and almost running to my room, where I immediately got out all the relics of her which I possessed, including some hair, all her notes and letters, and ambrotypes on glass. The former I made a fire of, the latter I actually crashed beneath my heel, in a sort of fierce joy of revenge and punishment. I now loathed and despised her altogether, and as for myself I felt as if a load of disease had suddenly been removed from me. That was the end. I never spoke to her or wrote to her again in all the subsequent years, and I have never had a single moment of loving thought towards one who for so many months entirely filled my

---

[16] Ibid. (p. 142).

heart. In fact, I have always rather hated her memory, though now I can see that I had gone unnecessarily far in that direction. At any rate, from that happy morning onward I regained possession of my own proper soul, and have never since fallen into any similar trap.[17]

Strikingly, this description does not refer to any *external* stimulus that triggers the sudden change. Maybe there was a thought, an imagination, a memory, but the man's report does not explicitly mention it. Apparently, some internal process took place, not gradually but suddenly and rather unpredictably. James understands it as "an unusually clear example of two different levels of personality, inconsistent in their dictates, yet so well balanced against each other as for a long time to fill the life with discord and dissatisfaction."[18] In that context, he introduces an intriguing concept, "unstable equilibrium," which may account for the *internal tension* that precedes the sudden reversal: "At last, not gradually, but in a sudden crisis, the unstable equilibrium is resolved." This happens so unexpectedly that it is as if "some outside power laid hold on me."[19] In DST terms, there was a sudden change in his positioning toward the woman: from admiration to hate, preceded by an internal positioning of self-accusation. Apparently, these emotions were growing in himself, but they were not strong enough to generate the reversal, so that the man's self was, for some time, in a state of unstable equilibrium. Later, without a clear external stimulation but with an internal preparation, a dominance reversal, from admiration to hate, took place.

On a most basic level, I-positions are forms of energy that are dynamically related to other positions in the self and others. As placed in the context of other positions and dynamically related to each other, positions can provide energy (force) to each other, so that the energy of one position can be transferred to another position, a process that in DST is called "transpositioning."[20] In order to understand this process, it is insightful to return to a passage in James's work where he addresses the theme of "energy." He designates the group of ideas to which a person is devoted as the "*habitual centre of his personal energy*."[21] It makes a great difference, he observes, whether a particular set of ideas become central or remain peripheral in the self. When a person is "converted," this means that ideas that were previously peripheral in their consciousness take up a central place and then become the habitual center of their energy. Apparently, a

---

[17] Ibid. (p. 143).   [18] Ibid.   [19] Ibid.
[20] This concept was introduced in DST by van Loon (2017).
[21] James (1902/2002, p. 155, emphasis added).

peripheral position, or "background position" in DST terms, may later become dominant in somebody's self-system. However, I want to take James's formulation one important step further. I propose that the central idea not only *follows* the preceding idea but also *receives its energy*. In DST terms, this means that the preceding position energizes the following one. When we apply this insight to the man who was falling out of love, this means that his anger and hate were already prepared during the phase of his adoration of the woman, but his implicit dissatisfaction was not intense enough to move to the foreground and take up a central place in his position repertoire. However, as soon as the dominance reversal took place, the energy of the initial love and admiration was *transferred* to an intense anger and hate. In other words, there was a transpositioning of his energy from love to hate. Rather than a succession of two independent states of mind, the first form of positioning gave energy and impetus to the second one. In a similar way, I assume that what we generally consider as "good" or "bad" can be subjected to a process of transpositioning, which implies that they have the potential of energizing each other (elaborated in Chapters 4–6).

Collective Dominance Reversal: Bakhtin's Description of Carnival

Whereas James treats conversion and reversal on the individual level, Bakhtin studies the reversal experience primarily on the collective level, where we can see, in DST terms, the workings of we-positions and the way they organize I-positions. He does so by delving deeply into the phenomenon of carnival, which, in his view, has its deep roots in the primordial order and thinking of human beings, and he therefore considers it as "one of the most complex and most interesting problems in the history of culture."[22] I include it here as an additional example of the highly dynamic nature of the process of transpositioning.

Carnivalistic life, understood as the sum total of all diverse festivities and rituals of a carnival type, is life drawn out of its usual rut, "turned inside out," and it shows "the reversed side of the world."[23] The laws, prohibitions, and restrictions of the rigidly organized class society are suspended during carnival. The hierarchical structure, including its terror, social pressure, and reverence to authorities, gives way to free and familiar contact among people

---

[22] Bakhtin (1984, p. 122).   [23] Ibid. (p. 122).

in the open space of the carnival square.[24] Carnival is the time for acting out, in a "half-real and half-play-acted form,"[25] a different mode of interaction among individuals, who now have the freedom to enter a world that is counterposed to the all-powerful sociohierarchical structures that reign over everyday life. Behaviors, gestures, and discourses are *liberated* from the authority of hierarchical positions, such as social standing, rank, age, and possessions. From the perspective of noncarnival life, this form of interaction is considered eccentric and inappropriate. However, this eccentricity and, with it, the breaking of social codes permit the expression and revelation of "the latent sides of human nature."[26]

A clear example of dominance reversal of positions is the carnival act of the mock crowning and subsequent decrowning of the carnival king (in the present time it can also be a carnival queen), a ritual that, in one form or another, Bakhtin has found in all festivities of the carnival type. In its most elaborate form, it is part of the Roman saturnalia (Figure 1.3),[27] the European carnival, and the festival of fools. In the latter type, the official king was replaced by mock priests, bishops, or popes. Crowning/decrowning is an ambivalent ritual of dual nature as it expresses the creative power of change and renewal and the joyful relativity of structure, order, authority, and hierarchy. Crowning is ambivalent from the very start, as it already contains the idea of immanent decrowning. The one who is crowned, a slave or jester, is the antipode of a real king and symbolizes the inside-out world of carnival. The symbols of authority are handed over to the newly crowned king, and the extravagant clothing in which he is dressed expresses the eccentricity of this way of life. All carnival symbols, among which are many symbols of death, include within themselves a perspective of negation or vice versa. "Birth is fraught with death, and death with new birth."[28] Carnival marks the transition from the death and darkness of the winter to the new life and light of the upcoming spring.

In the carnivalistic world, crowning and decrowning are inseparable, and as parts of a duality they transform from one into the other. If they would be separated from each other, they would completely lose their carnivalistic meaning. This dual nature is at the heart of the carnival. As Bakhtin writes:

---

[24] In the Middle Ages, the square was a dominant place in cities and villages where festivities took place and punishments were demonstrated en plein public.
[25] Bakhtin (1984, p. 123).   [26] Ibid. (p. 123).
[27] The saturnalia was the ancient Roman festival of Saturn in December, a period of general merrymaking and the predecessor of Christmas.
[28] Bakhtin (1984, p. 125).

Figure 1.3   Roman saturnalia.
Source: Public domain, via Wikimedia Commons.

We must consider again in more detail the ambivalent nature of carnival images. All the images of carnival are dualistic; they unite within themselves both poles of change and crisis: birth and death (the image of pregnant death), blessing and curse (benedictory carnival curses which call simultaneously for death and rebirth), praise and abuse, youth and old age, top and bottom, face and backside, stupidity and wisdom. Very characteristic for carnival thinking is paired images, chosen for their contrast (high/low, fat/thin, etc.) or for their similarity (doubles/twins). Also characteristic is the utilization of things in reverse: putting clothes on inside out (or wrong side out), trousers on the head, dishes in place of headgear, the use of household utensils as weapons, and so forth. This is a special instance of the carnival category of *eccentricity*, the violation of the usual and the generally accepted, life drawn out of its usual rut.[29]

[29] Ibid. (p. 126, emphasis in original).

In his extensive exposition of carnival, Bakhtin also refers to the image of fire as another indication of the ambivalent nature of the ritual. He considers fire as ambivalent in the sense that it simultaneously destroys and renews the world. In many European carnivals, there was a vehicle adorned with gaudy carnival trash, and this vehicle was called "hell." At the close of the festival, this "hell" was triumphantly set on fire. A characteristic expression of this dual nature is also found in Roman carnival, in the ritual of "*moccoli*": Participants carried a lighted candle and tried to put out another's candle with a cry of "*Sia ammazzato!*" ("Death to thee!"). During "*moccoli*," a boy extinguished his father's candle with the cheerful carnival cry: "*Sia ammazzato il Signore Padre!*" ("Death to thee, Signor Father!").[30]

The significance of carnival becomes evident when one realizes that the people in the large cities of the late Middle Ages (e.g. Rome, Naples, Venice, Paris, Lyon, Nuremberg, Cologne) lived a full carnival life on average for three months out of the year and sometimes even more. With a certain reservation, Bakhtin adds that a person of the Middle Ages lived, as it were, two lives. One was the official life, "monolithically serious and gloomy, subjugated to a strict hierarchical order, full of terror, dogmatism, reverence, and piety." The other was the life of the carnival square: "free and unrestricted, full of ambivalent laughter, blasphemy, the profanation of everything sacred, full of debasing and obscenities, familiar contact with everyone and everything." Both lives were legitimate but separated by strict temporal boundaries (e.g., the beginning and ending of carnival).[31] However, *on the energetic level,* the precarnival, carnival, and postcarnival phases were intensely interconnected. The preceding phase of order and authority gave energy and impetus to the subsequent stage of chaos and anarchy and, vice versa, the free expression, obscenities, and debaucheries of the carnival led to the reconfirmation and restabilization of law and order in "normal life." Carnival and its preceding and following stages were involved in the transference of energy, or, in other words, in a process of transpositioning.

Dominance Reversal: Basic Similarity between James and Bakhtin

Recall that in James's description of falling out of love we see, in DST terms, a process of repositioning, from admiration to hate, that occurred on the individual level. In Bakhtin's portrayal of carnival life, we witness a

---

[30] Ibid. (p. 126). [31] Ibid. (pp. 129–130).

repositioning from a strictly hierarchical organization of society into a playful and leveling contact of everybody with everybody, as a change on the level of we-positions. In both instances, there is a reversal of positions. However, in order to examine extensively the commonality and differences of the two phenomena, a more detailed comparison is needed.

Let's go back to James's analysis of the transference of energy in the self. When a person is "converted," this means that previously peripheral ideas take over the central place and then become the main center of energy. In DST terms, a peripheral or background position becomes dominant in somebody's self-system. In the case of the man who was falling out of love, this means that his anger and hate were already present on an implicit level during the phase of his admiration of the woman, but his dissatisfaction was for some time not intense enough to move to the foreground and take the dominant place in his position repertoire. As soon as the dominance reversal took place, the energy of the initial position of love and admiration was transferred to its opposite in the form of intense anger and hate. His love was not simply succeeded by his hate, as if they were separate successive positions with their *own* energies only. Within a particular period of time, the intensity of his love was followed by the equal intensity of his hate. The intensity of his energy invested in his preceding love gave energy to his following hate and *continued* in it. The energy of the first position (adoring her) was transferred to the energy of the second one (loathing her). *What we generally consider as morally "good" (e.g. love) and "bad" (e.g. hate) can be subjected to a process of transpositioning, implying that one position can energize the other.*

A similar but not identical process takes place in the ritual of carnival. The energy of the strongly hierarchical and centralized precarnival period alternates with the anarchic, decentralized energy. The first one is transferred to the second one and vice versa. In his treatise of the process of crowning and decrowning, Bakhtin wrote: "The ritual of decrowning completes, as it were, the coronation and is inseparable from it ... And through it, a new crowning already glimmers. *Carnival celebrates the shift itself, the very process of replaceability,* and not the precise item that is replaced."[32] And he adds that "crowning and decrowning ... *pass one into the other;* in any absolute dissociation they would completely lose their carnivalistic sense."[33] In DST terms: Two opposite positions can, under particular circumstances, pass their energy to one another so that piled up

---

[32] Ibid. (p. 125, emphasis added).   [33] Ibid.

tensions can be reduced. The celebration of carnival creates a space in the self where the juices of life can flow freely.

Hell and, in particular, wishing somebody to hell would be considered as morally bad in a society that emphasizes love for one's fellow human being. However, recall the example of the vehicle called "hell" adorned with gaudy carnival trash, which at the close of the festival was triumphantly set on fire. And what about the cry "*Sia ammazzato!*" ("Death to thee!") shouted by the participants involved in joyful carnival ceremonies and the boy who, during "*moccoli,*" extinguished his father's candle with the cheerful carnival cry: "*Sia ammazzato il Signore Padre!*" ("Death to thee, Signor Father!")? During noncarnival time, shouting "Death to you, Father!" (with or without a candle) would be perceived as morally bad. However, during carnival, such a cry would be experienced, even by the father, as playful and acceptable. Living in a strictly hierarchical society, which, in Bakhtin's terms, is monolithically serious and gloomy, full of terror, dogmatism, reverence, and piety, tension and surmounting energy were built up, preparing a reversal from order to anarchy. In other words, behavior that was considered morally bad during precarnival times was evaluated as permissible during carnival. Yet, the healthy aspect of this reversal is that its eccentricity "permits – in concretely sensuous form – the latent sides of human nature to reveal and express themselves."[34] The built-up tension resulting from a period of rigid societal (and personal) order finds expression in a carnivalistic outburst, a temporally limited ritualistic revolution that functions, in a permissible form, as a confirmation of the stability of the moral order of the postcarnival period. Throughout history and continuing into our time, carnival has been a shining example of the moral middle ground, where good and bad coexist to the benefit of self and society.

The Jester as Middle Ground Character

During the medieval and Renaissance eras, a jester (Figure 1.4), a character engaging in foolish acts, was part of the household of a nobleman or a monarch. They were employed to entertain guests at the court and also to amuse common folk at fairs and town markets. Jesters often wore brightly colored clothes and eccentric hats in motley patterns. They entertained their audience with a wide variety of skills: songs, music, telling jokes, and puns, employing imitations and stereotypes. They were permitted to

[34] Ibid. (p. 123).

Figure 1.4   Jester.
Source: H. Armstrong Roberts/ClassicStock/Getty Images.

ridicule and insult monarchs, kings, politicians, and high-status members of the church, acts that were not permitted to any other citizen.

An example of the freedom to insult was the Persian (now Iranian) jester Karim, who could ridicule the whole court, including the Shah. When in a meeting the Shah asked whether there was a shortage of food in his country, the jester answered: "Yes, I see your majesty is eating only five times a day."[35] As this example illustrates, the jester's remark represents a coalition of two forms of positioning: insulting and addressing his target with a joke. Whereas the insult gives expression to a latent criticism, the joke makes the audience defenseless, even the Shah. As a character located at the moral middle ground of his community, the jester employs a fusion

[35] Otto (2001, p. 241).

of insulting and joking that, in their combination, works as a coalition of positions. This places the jester in the privileged position of addressing the powerholder and confronting him with an ambiguous remark or "offensive" act without the risk of being punished.[36]

Today, the jester is found in different formats of medieval reenactment, in fairs and entertainments, including carnival performances. During the Burgundian and the Rhineland carnivals, cabaret performances, presented in local dialect, are organized. In Brabant, one of the southern provinces of the Netherlands, this person is called a "*tonpraoter*" (ton speaker; one who is producing his jokes in or on a barrel). In Limburg (the most southern province of the same country), this person is named "*buutteredner*" (ton orator). They perform cabaret speeches covering many current issues that are well known to the local audience. Typically, celebrities from local and regional politics are mocked, ridiculed, and insulted. The orators can be considered as characters temporarily located at the middle ground of good and bad, as they may use primitive language, allusions, suspicions, and insults that, in noncarnival times, are not allowed to be expressed publicly.

When I was young, I often joined in with the carnival in Maastricht, the largest city in the south of the Netherlands. Wandering around in an extraordinary costume with an ugly mask on my face and drinking glasses of beer, one after another, together with friends, I have vivid memories of a custom named "telling the truth." This ritual allowed you to insult someone else, in particular about their moral weaknesses, misbehaviors, strange appearance, or anything that would be inappropriate to express in everyday life. Although the insult could be painful, the addressee was not expected to become angry but had to suffer the insults with a benevolent smile and, of course, with some cruel joke in return. When somebody was masked, the addressee was not allowed to remove the mask from their opponent's face. They could guess who the speaker was who addressed them, often with a disguised voice, but they were not permitted to ask their identity. It was a comedy of laughing, ridiculing, and being ridiculed, coalitions of being playful and offending at the same time. Good and bad were, during the temporally limited carnival time, not sharply distinguishable but rather combined as constitutive parts of a moral middle ground.

---

[36] For a more elaborate review of jesters in a variety of countries and cultures, including Shakespearean wise fools, Till Eulenspiegel, and Erasmus's *Plays of Folly*, see Otto (2001).

The Concept of Transpositioning: The Transfer of Energy

Because the concept of transpositioning plays a central role in the book as a whole, I want to dive somewhat deeper into its meaning and potential. As I have argued in the preceding sections, a commonality between the phenomena of falling out of love and carnival is the transfer of energy, described as a process of transpositioning. This commonality explains that the energy of the preceding phase is transferred to the subsequent phase and gives it force and impetus. However, the process of transpositioning has the potential of doing more than the simple transfer of energy alone. It is also possible that the *specific* experiential quality of one position is transferred to the subsequent position, with the effect that the subsequent position receives, to a stronger or lesser degree, the specific experiential quality of the preceding one, resulting in a new hybrid combination.

It makes sense to make a comparison between the process of transpositioning and Freud's well-known concept of transference. He most clearly defined this term in his paper "The Dynamics of Transference,"[37] where he explained that certain past "role models" could affect the later relationship of a patient with their physician in a psychiatric/psychotherapeutic setting.[38] A simplified everyday example is that you may transfer the original feelings or desires you had in relation to one of your parents to a new boss. In such a case, you attribute your parental feelings – positive or negative ones – to this new person. In this example, the energy originally directed to the parent subsequently influences the energy directed to the boss. However, the specific way the boss is experienced is not neutral but "colored" by the specific experiential quality you originally had in the relationship with your parent. What does this mean for the processes of positioning and transpositioning?

Let's take the example of enjoying a dinner. When you are hungry and have dinner, you feel it as an enjoyable experience. After finishing your meal, your appetite has gone. This is very different in the case of the gourmand who is proud of being a connoisseur of food and drink and is focused on the discriminating enjoyment of them. The gourmand has a hearty appetite for good food and drink, and they are quite knowledgeable about the history and rituals of haute cuisine. The gourmand is not simply having dinner but adds an artistic quality to it that affects the specific nature of enjoying the food. This artistic quality garnered the interest of a group of researchers[39] who wanted to know how visual factors, such as the

---

[37] Freud (1958).   [38] Parth et al. (2017, p. 167).   [39] Michel et al. (2014).

color and balance of the elements on a plate, affect a diner's perception and enjoyment of the food. They offered their participants a salad arranged in three different presentations: a simple plated one with all of the elements of the salad tossed together, another one with the elements arranged to look like a painting of Kandinsky (the artist's name was not mentioned to the participants), and a third arrangement in which the elements were organized neatly but in a nonartistic manner. Interestingly, the results revealed that the participants considered the Kandinsky-inspired version as more artistic and were willing to pay more for this arrangement on their plate. Moreover, after finishing their meal, they gave higher tastiness ratings for the art-inspired presentation. Therefore, the researchers concluded that their findings were in support of the common assumption that we eat with our eyes first.

In this research, at least two I-positions were involved: "I as enjoying a dinner" and "I as artistic." The latter position enhanced the experiential quality of the former one. The taste and enjoyment of the food were enhanced by the artistic perception. The enjoyer of the dinner did not simply appreciate the artistic pattern of the plate. Rather, the participants became "artistic enjoyers" in the style of a gourmand. The specific constellation of the elements of the plate changed the way they enjoyed the food. The enjoyer of food and the art lover came together in a *coalition* in which the mixture of the two positions resulted in a "hybrid" experience that can only be understood as a Gestalt that is more than the sum of its parts. This combination was the result of a process of transpositioning in which, due to their *specific* contributions, the two positions changed as parts of a special, enjoyable experience. At the end of this chapter and in Chapter 4 in particular I will apply the process of transpositioning to processes that take place on the moral middle ground.

Recapitulation

At the beginning of this chapter, I presented the ideas of James on the self and Bakhtin on dialogue as sources of inspiration for DST. In order to give an additional push to the theory, I selected two phenomena that are central in their work: James on conversions and Bakhtin on carnival. I did so with the intention to provide a theoretical basis for the understanding of the concept of dominance reversal in the processes of positioning and repositioning. My purpose was to show that the energy of the position before the reversal is transferred to the one that follows it. Positions do not follow each other as purely successive moments in a row; they have the potential to energize and vitalize each other in a process of transpositioning.

But how is this energizing process related to the notion of the moral middle ground? Precisely on that point Bakhtin's portrayal of carnival ritual adds a significant dimension to James's reversal description. Let's compare: In the example of falling out of love, we saw a sudden, relatively unpredictable dominance reversal from love to hate. Without any apparent causal stimulation, the man, while walking to his work, suddenly decided to return to his house and destroy all of his possessions related to his lover. Whereas previously he adored and admired his lover as a good angel, he despised her later as a bad lucifer. Certainly, his description showed signs of discomfort and tension before the reversal, as he secretly knew that she was unfit as his partner, but this knowledge was latent and not yet dominant in his mind. Only after the dominance reversal did his hate toward her came to a full and unrestricted expression. The preceding energies, including the latent tensions, oriented to the "good woman" were transferred to the "bad woman." However, in this description there is no sign of a middle ground where good and bad coexist. This is remarkably different from the carnival example, where we saw a temporally and spatially organized middle ground where it is no longer possible to separate good and bad or simply see them as mutually exclusive opposites. They go together in a well-organized *coalition* producing a *new quality* (e.g. playful insulting, or "Death to thee, Signor Father!") that provides an emotional outlet for tensions built up in the everyday, restrictive, hierarchical society. What is usually considered as morally "bad" does not simply disappear but has a role to play that contributes to the vitality of self and society. As parts of this coalition, and as long as they can get along well with each other, good and bad don't function as enemies but as a pair, of which the components energize each other and are involved in a process of transpositioning.

In the present chapter, I referred to the phenomenon of carnival as a prelude to an exposition of the moral middle ground, the central concept in this book, My intention is to explore this middle ground and its potentials on a broader and deeper level in the next chapters, particularly in Chapter 4.

Practical Implications

If we accept the existence of a middle ground, including its positional dynamics, it has some significant implications. In my view, the main one is avoiding any sharp separation between mutually excluding definitions of good and bad. Let's explore some real-life examples that show not only the existence of a middle ground, but also its *open boundaries to the realms of*

good and bad. With these examples, I want to demonstrate, in a preliminary way, that the middle ground is not a sharply delineated area, clearly
separated from what is evaluated as good or bad, but that its boundaries are
highly permeable; that is, positions in this area are highly dynamic in the
sense that they can fluidly move to one or the other side.

Sabotage Is Forbidden but ...

On September 27, 2016, Greenpeace activists closed off access to imports
and exports from the palm oil trader IOI, one of Malaysia's biggest
conglomerates, in the port of Rotterdam.[40] This blockage was preceded by
a report by Greenpeace mentioning that international palm oil companies
were involved in forest destruction, peatland fires, and child labor. Two
Indonesian men who were directly affected by forest fires blocked access to
the refinery together with eight activists. The Greenpeace ship *Esperanza*
moored to the dock at the back of the Rotterdam refinery and prevented
palm oil from being unloaded from incoming oil tankers. For sure, this
blockage was illegal in the country where it happened and had economic and
financial consequences for IOI and the involved traders. Was this action
good or bad from a moral perspective? It may be evaluated as good by
Greenpeace but as bad by the trading partners. However, from a broader
moral perspective good and bad are not clearly separated in this case but
rather represent a moral coalition. Any conclusion about its moral nature
would require discussion and dialogue, implying both agreements and
disagreements. But the moral judgment was not clear from the onset. This
would be different if Greenpeace (or any organization with similar purposes)
and IOI representatives could find a solution to the problem via negotiations. In that case, the action would shift to the side of moral good.
However, suppose Greenpeace decided to sink the ship, resulting in casualties; then the action would shift to a judgment of "morally bad." In the latter
two possibilities, the validity of moral judgments in the community where it
happened would be less problematic than in the case of the moral middle
ground where good and bad coexist as a coalition of two positions.

Stealing Is Forbidden but ...

Robin Hood, a legendary heroic outlaw originally depicted in English
folklore of the late Middle Ages, was admired as a highly skilled archer

---

[40] www.marineinsight.com/shipping-news/greenpeace-blockades-palm-oil-trader-ioi/.

and swordsman. One of the reasons for his immense popularity across the centuries is the influence of his stealing from the rich and giving to the poor, an action that continues to inspire discussions and debates today. The image of a noble bandit who fights for justice by acting against a corrupt system for the benefit of the oppressed appeals to many people. There are many versions of this story portrayed in films and literature,[41] and there is even doubt as to whether Robin Hood ever existed. Purely as an invitation to reflection, let's take the version in which he is portrayed as a hero who returned the property of the poor that the rich had taken from them by imposing improper taxes and by outright theft. Robin Hood returned the goods to the poor to help them out of poverty. He did not steal from those who were rich because they had accumulated their wealth. His targets were only those individuals who had accumulated their wealth from human misery.[42]

From a utilitarian perspective, which claims that it is morally right to seek the greatest good for the greatest number of people, many of Robin Hood's deeds could be evaluated as acceptable because, compared to the gains by the poor, the losses of the few rich were insignificant. However, Kantian ethics would regard stealing as inherently wrong. Such a contradiction can evoke hot debate and controversy. When reading about Robin Hood, I remembered the national commotion caused by one of our bishops in the Netherlands, Tiny Muskens, with his public statement that stealing was, in particular circumstances, acceptable: "The catholic morality has always made clear that, when you are so poor that you cannot live, you are then allowed to take away a bread from the shop."[43] As this example suggests, there are circumstances in which it is difficult to separate moral good and bad. In the bishop's view, even Catholic morality permitted, in special circumstances, limited or necessary forms of theft.

Imagine a hypothetical situation in which Robin Hood asked the rich to do something to benefit the poor, and they agreed with his request to turn over part of their wealth to the poor. In that case, the action would shift from the middle ground to the realm of good. However, if he killed rich landowners, as some sources[44] reveal, then the action would shift from the middle ground to the realm of moral bad.

---

[41] A recent example of the Robin Hood legend is *Sherwood*, an American computer-animated science fiction web television series created by Diana Manson and Megan Laughton that premiered on March 6, 2019, on YouTube Premium.
[42] Interpretation by Dennis Manning, www.quora.com/Didnt-Robin-Hood-steal-from-the-rich-and-give-to-the-poor/answer/Dennis-Manning-9.
[43] Muskens (1996).   [44] Hilton (1958).

Fraud Is Forbidden but ...

Perhaps you are familiar with the case of Dr. Ozel Clifford Brazil, a black minister who committed fraud in order to send 18,000 young African American people from Los Angeles's inner-city neighborhoods to college. He succeeded, over a period of more than fifteen years, to help students get into college and university, and he claimed that 98 percent of them ended up getting their degrees. He advised students to sever all legal ties with their parents if that would put them in a better financial position. In some college applications he mentioned only the lower-income earner of two parents while not mentioning the income of the other parent. None of what Brazil did ever benefited him personally. The downside of his generous help was that in 2003 he was sentenced to three and a half years in prison for financial aid fraud. Moreover, he also ended up having to pay restitution of nearly three-quarters of a million dollars.[45]

In this case too we notice a gradual transition to both moral sides. Suppose that Brazil had found a loophole in the law that allowed him to help disadvantaged students to go to college. His actions would then lean to the moral good. However, if his actions were planned and realized in the service of his own financial benefit, then we would be inclined to say that he deviated in the wrong direction.

I give these brief sketches not only to illustrate the existence of a moral middle ground, but also to demonstrate that the boundaries in the directions of both good and bad are highly permeable. But what is the practical advantage of assuming the existence of such a middle ground as a welcome element in our moral considerations? An argument for this can be found in the way moral discussions seem to degenerate into moral clashes in an increasingly polarizing society.[46] With Tim Dean, Honorary Associate in Philosophy of the University of Sydney, I agree that there is not a lack of morality in the world, but rather too much.[47] The way we tend to think and talk about morality, often limited by the social, political, or ideological groups to which we belong, puts serious limits on our ability to engage with views other than our own. The moral "bubbles" in which we are locked up make it hard to manage diversity and disagreement and to provide space for alternative moral views. As a consequence, we face a great struggle in finding appropriate responses to a *multiplicity of moral positions* (see also Chapter 2), and overcoming this is crucial in a globalizing and digitalizing world. Moral tribalism and its associated rigid

[45] Price Pierre (2014).   [46] Phillips (2022).   [47] Dean (2018).

boundaries often lead to moral clashes that produce suffering and moral unrest, which have their origins in the conviction that our moral norms have a universal pretention, in the sense that everybody *should think as we do*. In a highly interdependent society in which we have to live together with other social, cultural, political, ethnic, sexual, and gender groups, any form of moral tribalism is increasingly infeasible.

Far from having the pretention that the present book provides any "solution" to this problem, I propose that the acceptance of a middle ground as an element in our moral discussions has one great advantage: It stimulates debate and dialogue that offer the potential of relativizing any sharp and rigidly closed moral position both in the relationships among people and within the domains of our own selves. If the middle ground is allowed in moral discussions, it can work as a buffer against hard clashes between convictions of good and bad because it "makes us think" and stimulates dialogue with others and within ourselves. The moral middle ground is loaded with uncertainty, contradiction, and ambivalence (see Chapter 5), as it is located in a field of tension *between* positions evaluated as good or bad, exemplified by the three examples presented above. Pausing on this middle ground makes it difficult to give a quick and fixed answer to moral problems, reveals the existence of a space that resists any sharply differentiated thumbs-up or thumbs-down gesture, and goes beyond any simplifying and dichotomous like or dislike, often used as "moral knives."

Summary

I started this chapter with a summary of DST and its historical forerunners. The works of the two main authors who inspired this theory were outlined: William James on the self and Mikhail Bakhtin on dialogue. The two terms, self and dialogue, are combined in the concept of the dialogical self.

To demonstrate the flexibility of the processes of positioning and repositioning and the associated transference of energies, I introduced the concept of dominance reversal, illustrated by James's description of "falling out of love" and Bakhtin's exposé of carnival. I argued that the carnival ritual provides a basis for the conceptualization of a moral middle ground and the process of transpositioning. The main practical implication of this chapter is the significance of recognizing that, via this middle ground, sharp distinctions between good and bad can be transcended and that moral positions can work together in productive coalitions.

To illustrate this, I analyzed some controversial events, referring to sabotage, stealing, and fraud, in order to demonstrate that there exists, in particular circumstances, a moral middle ground in which good and bad positions form coalitions that have a specific quality that is not reducible to any one of its components. Analyzing these examples, I clarified that moving onto the moral middle ground opens up the boundaries to the sides of both moral good and bad. Recognition of a middle ground has the potential of buffering the clashes between individuals and groups that implicitly assume that good and bad are sharply differentiated and mutually exclusive. Moreover, allowing uncertainty and contradictions, as necessarily associated with the moral middle ground, has the advantage of stimulating debate and dialogue both within the self and between social groups in society at large.

CHAPTER 2

Embracing Bad as Good via Internalization

Hypocrisy is the homage vice pays to virtue.

Francois de La Rochefoucauld[1]

My specific interests in this chapter are philosophies and worldviews that, in strong opposition to the morality of the established institutions of their time, elevate bad to the level of goodness or even holiness, and in doing so they illustrate the surprising *flexibility* of moral definitions. As prominent examples of such revolutionary worldviews, I analyze the works of three authors who propose a radical dominance reversal of "bad," as defined by the societies in which they live, into what they define as "good." They do not remove, sublimate, or change an action as bad, but worship it just because, in their view, it holds value in itself. In his autobiographical work *The Thief's Journal* (1949), the French novelist Jean Genet appropriates Christian concepts to pursue alternative forms of "sainthood," celebrating theft, betrayal, and homosexuality as "virtues" instead of vices. Similarly, in his novel *The 120 Days of Sodom* (1785), philosopher Marquis de Sade worships crime as "the soul of lust." In addition, I analyze *The Satanic Bible* (1969), the codification of the Church of Satan, a religious organization dedicated to satanism established in San Francisco in 1966 by Anton Szandor LaVey. I analyze these works from the lens of Dialogical Self Theory (DST) as the primary conceptual framework of the present book. The conclusion is that these works advocate the worship of lust as a liberating act of "anti-positioning" against the dictates of the official religious institutions, which are accused of suppressing the vitality of bad in the self and preaching a hypocritical morality. I then explore more deeply the phenomenon of hypocrisy from the perspective of the psychology of morality and its relationship with moral multiplicity. Finally, some practical implications of the chapter will be outlined.

---

[1] Brainy Quote, November 29, 2022.

Figure 2.1   French author Jean Genet (1910–1986).
Source: Hulton Archive/Getty Images.

Jean Genet and His Sainthood

Jean Genet (1910–1986; Figure 2.1)[2] was a French novelist, playwright, poet, essayist, and political activist. He was born to a twenty-two-year-old unwed mother and abandoned by her when he was thirty weeks old. He was placed with foster parents in a small village in the Morvan, a poor region in east-central France. At the age of thirteen he was sent to an educational center run by the public welfare system, from which he immediately ran away. After a series of problems in homes and institutions and arrests for theft, he was finally consigned, at the age of fifteen, to the penal institution of Mettray. It was there that he began to realize his destiny as a writer and as a homosexual and where he embarked upon

---

[2] For biographies of Genet, see White (1993); Barber (2004). For a summary, see de Courtivron (1993).

the themes of honor and treason, domination and submission, authenticity and illusion as main issues of his writings. In *Miracle of the Rose* (1946), he gave an account of his experiences during a period of detention. He wrote this work in the solitude of a prison cell, on pieces of white paper the penal authorities furnished the convicts for making paper bags. This was followed by a period in which he traveled as a vagabond, thief, and prostitute across Europe, as recounted in *The Thief's Journal* (1949). As one of his biographers notes about Genet's life during the 1930s: "In every place he traverses, Genet steals: he cracks open the offerings-box in churches, offers himself for prostitution to older homosexuals and then robs them, and plans burglaries or drugs robberies with his associates."[3]

In 1949, Genet was threatened with a life sentence after a series of convictions. However, the famous French artist Jean Cocteau and philosopher Jean-Paul Sartre successfully petitioned the French government to prevent the sentence. In May 1967, three years after the suicide of tightrope-walker Abdallah Bentaga, one of his most favorite lovers, Genet himself attempted, after a period of depression, to commit suicide in an Italian hotel room with an overdose of sleeping tablets combined with alcohol. In a state of coma he was taken to a hospital, where he was eventually reanimated and where he recovered. Facing an imminent death after a diagnosis of cancer, Genet continued to travel, stubbornly refusing to stay in one place. While facing death, he finally returned to Paris, where he spent the last weeks of his life. Out on the streets of contemporary Paris, the traces of Genet's life and obsessions are still tangible: the Tarnier clinic, where he was born as an unwanted bastard in 1910; the walls of the Santé prison, where he was imprisoned several times between 1937 and 1943; and Jack's Hotel, where Genet died as an anonymous customer in 1986.[4]

As an ardent and restless traveler, Genet visited many places in the world, not only many cities in Europe, but also in Africa, where he claimed to have joined the French Liberation Movement. He traveled to the United States, where he came into contact with the Black Panther movement, and to Palestine, where he had a brief meeting with Yasser Arafat. His persistent drive to political action and alliances was also exemplified by his support of the German Rote Armee Fraktion (Red Army Faction) terrorist movement.[5] He was not only a restless loner in search of like-minded spirits, he also was an agitated wanderer in the space of his own mind. In terms of DST, he was continuously jumping through a

---

[3] Barber (2004, p. 63).   [4] Ibid. (p. 146).   [5] White (1993).

contrasting and conflicting multiplicity of I-positions: from an abandoned child to criminal, traveler, homosexual, revolutionary, novelist, filmmaker, and playwright, never abandoning his manifold creativity.

Most central in Genet's life was his self-proclaimed position as a criminal that was not only dominant in his own life, but also reflected his view on the education of youngsters. This became particularly evident in a censored radio script *The Criminal Child* from 1949, in which he complained about the efforts of well-meaning reformers to soften the strict living conditions in the penal colony of Mettray, where he himself was forced to stay after his arrest in 1926. Genet made it very clear that he admired Mettray as cultivating the violence of the young male inmates. He saw cruelty and violence as the poetic expression of the youngsters' affirmation of evil and rebellion. Obedience to the rules of the prison system would erase their individual differences. In contrast, rebellion would sharpen their individuality. Instead of being raised as interchangeable sheep, each of them should become a distinct hero-criminal. For Genet, crime itself was beautiful, and therefore he supported the cruelty of the unreformed prison system that would turn young people into hardened criminals. Genet clearly described his position as follows: "As for me, I've chosen; I will be on the side of crime. And I'll help children not to gain entrance into your houses, your factories, your schools, your laws and holy sacraments, but to violate them."[7]

Genet's radical and fierce anti-positioning against existing society as a whole was clearly revealed in an interview after the murder of President Kennedy, in which he expressed his sympathy with Lee Harvey Oswald, Kennedy's assassin: "Not because I have a particular hatred for President Kennedy; he doesn't interest me at all. But this solitary man who decided to oppose a society as strongly organized as the American society and even as Western society or even as every society in the world that rejects Evil." And he added: ". . . ah yes, I'd rather be on his side. I sympathize with him, but as I would sympathize with a very great artist who would be alone against all society, neither more nor less, I am with every man alone."[8] As this and other quotations suggest, Genet presented himself as an ardent advocate of the promotion of crime, but his defense of evil was not the expression of an isolated position in his repertoire. It was the *coalition* of evil and art, in the sense of being a novelist and playwright, that worked for him as an exaltation of his criminality.

---

[6] Genet (2020).   [7] Ibid. (p. 72).   [8] Ibid. (p. 243).

This exaltation and the radical reversal of good and evil is even expressed in a coalition of acting as a criminal and addressing himself as a saint:

> Though saintliness is my goal, I can not tell what it is. My point of departure is the word itself, which indicates the state closest to moral perfection. Of which I known nothing, save that without it my life would be vain. Unable to arrive at a definition of saintliness – no more than of beauty – I want at every moment to create it, that is, to act so that everything I do may lead me to what is unknown to me, so that at every moment I may be guided by a will to saintliness until the time when I am so luminous that people will say, "He is a saint," or, more likely, "He was a saint."[9]

From this quotation it becomes clear that Genet doesn't act from one position only, I as a criminal, although it occupies the central place in his repertoire of I-positions. By combining it with I as a saint, he heightens it to the highest moral level and gives it a personal expression. Via a coalition of the criminal with the saint position, he realizes a radical reversal of the criminal position, regarded as despisable by the society in which he lives, but exalted to holiness in his personally constructed self. On a positional level, Genet's reversal in his private life is similar to the reversal phenomenon during carnival, as described in Chapter 1. Whereas carnival allows an officially permitted dominance reversal from a slave to a king as a ritual at the collective level, Genet aspires to a reversal from an officially despised criminal to saint as part of his idiosyncratic life project. Transferring energy from the saint position to the criminal position confirms and strengthens the latter one, including its subpositions (thief, male whore, gangster). In this way, he receives "sacrificing grace," which gives an extra boost to the vitality of his criminal position and to his self as a whole.

It should be noted that there is also a significant difference between coalitions in Genet's case and those in the treatment of carnival (Chapter 1). Whereas carnival allows for the emergence of coalitions of good and bad on the moral middle ground, for Genet coalitions are in the service of a reversal of bad into good, and therefore there is no moral middle ground in his case. The same applies for the reversals that are basic to the conceptions of Marquis de Sade and Anton LaVey, as will be discussed later in this chapter.

The analysis of Genet's self-construction in terms of coalitions of positions can further be deepened by examining the role of others-in-his-self defined in DST as external positions, extended as they are to the

---

[9] Genet (2004, p. 96).

outside world. More insight into that topic can be gained when we take philosopher Jean-Paul Sartre's profound analysis of Genet's life project as a guide.

Sartre on Genet

Before we move to Sartre's analysis, let's have a look at what happens inside's Genet's mind when he is involved in his act of stealing. In his account, there are some elements referring to the relationship between his position as a burglar and his mental appropriation of the owner of the stolen material:

> And what happens during a burglary? Having broken the lock, as soon as I push the door it thrusts back within me a heap of darkness, or, to be more exact, a very thick vapor which my body is summoned to enter. I enter. For a half hour I shall be operating, if I am alone, in a world which is the *reverse* of the customary world. My heart beats loudly. My hand never trembles. Fear does not leave me for a single second. I do not think specifically of the proprietor of the place, but all my gestures evoke him in so far as they see him. I am steeped in an idea of property while I loot property. I recreate the absent proprietor. He lives, not facing me, but about me. *He is a fluid element which I breathe, which enters me, which inflates my lungs.* The beginning of the operation goes off without too much fear, which starts mounting the moment I have finally decided to leave. The decision is born when the apartment contains no more secret corners, *when I have taken the proprietor's place.*[10]

Compare this quotation with the portrait of Genet presented by his autobiographer, Stephen Barber, who depicts *The Thief's Journal* as a book of profound solitude, in which Genet recounts his travels on foot across Europe in the 1930s. Although he encounters various criminals with whom he has sexual relationships, he constructs for himself "an isolation cell" around his body, "since only that profound separation from every other human being can enable him to compound the aura of abject glory through which he survives."[11] However, as Genet's own description of his burglary suggests, he identifies with the absent but imagined proprietor, to such a degree that he *becomes* this person that is internalized as an external I-position in his extended self. Precisely at this point, Sartre's treatment in his celebrated book *Saint Genet: Actor and Martyr*[12] gives us a clue to unravel the complexities of Genet's mysterious inner world. Sartre poses

---

[10] Ibid. (p. 71, emphases added).   [11] Barber (2004, p. 62).   [12] Sartre (2012, emphasis added).

this intriguing question: "Why does he demand disgust and rebuffs, the other's indifference, the tortures of jealousy and, in the end, the despair that comes from the certainty of not being loved?" Sartre then supposes: "And yet he must have something to gain by this. What is behind it all? For Genet [in Sartre's view], the answer is clear: love is a magical ceremonial whereby the lover *steals the beloved's being in order to incorporate it into himself*..."[13] When we accept this interpretation, Genet is not only a thief of materials, making them his property, but he "steals" even the beings he loves in order to transform them into external I-positions in his self. In Sartre's terms: "It is not so much the skin, the hardness of the muscles, the hair, the odor which stagger him and flood him with desire. It is, of course, all that, but all that as an embodiment of being, of his being. In that other who resembles him – or rather resembles what he would like to be – he at last sees himself as others see him." And he adds, "In loving that indifferent charmer with his body and soul, the abandoned child fulfills his impossible dream of being loved. For since he is the Other, it is he, he alone, who *is loved in the Other*."[14] By *becoming* this position in his extended self, he experiences a form of self-love that he felt was lacking since his birth. For Genet, this interiorized other receives even a religious meaning. In his own terms, "In this way, I seem to recognize that over the act of stealing rules a god to whom moral actions are agreeable. These attempts to throw out a net, on the chance that this god of whom I know nothing will be caught in it, exhaust me, excite me and also favor the religious state."[15]

In Sartre's view, ever since his birth Genet has been "the unloved one, the inopportune, the superfluous. Undesirable in his very being, he is not that woman's son but her excrement."[16] He felt rejected and left by his mother, who wanted no longer to see her unnatural son. And with masochistic pleasure, Genet later compares himself to filth, to a waste product. The abandoning of a child signifies a radical condemnation. But Genet reacted to his condemnation by effecting an ethical and generalized inversion. He was, as he said, "turned inside-out like a glove."[17] The striking thing is that his erotic humiliations as a homosexual and his occupational risks as a thief were tinged with an aura of the sacred, which finds its expression as a coalition of I-positions: "the eternal couple of the criminal and the saint."[18] In this way Genet succeeded in escaping from the I-prison in which he was condemned to stay from the beginning of his

[13] Ibid. (p. 83, emphasis added).   [14] Ibid. (p. 86, emphasis in original).
[15] Genet (2004, p. 10).   [16] Sartre (2012, p. 8).   [17] Ibid. (p. 81).   [18] Ibid. (p. 8).

Figure 2.2   Portrait of Donatien Alphonse François de Sade by Charles Amédée Philippe van Loo. The drawing dates to 1760, when Sade was nineteen years old.
Source: adoc-photos/Corbis via Getty Images.

life. In his own terms: "Saintliness means turning pain to good account. It means forcing the devil to be God. It means obtaining the recognition of evil."[19] The coalition of criminal and saint enabled him to transfer pain to moral goodness.

Marquis de Sade: Over-Positioning of Sex

"Imperious, choleric, irascible, extreme in everything, with a dissolute imagination the like of which has never been seen, atheistic to the point of fanaticism, there you have me in a nutshell, and kill me again or take me as I am, for I shall not change."[20] This frequently cited self-characterization of Marquis de Sade (1740–1814; Figure 2.2) may be one of the reasons why his work is perceived by some as an incarnation of absolute evil, as it advocates the unleashing of one's instincts even to the

[19] Genet (2004, p. 94).
[20] Quoted by Simone de Beauvoir in her introduction to Sade's *The 120 Days of Sodom*. See Marquis de Sade (1966, p. 12; pagination starts from the cover).

point of crime, whereas others admire him as a champion of total liberation through the satisfaction of desires in all forms. His celebration of
excessive sexual aberrations may well explain why his writings were banned
in France until the 1960s.[21]

Donatien Alphonse François de Sade was the son of the Comte de Sade,
an aristocratic landowner in the south of France. His mother was a lady-in-
waiting (court lady) to the Princess of Condé. Little Donatien was born
into a privileged background, and, as the only boy in the family, he was
doted on by a paternal grandmother and five aunts. In his early years,
however, the most important influences were his father and his paternal
uncle, the Abbé Jacques François de Sade, both of whom had a preference
for a libertine lifestyle. Between the ages of ten and fourteen, he attended
the Jesuit school of Louis-le-Grand in Paris, where he was trained by a
young, gentle, and highly intelligent teacher, the Abbé Amblet, who
taught him reading, arithmetic, geography, and history. At this school,
the young Marquis became skilled in classical rhetoric and debating.
In 1754, he began a military career, which he abandoned in 1763. In that
year he married (arranged) Renée-Pélagie de Montreuil, the daughter of a
high-ranking bourgeois family, a marriage that produced two sons and
a daughter.[22]

Just five months after the wedding, however, Sade was arrested for the
crime of debauchery, for which he became imprisoned. He was accused of
shocking a young Parisian prostitute with talking about masturbating into
chalices and thrusting communion hosts into vaginas. Moreover, he had
frightened her with whips and other instruments. After three weeks of
imprisonment, he continued his debauchery by committing a number of
similar acts, including the flagellation and buggery of prostitutes and the
sexual corruption of young women.[23]

In 1768, the first public scandal erupted through his affair with Rose
Keller, a thirty-six-year-old beggar-woman from Alsace, who accused Sade
of subjecting her to acts of libertinage, sacrilege, and sadism in his house at
Arcueil. According to her, he locked her up and abused her sexually. She
escaped and related Sade's unnatural acts and brutality to persons in the
neighborhood and showed them her wounds. As a defense, the Marquis
claimed she was a prostitute who had been well paid for her services.
Nevertheless, he was imprisoned for six months. His sentences, however,

---

[21] "Marquis de Sade," in *Encyclopedia Britannica*, www.britannica.com/biography/Marquis-de-Sade,
retrieved February 15, 2022. The colloquial term "sadism" is derived from Sade's name.
[22] Phillips (2005).   [23] Ibid. (p. 4).

did not stop his extravagant behavior. Four years later, in 1772, he and his valet organized a party with a number of young prostitutes in Marseilles. One of the women became seriously ill, which led to the suspicion that the Marquis had poisoned them, and the case was reported to the authorities. It appeared that Sade had given the prostitutes pastilles containing Spanish fly, a well-known aphrodisiac, with the intention of causing flatulence. Given Sade's fixation on the female buttocks and excrement, this effect undoubtedly gave him a perverse thrill. As the situation became more dangerous to them, the two men escaped to Italy so that they were out of reach of the French authorities. In their absence, Sade and his valet were condemned to death for crimes of sodomy and attempted poisoning. Their bodies were symbolically burned in effigy.[24]

As expressed in his Last Will and Testament of 1806, Sade wished to be buried in an unmarked grave: "... the traces of my grave may disappear from the face of the earth as I trust the memory of me shall fade out of the minds of all men save nevertheless for those few who in their goodness have loved me until the last and of whom I carry away a sweet remembrance with me to the grave."[25] Sade died of a pulmonary disease at the age of seventy-four. At the behest of his son, Armand, he was buried with full Christian rights in the small asylum cemetery of Charenton, where he had lived during the last year of his life. No trace remains of his grave today.

The 120 Days of Sodom: Cruelty Guided by Reason

Among Sade's main works is *Justine: The Misfortunes of Virtue* (originally printed in French in 1779), in which he describes the misfortunes suffered by the heroine from her failure to recognize that God is evil and that wickedness is the source of human activity. A parallel work is *Juliette: Or the Prosperities of Vice* (1797), in which the protagonist, Juliette, is involved in increasingly horrific manifestations of sexual violence, but unlike Justine she has a happy life. In these works the reader finds numerous references to contemporary philosophers such as Diderot, Montesquieu, Rousseau, Molière, and Machiavelli, signs of Sade's erudition that support his philosophical message.[26]

His philosophical message was also exposed in another main work, *The 120 Days of Sodom*, which he wrote when he was imprisoned in the Bastille

---

[24] Ibid. See also "Marquis de Sade," in *Encyclopedia Britannica*, www.britannica.com/biography/Marquis-de-Sade, retrieved February, 16, 2022.
[25] Phillips (2005, p. 112).   [26] Ibid. (p. 102).

in 1785. It was written down in microscopic handwriting on long, narrow rolls of paper that he glued together into a roll that eventually became forty-nine feet long and that he kept hidden in a hole in the wall of his cell. Then, ten days before the storming of the Bastille in 1789, Sade was suddenly moved to another fortress, and he had no opportunity to take his manuscript with him. To his great regret, he never saw *The 120 Days* again. However, later the manuscript was discovered and remained in private hands until the early twentieth century, when the German psychiatrist Dr Iwan Bloch published a first limited edition of the work.[27]

In *The 120 Days of Sodom*, four rich, libertine protagonists indulge in a four-month-long orgy of depravity, rape, and murder. This takes place in a remote medieval castle, high in the French mountains and surrounded by forests, detached and isolated from the rest of the world. The four main actors, so-called libertines, represent the four sources of authority and power in eighteenth-century France: the nobility, the church, the courts, and high finance. The largely negative way Sade portrays them suggests that the work is intended to be read as a political satire. In Sade's view, the four main protagonists represent the lusts and perversions of bankers, lawyers, priests, magistrates, landowners, and military officers, all old, rich, and powerful. Four accomplished prostitutes, middle-aged women, act as storytellers and function as intermediaries in the story. They have the task to tell anecdotes of their perverse careers in order to inspire the four principal actors into similar acts of decadence. Eight studs (French: *fouteurs*, "fuckers") are chosen solely because of the impressive size of their penises and their sexual potency. Eight boys and eight girls aged from twelve to fifteen have been kidnapped, chosen because of their beauty. They are all virgins, and the four libertines' plan is to deflower them, vaginally and especially anally. The narration of the stories and the communal orgiastic activities instigated by these stories take place in a main hall, designed in the shape of an amphitheater. Each storyteller sits on a centrally positioned throne when it is her turn to narrate, while the four protagonists occupy seats in four separate recesses, listening to the narratives before they enact them.[28]

The question arises as to whether we see in this and other tales of Sade the unobtrusive expression of a sick mind obsessed by sex, horror, and crime or the existence of deeper philosophical motivations and inspirations that drive him. Or to put it otherwise: Are *The 120 Days* to be seen as the wild irrational delusions of a frustrated outcast or is his work based on

---

[27] Ibid. (p. 62).   [28] Ibid. (pp. 62–72).

reason, albeit an unusual conception of reason? Sade is quite explicit on this: "I have supported my deviations with reasons; I did not stop at mere doubt; I have vanquished, I have uprooted, I have destroyed everything in my heart that might have interfered with my pleasures."[29] He claims reason even as the fundament of his philosophy when he writes about the difference between virtue and vice: ". . . the first is illusory, a fiction; the second is authentic, real; the first is founded upon vile prejudices, the second upon reason; the first, through the agency of pride, the most false of all our sensations, may provide the heart with a brief instant's titillation; the other is a veritable mental pleasure-taking, and it inflames every other passion by the very fact it runs counter to common opinions."[30]

Sade's claim that his morality is founded on reason starts from the assumption that moral good is justified by the law of nature that prescribes that strength is good and weakness bad. This justification of natural reason requires a dominance reversal, the concept that was already discussed in Chapter 1 of the present book and in our exposition of Jean Genet. As Sade remarks:

> If one were to raise the objection that, nevertheless, all men possess ideas of the just and the unjust which can only be the product of Nature, since these notions are found in every people and even amongst the uncivilized, the Duc [one of his characters] would reply affirmatively, saying that yes, those ideas have never been anything if not relative, that the stronger has always considered exceedingly just what the weaker regarded as flagrantly unjust, and that it takes no more than the *mere reversal of their positions* for each to be able to change his way of thinking too.[31]

More generally, Sade plays with dominance reversal and even applies it to a reversal of the sexes: ". . . the girls were costumed as sailors, the little boys as tarts; the effect was ravishing, nothing quickens lust like this voluptuous little reversal; adorable to find in a little boy what causes him to resemble a girl, and the girl is far more interesting when for the sake of pleasing she borrows the sex one would like her to have."[32] However, far from any emancipatory ideal, this reversal seeks a purely pleasure-enhancing effect in the otherwise extreme masculine Sadean world as symbolized by the absolute dominance of the four main male protagonists and as expressed in such passing statements as ". . . the boy is worth more than the girl."[33]

---

[29] Quoted by Simone de Beauvoir in her introduction to Marquis de Sade (1966, p. 59; pagination starts from the cover).
[30] Marquis de Sade (1966, p. 75).   [31] Ibid. (p. 250, emphasis added).   [32] Ibid. (p. 413).
[33] Ibid. (p. 554).

At the same time, *The 120 Days* reflects the extreme sexism of the ruling class of eighteenth-century France as an expression of more general masculine power structures that continue to exist on a global scale in the world today.

Sade's Place in the History of Art and Philosophy

Certainly, it would be a misrepresentation of Sade's work if we would reduce it simply to an exposé of orgiastic sexuality and crime only or associate it stereotypically with the notion of "sadism," as this would neglect the importance of his contribution to art and philosophy over the centuries. In his book *The Marquis de Sade: A Very Short Introduction*, literary scholar John Phillips includes a highly informative chapter titled "Apostle of Freedom,"[34] in which he places Sade in the larger context of art and philosophy. In this section, I will refer to some of Phillips' insights, in particular to Sade as a precursor to postmodernism, which then will be followed by my interpretation of Sade from the perspective of DST.

Although largely ignored during the last two centuries, Sade's works continued to be read in private, and his influence on writers, artists, and thinkers throughout this period is undeniable. Even during the nineteenth century, when his reputation was at its lowest level, his shade hovered incessantly over all the century's major literary and philosophical movements. His works *Justine* and *Juliette* were secretly read and greatly admired by writers such as Gustave Flaubert, Charles Baudelaire, Algernon Swinburne, and many others. For the surrealist poet Guillaume Apollinaire, Sade was simply "the freest spirit who ever lived."[35]

Sade figures as a significant precursor of the work of sexologists and psychoanalysts such as Sigmund Freud and Richard von Krafft-Ebing, who were influenced by his systematic portrayal of what came to be known as "perversions." Likewise, Sade's scandalous yet unique elevation of the body over the mind precedes Nietzsche's emphasis on the Dionysian nature of human beings. Also, the poststructuralist philosopher Michel Foucault[36] expresses his appreciation of Sade when he critically discusses the disciplinary control of the body in the schools, prisons, and factories of the past centuries in service of a capitalist imperative that prioritizes work over leisure and renders the body as a commodity in the service of profit-making.

---

[34] Phillips (2005, pp. 112–122).   [35] Quoted by Phillips (2005, p. 116).   [36] Foucault (2015).

American feminist Camille Paglia assesses the reasons for Sade's neglect with verve: "The Marquis de Sade is a great writer and philosopher whose absence from university curricula illustrates the timidity and hypocrisy of the liberal humanities. No education in the western tradition is complete without Sade. He must be confronted, in all his ugliness."[37] On the other hand, the French philosophers and novelists Albert Camus and Raymond Queneau were examples of commentators who were merely critical of Sade. From a political perspective, Queneau saw in Sade's ideas a pre-configuration of Hitler's and Stalin's concentration camps.[38]

According to John Phillips, Sade's texts have much in common with postmodernism. From a postmodern perspective, textual meaning is not fixed and dictated by the author but constructed by the reader and the result of interaction between reader, text, and intertext. In such writings, readers may discover a plurality of potential selves and constructed meanings flitting from character to character and from situation to situation. Identifications with the characters of a novel take place in the minds of individual readers rather than being preinscribed into the text, so that imagined dialogue with the characters of the text becomes possible. Because dialogue is inherently pluralistic, it works against the creation of a single, unified point of view. Sade's prose works offer a multiplicity of voices, physically represented on a stage as exemplified by the amphitheater in *The 120 Days of Sodom*. This multiplicity can be found abundantly in the Sadean text, which mixes and confuses genres, with fading boundaries between comedy and tragedy to which some readers will react with aversion, others with laughter. The text ripples with inconsistencies and contradictions that keep it open to multiple interpretations and accessible to dialogically responding readers. Therefore, Phillips continues, Sade's writings cannot really be considered pornography in a limited sense of the term. In spite of their extremes of obscenity and violence, their erotic potential is interwoven with irony, parody, and satire. In this way, "Sade created a corpus of writing of astonishing breadth and unparalleled complexity that shines a light into those dark corners of the human psyche from which most of us would prefer to avert our gaze."[39] He does so with skill, erudition, playfulness, and humor, qualities that entitle him to a place in the Western literary and philosophical tradition, according to Phillips. This apparent multiplicity that can be found in the reading and interpretation of his texts does not contradict my thesis that, *basically*, both in his life and works Sade puts his full weight on a personal project that aims for

---

[37] Quoted by Phillips (2005, p. 116).   [38] Phillips (2005, p. 117).   [39] Ibid. (p. 121).

the reversal of what is seen as moral bad into a personalized moral good. This brings us back to DST.

Sade and Genet from the Perspective of Dialogical Self Theory

In both authors, Genet and Sade, we see elements of a *reversal* from moral bad, as defined by the mainstream moral standards of their time, into what they defined themselves as moral good. Genet did this, for example, in his plea for the penal colony Mettray as a place for cultivating the violence of young boys and his sympathy with the murderer of President Kennedy. Sade aimed at a reversal of virtue and vice: ". . . the first is illusory, a fiction; the second is authentic, real." Moreover, he acted as a reversal of Kant by using reason not as a path to moral good but, instead, as a basis for realizing the moral bad: ". . . the first [virtue] is founded upon vile prejudices, the second [vice] upon reason."

However, this reversal, including the intensification and justification of moral bad, was supported by *coalitions*. Genet elevated his criminal behavior to saintliness, as expressed in Jean-Paul Sartre's qualification of "the eternal couple of the criminal and the saint." Recall also Genet's own words: "Saintliness means turning pain to good account. It means forcing the devil to be God. It means obtaining the recognition of evil." Sade also was very explicit about the coalition of crime and pleasure: "Crime is the soul of lust. What would pleasure be if it were not accompanied by crime? It is not the object of debauchery that excites us, but rather the idea of evil."[40] Moreover, I believe that the main reason that both authors have received the attention and even appreciation of artists and scientists is in the coalition of crime and art as expressed in their otherwise shocking productions.

Such coalitions enable the self to become involved in a process of *transpositioning*, transferring energy form the one to the other I-position. In Genet's case, the transference of energy from a saint position to a criminal position further confirmed and strengthened his desire for excitement via crime. In Sade's writings, we can see a similar process of transferring energy from artistic creation to pleasure. In Beauvoir's terms: "He subordinated his existence to his eroticism because eroticism appeared to him to be the only possible fulfillment of his existence. If he devoted himself to it with such energy, shamelessness, and persistence, he did so

---

[40] Genet, quoted by Simone de Beauvoir in her introduction to Marquis de Sade (1966, p. 44; pagination starts from the cover).

because he attached greater importance to the stories he wove around the act of pleasure than to the contingent happenings ..."[41]

This transfer of energy stimulates a process of *over-positioning*: The energy was concentrated on one main position, crime in Genet's case and sexual excitement for Sade. They got into a state of overdrive by reaching a high degree of exaggeration of their main positions in order to reach unrestrained levels of pleasure and excitement as exclusive moral purposes. Because their energy was focused on their main position, not much energy was left for engagement in alternative moral purposes. This excessive and exclusive concentration, with the simultaneous lack of any effective counter-position, made them (creative) fanatics in their own realms.

As advocates of the reversal of bad into good, the two authors clashed systematically and frequently with the moral codes of the societies in which they lived and could only survive via a process of *anti-positioning*. They became complete outsiders in their communities and could maintain and develop their identities only via fierce opposition to mainstream institutions and moralities. Genet was a wandering loner in search of like-minded individuals or groups, such as the Black Panther movement in the USA, the Palestine Liberation Organization, and the Rote Armee Fraktion in Germany. Later in his life, Genet remarked that all of his five novels had been written in prison, the price for his systematic anti-positioning.

Sade not only rejected religious dogma, but also all of the social and moral directives that derive from it. He became furiously engaged in the defense of atheism as a necessarily vigorous anti-positioning to the oppressive theism of his society. As he was regarded by the authorities and the people of his time as dangerous and subversive, he had to suffer persecution that often involved imprisonment, torture, and even the threat of execution. His position as a rebel and iconoclast impelled him to propagate his personal mission, for which he had to spend the best part of his adult life in prison.[42]

Anton LaVey and the Church of Satan

In their book *The Invention of Satanism*, Dyrendal, Lewis, and Petersen[43] show that the idea of a sinister, antihuman force allied with powers of darkness has been prevalent in nearly all known human societies. One of

---

[41] de Beauvoir, introduction to Marquis de Sade (1966, p. 20).   [42] Phillips (2005).
[43] Dyrendal et al. (2016).

the most malevolent forms is the idea of the "night witch" as an antihuman power, often depicted as part of an upside-down society of dark beings. The values and goals of this dark society are the opposite of the prevailing norms, as they invert sacredness and attempt to corrupt or destroy everything of value. Often these witches have been accused of spreading disease, killing children and cattle, promoting sin, and being affiliated with evil forces outside the community.

In their profound discussion of satanism, Dyrendal and colleagues distinguish two main categories: esoteric and rationalist versions. *Esoteric satanism* is theistic and is inspired by the esoteric traditions of Paganism, Western Esotericism, Hinduism, and Buddhism, among others, culminating in a religion of self-actualization. The existence of Satan is usually formulated in platonic or mystical terms, although he is not necessarily worshipped as a literal entity. Rather than a god to be worshipped, Satan is understood as a principle to be followed as a path to individual enlightenment.[44]

Rationalist satanism is explicitly atheistic, materialistic, and hedonistic. Representatives of this tradition consider Satan as a symbol of rebellion, carnality, and individual empowerment. Their materialist philosophy is fertile soil for the formation of an alien elite that pursues indulgence, vitality, and rational self-interest. Although ritual practices are performed and forms of diabolical anthropomorphism play some role from time to time, they function as metaphorical and pragmatic instruments of self-realization. Rational satanism embraces science, philosophy, and intuition as sources of authority and considers nonconformity as the highest goal of the individual.[45]

Looking at the current landscape, it is notable that satanism was practiced in the late 1960s and early 1970s in a variety of subcultural streams. It coincided with the emergence of the counterculture of that time, including the early New Age, the rise of the Human Potential Movement, the sexual revolution, the salience of leisure and consumption, flower power, and the revolutionary tendencies in mass higher education. All of them are incorporated in the makeup of satanism, which can be portrayed as a subcurrent within that milieu, rising as a dark or sinister counterculture as part of Western "occulture."[46]

A most remarkable figure who gave, from the 1960s onward, organizational form to modern rationalist satanism was Anton LaVey (1930–1997; Figure 2.3), an American author and musician born of an American father

---

[44] Ibid. (p. 6).   [45] Ibid.   [46] Ibid. (p. 3).

Figure 2.3   Church of Satan founder Anton LaVey.
Source: Bettmann/Getty Images.

and a mother of Eastern European origin. He was the subject of numerous articles in news media throughout the world, and he also appeared on many talk shows and in feature-length documentaries. According to some sources, he left high school to join a circus and subsequently worked, among other occupations, as a psychic and as a nightclub organist. He gained local celebrity in the San Francisco area as a dark, mysterious figure who rejected traditional Christian morality as hypocritical. He founded the Church of Satan on Walpurgis Night on April 30, 1966, and called himself its high priest. Three years later he published *The Satanic Bible*, his most influential work, in which he depicted the teachings and rituals of his church as a reversed religious institution.[47]

The Satanic Bible

LaVey's main work, *The Satanic Bible*, is a collection of essays, observations, and rituals, considered as the foundation of the philosophy and dogma of the Church of Satan. The "black pope" of this church, as he was

[47] *Encyclopedia Britannica*, www.britannica.com/biography/Anton-LaVey, May 14, 2022.

sometimes called in newspapers, praises the virtues of exploring one's own nature and instincts. He and his organization of contemporary Faustians presented themselves in two strikingly new identities. First, they sacrilegiously represented themselves as a "church", a term previously reserved for the branches of Christianity. Second, their black magic[48] was practiced openly instead of underground. In his works, LaVey realizes a radical reversal from what he considered as the false altruism of the mandatory love-thy-neighbor attitude and presents satanism as a blatantly selfish, brutal philosophy based on the belief that human beings are inherently selfish, violent creatures and that life is a Darwinian struggle for survival. This act of turning religion upside down is clearly expressed in the following text that is typical of his rebellious writing style:

> The first book of the Satanic Bible is not an attempt to blaspheme as much as it is a statement of what might be termed "diabolical indignation". The Devil has been attacked by the men of God relentlessly and without reservation. Never has there been an opportunity, short of fiction, for the Dark Prince to speak out in the same manner as the spokesmen of the Lord of the Righteous. The pulpit-pounders of the past have been free to define "good" and "evil" as they see fit, and have gladly smashed into oblivion any who disagree with their lies – both verbally and, at times, physically. Their talk of "charity", when applied to His Infernal Majesty, becomes an empty sham – and most unfairly, too, considering the obvious fact that without their Satanic foe their very religions would collapse. How sad, that the allegorical personage most responsible for the success of spiritual religions is shown the *least* amount of charity and the most consistent abuse – and by those who most unctuously preach the rules of fair play! For all the centuries of shouting down the Devil has received, he has never shouted back at his detractors. He has remained the gentleman at all times, while those he supports rant and rave. He has shown himself to be a model of deportment, but now he feels it is time to shout back. He has decided it is finally time to receive his due. Now the ponderous rule books of hypocrisy are no longer needed. In order to relearn the Law of the Jungle, a small, slim diatribe will do. Each verse is an inferno. Each word is a tongue of fire. The flames of Hell burn fierce . . . and purify![49]

LaVey emphasizes that the satanic religion has not merely taken the coin but has flipped it completely over. He is entirely and radically devoted to a reversed doctrine that he presents as a satanic philosophy that is not a white-light religion but a religion of the flesh, the mundane, the carnal,

---

[48] Black magic involves practices associated with the devil or with evil spirits (*Encyclopedia Britannica*, www.britannica.com/dictionary/black-magic, retrieved June 8, 2022).

[49] LaVey (1969, p. 15, pagination starts from the cover).

Figure 2.4   The Sigil of Baphomet is the official symbol of LaVeyan satanism and the Church of Satan.
Source: Maksym Malcev/iStock/Getty Images Plus.

ruled by Satan and embraced as the personification of the "Left Hand Path" (Figure 2.4).[50]

Like in the lives and works of Genet and Sade, we see in LaVey's case elements of a radical *reversal* from moral bad, as defined in the society in which he lives, into moral good. In his own words: "The seven deadly sins of the Christian Church are: greed, pride, envy, anger, gluttony, lust, and sloth. Satanism advocates indulging in each of these 'sins' as they all lead to physical, mental, or emotional gratification."[51] This reversal, including the intensification and justification of moral bad, is supported by *coalitions*. Similar to Genet, who celebrated his position as a criminal as a coalition with his position as a saint, LaVey uses religious terminology to heighten his identity as a worshipper of the carnal: "Say unto thine own heart, 'I am mine own redeemer.'"[52] And he aspires to be "the true worshipper of the highest and ineffable King of Hell!"[53] Like in Genet's and Sade's works, these coalitions allow him to become engaged in a process of *transpositioning*, transmitting the energy of worshipping to his infernal position in order to breathe extra life in it.

LaVey arrives in a process of a structural *over-positioning* of his nonconformity by recommending satanism as a selfish, brutal view of life, guided by the belief that human beings are essentially violent.[54] Finally, like

[50] Ibid. (p. 28).   [51] Ibid. (p. 25).   [52] Ibid. (p. 19).   [53] Ibid. (p. 91).
[54] Burton H. Wolfe in his introduction to LaVey (1969).

Genet and Sade, he is involved in a process of *anti-positioning* toward the morals of Christianity, as expressed in statements such as: "The pulpit-pounders of the past have been free to define 'good' and 'evil' as they see fit, and have gladly smashed into oblivion any who disagree with their lies."[55] As an advocate of the reversal of bad into good, LaVey systematically and necessarily clashes with the moral codes of the societies in which he lived.

Hypocrisy as a Challenge to the Mores of the Time

In the works of Genet, Sade, and LaVey, we find explicit or implicit criticisms of hypocrisy as a detestable aspect of the morality of their societies. Elaborating on this criticism, I will examine the phenomenon of hypocrisy as discussed in moral psychology and examine it from the perspective of moral multiplicity.

Writing about Genet's life and work, Jean-Paul Sartre notes that he (Genet) is living in a "strange society" in which individuals retain the trappings of striving for order and wish to disorganize it at the same time. Precisely because of "this hypocrisy," society presents an appearance of morals, values, rites, and prohibitions.[56] Criticism of society's hypocrisy is also apparent in Sade's work, as he savagely rejects the idea of submission to society's rules and he detests the hypocritical resignation that is adorned with the name of virtue. In submitting to these rules, people renounce both their authenticity and their freedom.[57] Most explicit is the theme of hypocrisy addressed by LaVey, who observed, from a young age onward, that "the Christian church thrives on hypocrisy, and that man's carnal nature will [come] out no matter how much it is purged or scourged by any white-light religion."[58] As a vital alternative he contends that Satan represents "undefiled wisdom, instead of hypocritical self-deceit!"[59] According to LaVey's commenters, his work breathes a "consuming disgust for hypocrisy."[60]

Hypocrisy is not only a serious topic in counter-ideologies, like those of Genet, Sade, and LaVey; it has also gained the interest of researchers in the field of moral psychology.[61] Paying attention to their research findings has the distinct advantage that we can learn how hypocrisy functions in the

---

[55] LaVey (1969, p. 15).   [56] Sartre (2012, p. 177).
[57] de Beauvoir, introduction to Marquis de Sade (1966, p. 72).   [58] LaVey (1969, p. 7).
[59] Ibid. (p. 57).   [60] Dyrendal et al. (2016, p. 83).   [61] Ellemers et al. (2019).

everyday lives of ordinary people and what means are available to reduce it (see the "Practical Implications" section at the end of this chapter).

In an influential study in the field of moral psychology, Batson and colleagues[62] started their experimental research by wondering whether the truism "moral principles motivate moral action" is really true. Although this maxim undergirds much teaching, preaching, parenting, and politicking, is there any evidence demonstrating that people who learn to value moral responsibility are more likely to act accordingly? In their doubts about the answer to this question, the researchers referred to some astute observers of the human condition such as the writers Jane Austen, Charles Dickens, and Mark Twain, who, like Genet, Sade, and LaVey, noted that highly valued morals often serve another master, one who provides convenient and high-sounding rationalizations for one's self-interest. Intrigued by these considerations, the investigators provided their research participants with two tasks: a so-called positive consequences task in which each correct response earned a raffle ticket and a neutral consequences task that was described as rather dull and boring in which each correct response delivered nothing worthwhile. Participants were free to assign the tasks to themselves or to another participant. It was found that sixteen out of the twenty participants assigned themselves to the positive consequences task, even though in retrospect only one of them said it was moral to do so. Apparently, the actual behavior of the participants was not in agreement with their avowed moral norms. On the basis of this study and review of other research projects on the discrepancy between moral beliefs and behavior, the investigators concluded: "Given that, on the one hand, participants tended to express great adherence to moral responsibility in their self-reports ... and that, on the other hand, when possible they acted in a way that had the surface appearance of morality yet still served self-interest, the label moral hypocrisy seems accurate – even unavoidable."[63]

Similarly, other researchers[64] became interested in another unsettling type of hypocrisy described as individuals' tendency to evaluate their own moral transgressions as substantially different from the same transgressions enacted by others. To investigate this assumption, they assigned their subjects to two different experimental conditions. In one of them, the subjects were required to distribute a resource (time and energy) to themselves and another person. They could do so either fairly (through a random allocation procedure) or unfairly (selecting the better option for themselves). After this manipulation, they were asked to evaluate the

[62] Batson et al. (1997).   [63] Ibid. (p. 1346).   [64] Valdesolo and DeSteno (2007).

fairness of their own actions. In the other condition, participants viewed a collaborator of the researcher acting in an unfair manner and subsequently evaluated the morality of this act. Hypocrisy was defined as the discrepancy between the judgments of the same unfair behavior when committed by the self or by the other. It appeared that individuals perceived their own unfairness to be less objectionable than the same unfairness enacted by another person, a finding that suggests that the individuals applied, hypocritically, moral evaluations of themselves that were not in line with the ones they applied to others.[65]

Moral mandates are typically formulated at an abstract level, as illustrated by LaVey's criticism of the mandatory love-thy-neighbor attitude. This awareness stimulated research[66] in which abstract and concrete notions of morality were compared. Why is this difference relevant? When we think about actions and events in a concrete and specific manner, we tend to concentrate on the specific details of the situation and are focused on the immediate experience. Conversely, if we think in a more abstract and general manner about a certain action or event, we focus on more global, overarching features that are more distant from the specific situation. An example might be illustrative. Participants in this kind of research were informed that, during an unexpectedly difficult exam, an opportunity arose to dishonestly copy some answers from another particularly bright student, without the risk of being caught. It was found that participants with a concrete focus (it happens here and now) found cheating equally acceptable for themselves as for others, meaning that they did not show hypocrisy. Yet, participants with an abstract focus (it happens at some future point in time) believed cheating was more acceptable for themselves than for others, suggesting that participants with an abstract focus showed a higher degree of hypocrisy. The author of this study[67] concludes with a general warning. He hypothesizes that people who routinely think in an abstract manner about moral issues are more susceptible to hypocrisy. This is particularly disturbing as it suggests, in his view, that officials who routinely base their behavior on an abstract set of rules, such as judges, police officers, or priests, are themselves the most susceptible to hypocrisy.

So far, I have presented three instances of the reversal of bad into good as a central theme in the works of Genet, Sade, and LaVey. All three of them, with LaVey's voice being the most pronounced, criticize hypocrisy

---

[65] For a treatment of hypocrisy in relation to the modularity of the mind, see Kurzban (2010).
[66] Lammers (2011).   [67] Ibid.

as a basic problem in mainstream religion and in the morals of their time. As a protest, they proposed the exaltation of moral bad as an equally one-sided alternative. In the following, I will argue that there is not simply one moral position at work in the self but rather a multiplicity of positions, in agreement with the basic thesis of DST that understands the self as a dynamic multiplicity of relatively autonomous I-positions in the society of mind, with the potential of dialogical relationships among them. Following this path, I will examine the nature of moral multiplicity and arrive at the conclusion that, perhaps to the surprise of some readers, *a certain degree* of hypocrisy is unavoidable when one finds oneself in the field of tension of moral multiplicity.

What is judged as immoral in one situation is permissible in another one

One of my neighbors has the key to my house and takes care of my mailbox and plants when I'm gone for a couple of days. Suppose that on my return I notice that one of the ten bonbons on my table had been removed. In this case, I would not mind; rather, I would smile, because this act of my neighbor would be for me within the realm of the permissible.

A few years ago, I was standing in a supermarket in front of a large bowl of delicious-looking, multicolored sweets for sale. I could not resist the temptation to take one in my hands and was about to bring it to my mouth when suddenly, like a jack-in-the-box, a staff member of the supermarket appeared next to me and shouted: "We should not do that!" Entirely embarrassed and shameful, I asked her, after a short moment of hesitation: "Should I put it back?" "Yes!" she said adamantly. Although the financial value of the tiny sweet in the supermarket was less than the value of the precious bonbon on my table, I was aware that I had broken the rules. Apparently, the general command "you shall not steal" is highly flexible, often implicit, and, in its behavioral implications, situation-dependent to a significant degree.

Moral Multiplicity and the Problem of Hypocrisy

Social psychologists[68] have proposed a *moral-pluralistic approach* that allows us to see that we often find ourselves in situations in which *different* moral positions (they call it "values") are salient and that these positions can often come into conflict interculturally, interpersonally, and even intrapersonally. An important implication of this approach is that enacting

---

[68] Graham et al. (2015).

upon one specific moral value might not be a normatively desired end goal for all people in all situations.

A most simple example of the simultaneity of conflicting moral positions is the phenomenon known as telling "white lies."[69] For example, people might tell their host that the meal they prepared was "great" or compliment a hairdresser that they like their unexpected "new look." Or Annabelle might invite her friend to have a look at the painting she has just finished. The friend thinks: "This is something my two-year-old daughter could make!" But she says: "Ah, your paining looks like a Paul Klee!" These little white lies that hide one's true evaluations are commonly told to ensure that the contact with an interaction partner proceeds smoothly without negative consequences for the relationship. That such lies are not infrequent was demonstrated in a consumer research project in which investigators administered a survey to restaurant guests. It appeared that 85 percent of the guests admitted to telling white lies when their dining experiences were not satisfactory but in fact told the server that their experience was good.[70]

What we usually call "tact" requires, certainly in situations of political disagreement and conflicts of interest, a subtle balance of being honest about one's purposes but, at the same time, avoiding any insult. This is well expressed in a statement ascribed to Winston Churchill: "Tact is the ability to tell someone to go to hell in such a way that they look forward to the trip."[71]

Telling white lies is a useful example of moving on the middle ground as the main theme of this book. Telling a white lie is located in a field of tension between honesty as a moral good and lying as morally rejectable. In the white lie scenario, good and bad coexist and even are reconciled. They allow the individual to keep the social relationship intact with only minimal dishonesty. The white lie is an acceptable coalition between two different positions: I as (slightly) dishonest and I as friendly.

In this context, we can ask: How are these findings related to hypocrisy? And, more crucially: What is the relationship between moving on the moral middle ground and hypocrisy? In order to answer this question, we have to realize that, as long as one is standing on the middle ground, there are at least two positions involved. In the example of white lies, one wants, at the same time, to be honest and friendly, but, as long as one is at this juncture, it is impossible to be either fully honest or fully friendly. One has

[69] Argo and Shiv (2012).   [70] Ibid.
[71] Goodreads, www.goodreads.com/quotes/33365-tact-is-the-ability-to-tell-someone-to-go-to.

to, at least to some extent, concede to the moral requirements of both positions, resulting in a compromise in which the values of both positions are only *partly* realized. As none of the values can be expressed fully, a certain degree of hypocrisy is unavoidable. One values honesty highly, but in the actual behavior one is not fully honest. Or, one wants to be friendly to others, but one is not completely friendly.[72]

Also, at the societal level, a compromise between different moral principles is, in specific situations, inescapable. Take the example[73] of a finance minister who has compelling reasons to devaluate the currency of the country. This measure has been prepared in deep secret in order to prevent speculators on the money market abusing their foresight. However, a journalist, who has a suspicion about what is going to happen, asks the minister if she is planning a currency devaluation. The minister, who may be a very truthful person, firmly denies this. And surprise! The next day the devaluation actually takes place. So, it is clear that she lied. Yet, whereas in other cases a discovered lie of the minister would cause great commotion, both the public and the parliament have full understanding of the minister's course of action. If the minister had acted on the principle that one should always and everywhere speak in full honesty, she would later be accused of having damaged the country's welfare. Apparently, there are *specific* situations in which a person in this particular position has to get their hands dirty.

The "dirty hands problem" has been, in sociological circles, a much-debated issue since Max Weber's classic publication *Politics as a Vocation*,[74] in which he makes a distinction between the "ethic of ultimate ends" (sometimes also called the "ethic of conviction") and the "ethic of responsibility." In Weber's view, those who follow an ethic of ultimate ends act on the basis of their moral convictions. They don't feel responsible for the negative consequences of their actions because they are interested in keeping alive the flame of their pure (good) intentions. Weber considers the adherents of this ethic "quite irrational," as their actions do not take into consideration the possible outcomes of their behavior and decisions. By contrast, those who act according to the ethic of responsibility "take account of precisely the average deficiencies of people."[75] Hence, these politicians regard themselves as responsible for the potentially undesired effects of their actions (like in the example of the

---

[72] See Andersen and Hovring (2020) for a view that emphasizes the value of hypocrisy for dialogical relationships.

[73] de Valk (2003).   [74] Weber (1946, p. 120).   [75] Ibid. (p. 121).

finance minister who had strong reasons to lie, at that particular moment, to the journalist).

Later commentators[76] have noted that Weber's discussion of the distinction between the two kinds of ethic is rather complex. On the one hand, he sees an "abysmal contrast" between the two kinds of ethic, arguing that "it is not possible to bring an ethic of ultimate ends and an ethic of responsibility under one roof . . ."[77] On the other hand, he claims that the two ethical orientations "are not absolute contrasts but rather supplements."[78] The two ethics, therefore, "seem to be both reciprocally implied and incompatible."[79] This observation has important implications for the concept of the moral middle ground as the main theme of this book. As I have demonstrated at the end of Chapter 1, we may find ourselves, in some situations and under specific circumstances, in a field of tension where moral good and bad are contrasting and conflicting but, at the same time, go hand in hand in mutually complementing ways. Or, to be responsible in a particular situation, one has to consider the *consequences* of one's decisions or actions, which makes it necessary to make concessions to the values to which one is dedicated. In order to act in a responsible way, the finance minister in our example has to find a compromise between her moral values and the equally valid moral demands of the situation. This means that, in such situations, a certain degree of hypocrisy is inescapable. In situations where it is required, an optimal use of hypocrisy helps us to avoid two pitfalls. First, when moral values are absent, the politician, or any power-holder, is at risk of sliding down the path toward opportunism, self-interest, and moral transgression. When, on the other hand, they act, always and in every situation, purely on the basis of their moral principles, they have to face the undesirable and potentially immoral consequences of their actions and decisions. In other words, to act in a responsible way means we are, in some specific situations, placed on the moral middle ground, where we are challenged to find the most optimal combination of moral good and bad.

What I want to argue is that, in some specific situations, acting in full agreement with some moral principle, without considering the undesirable consequences of this conduct, can be damaging to society. Actually, this is also valid for everyday situations in which pure honesty could cause damage to a significant other, with the risk that the precious relationship with this person might be broken. Moreover, in many situations not one

---

[76] See Pellizzoni (2018) for a review.   [77] Weber (1946, p. 122).   [78] Ibid. (p. 127).
[79] Pellizzoni (2018, p. 199).

but various values are involved; not only honesty, but also care! This value may justify the use of a white lie if it is considered necessary in a particular situation.

In my view, political scientist David Runciman[80] arrives at a conclusion that is worthy of consideration in this context: We should accept hypocrisy as an actual fact of politics but without resigning ourselves to it, let alone cynically embracing it. Instead of trying to eliminate and reject every form of hypocrisy, he recommends *distinguishing between harmless and harmful forms of hypocrisy.* The range in between those is huge and extends far beyond political discourse. At one end we can place a politician who preaches peace and dialogue in the service of useful image-building but, at the same time, relentlessly and systematically murders his political opponents. At the other end we see a person who is "keeping up appearances" to preserve a precious relationship.

The Danger of Acting on the Basis of Just One Moral Position

What happens when one's behavior is guided by just one moral position? In an article on the "dark side of morality," Skitka and Mullen[81] discussed events like the September 11, 2001, terrorist attacks on the World Trade Center and the Pentagon. They wondered what could possibly motivate people to embark on such an incredibly horrific mission that involves not only a strong motivation to be a martyr for one's cause, but also a willingness to take the lives of untold numbers of innocent human beings. Without any doubt, the people at the front lines of these attacks had strong beliefs about their own cause. But what happened on the side of the American people?

Gallup polls in September 2001 indicated that many Americans were willing to forego numerous civil liberties or restrict the civil liberties of others in response to the terrorist attacks. The polls showed that 58 percent of Americans favored subjecting Arabs, including those who were US citizens, to more intensive security checks. Moreover, the polls indicated a widespread desire for vengeance: 92 percent of Americans supported taking military action and 65 percent endorsed going to war, even if it would be at the cost of American casualties.[82]

---

[80] Runciman (2008).   [81] Skitka and Mullen (2002).
[82] Ibid. Note that a Gallup poll taken at a later date might have given different results, since the time frame plays an important role here.

In their reflections on the responses of US citizens to the polls, the researchers[83] introduced the concept of "moral mandates," which they defined as "the specific attitude positions or stands that people develop out of a moral conviction that something is right or wrong, moral or immoral."[84] They propose that such moral mandates share the features of other strong attitudes – extremity, importance, and certainty – but they are imbued with moral conviction, which serves an added motivational and action component. Such conviction motivates them to strongly support waging war against nations that harbor terrorists or efforts to help those who were harmed by the attacks. Moral mandates are most likely to be expressed when people are under threat or when they feel the need to prove to themselves or others that their moral position is authentic.

At the time when I'm writing this book, the Russia–Ukraine war is already several months underway. Every day we are overwhelmed by an endless series of alarming messages and we – me and the people around me – are shocked by the continuous updates about atrocities and war crimes. The beginning date of this war, February 24, 2022, will be as deeply engraved in the memories of many of us as is the 9/11 terrorist attack. I wonder continuously what is going on in the mind of the man, President Putin, who decided to invade a sovereign state and not only kill many of the brave Ukraine soldiers and citizens, but also sacrifice many of his own innocent and ignorant fighters. What justifies in his mind all these atrocities, economic losses, and the far-reaching isolation of his country? (See Chapter 3 for an extensive exploration of Putin's worldview.) At this point, I restrict myself to the question regarding which positions might play a role in his justification of all these acts and consequences. I guess that at least three positions form a basis of his behavior: (1) Like many aggressors, he places himself in a *victim position* of the growing economic capacity of the EU and what he sees as the aggressively advancing NATO members that have enlarged their influence, even in countries that previously belonged to the Soviet Union; (2) as a response, he takes an *accusing position*, placing the EU and NATO as responsible for these developments, which allows him to take a strong anti-position and serves as a justification of his aggression and violence; and (3) he places himself in a *savior position*: Driven by the utopian ideal of restoring the Tsarist empire of the past and purifying the united Great Russia, he invaded successively Chechnya, Georgia, and Crimea, supported President Assad in Syria, and now has invaded Ukraine in order to "denazify" the country. Together, these positions

---

[83] Skitka and Mullen (2002).   [84] Ibid. (p. 37).

may serve as Putin's justification of a war that is apparently supported by a considerable part of Russia's population, indoctrinated by a propaganda machine that tolerates no counter-position in the form of dissidence or public criticism. Is he involved in a process of over-positioning, as we have already noticed in the cases of Genet, Sade, and LaVey?

We have seen over the course of history that utopian ideals demonstrate the far-reaching consequences of a lack of moral multiplicity. Utopian ideals typically start from good or noble intentions, but, after their institutionalization, they may transform, via a process of over-positioning, into "giant monsters." As history abundantly makes clear, many social, political, and religious utopias have nurtured the illusion of complete purity, goodness, and perfection as the *end position* of an idealized society. This final salvation might be realized by transforming the imperfect society into a heaven of ultimate redemption. The Christian belief expects to achieve this final aim by promising an eternal afterlife, a mission that has produced institutions that caused rampant wars and led to the extermination of heretics, legitimized by the moral conviction that they were inherently evil. Communism, in its protest against religion as the opium of the masses, painted the vistas of a class-free society of freedom but ultimately led to the mass executions of the Stalin regime. The supremacist ideology of Nazism envisioned an ideal society in which only one race, the Aryan race, was depicted as a superclass, but this ideal resulted in the disaster of the Holocaust. Neoliberal capitalism preached the message of salvation of the free market but has resulted in worldwide exploitation of the earth, poverty of large parts of the world's population, and sharp economic divides. Some trends in Islam consider the original teachings of Mohammed "holy," but in their political manifestation they produced the horrors of killing "unbelievers." (For Putin's utopic ideal, see Chapter 3.) Taken together, many generations are educated by institutions spreading beliefs in "pure religion," "pure race," "pure liberty," and even the "pure ideology of the free market," all of them propagated as moral goodness but associated with a simultaneous blindness to their shadowy sides. These shadows should not simply be considered as undesirable side effects of a valuable aim, but as potentials inherent to the original, mono-positional ideal. The problem with such ideals is that they lack moral multiplicity and the dynamic influence of counter-positions that prevent any conviction or moral mandate from succumbing to a process of over-positioning of the original impulse. When thinking about utopias and their moral mandates, it may be relevant to quote social psychologists Walter Mischel and Harriet Mischel, who remarked:

History is replete with atrocities that were justified by invoking the highest principles and that were perpetrated upon victims who were equally convinced of their own moral principles. In the name of justice, of the common welfare, of universal ethics, and of God, millions of people have been killed and whole cultures destroyed. In recent history, concepts of universal right, equality, freedom, and social equity have been used to justify every variety of murder including genocide.[85]

In order to avoid an unlimited process of over-positioning of the moral mandates of utopias and ideologies, the recognition and appreciation of moral differences, contradictions, and alternative points of view are needed as invitations to productive and innovative dialogue based on processes of positioning, counter-positioning, and repositioning (see Chapter 6).

At this point in the book, I want to emphasize that the recognition and awareness of the existence of a moral middle ground has the advantage that good and bad are brought close together so that they can "touch each other." This contact exists in the experience of conflict between them, seeing their contradictions, and feeling their tensions. Such contradictions might motivate people to "stand still" for a while to consider and reconsider the contradictions among their different moral positions and stimulate a dialogue that allows one to move from the one position to another and back so that there is opportunity for perspective change (for elaboration, see Chapter 5). This is very different from situations in which people adhere unthinkingly to abstract moral principles and, moreover, don't see the discrepancies between these principles and their actual behavior, as researchers in the field of moral psychology have demonstrated (described earlier in this chapter).

Practical Implications

On the practical level, I see three significant implications of this chapter for the development of human morality: the role of self-awareness, perspective-taking, and increasing moral multiplicity.

Self-Awareness

Explorations in the field of moral psychology show that self-awareness manipulations have been found to heighten awareness of discrepancies between one's own behavior and relevant personal standards, which has

---

[85] Mischel and Mischel (1976), quoted by Skitka and Mullen (2002, p. 39).

the effect of creating pressure to act in accord with standards. Researchers[86] have found that self-awareness leads to a decrease in transgressing behavior. When subjects were given the opportunity to cheat on an anagram task while seated in front of a mirror and listening to their own tape-recorded voice, they cheated much less (only 7 percent of them cheated) than participants who did the same task but were not made self-aware (71 percent cheated of those who did not observe themselves in a mirror). Building on this research, Daniel Batson and his team[87] became interested in the question of what would be the effect of self-awareness on hypocrisy. They used the same positive consequences task already described earlier in this chapter, in which each correct response gave the participants a reward. The participants were free to assign the interesting task to themselves or to another participant. The investigators found that having participants assign the tasks while facing themselves in a mirror eliminated the moral hypocrisy effect. In that condition, the participants assigned the task to the other and themselves in a fair way.

Such results are relevant to the notion of the I-position in DST. I-positions, like I as fair or I as cheating, have the possibility of making actors become self-aware of these positions and the behavior that is associated with them. The I of the I-position serves as a "mirror" for the self: Is it morally right to do this and is my behavior in concordance with my moral standards? The I-ness of the I-position provides an opportunity for self-evaluation, self-reflection, and correction of one's actual position and behavior in light of one's moral standards.

Perspective-Taking

In a later study, Batson and colleagues[88] were interested in the question of whether perspective-taking could be a profitable way of reducing hypocrisy. Their strategy was inspired by a range of religious teachers, moral philosophers, and moral psychologists, with the religious prescription of the Golden Rule as the most well-known moral device: "Do unto others as you would have them do unto you" (e.g. the gospel of Matthew in the New Testament: Matthew 7:12). This rule invites a form of perspective-taking in which you empathically place yourself in the other's position. Presumably, imagining how you would like to be treated provides the standard for how you should treat the other, leading you to consider the other's interests as well as your own. The investigators also referred to

[86] Diener and Wallbom (1976).   [87] Batson et al. (1999).   [88] Batson et al. (2003).

philosopher Mark Johnson,[89] who emphasized the moral significance of perspective-taking in his analysis of moral imagination and argued that moral insight and sensitivity require one to imagine how it is to stand in someone else's shoes. Similarly, they mentioned the work of developmental psychologist Lawrence Kohlberg,[90] who made perspective-taking or role-taking integral to his cognitive-developmental analysis of morality.

In their own research, Batson and colleagues[91] placed their subjects in a situation in which they could either accept a rewarding task (the already-mentioned positive consequence task) while the other participant received nothing or, as an alternative, change the assignment so they and the other both would each receive moderately positive rewards. In this situation, the results showed that imagining oneself in the other's position did significantly increase moral action. At the conclusion of a series of experiments, the investigators referred to a dimension that may be significant to moral behavior: the symmetry or asymmetry of the needs of self and other. Many situations of moral conflict are symmetrical, which means that your wishes and the wishes of the other are much the same. In such situations, putting yourself in the position of the other may not do much to help you to act in a moral way. You may focus on your own wishes, making it likely that you will ignore the wishes of the other, running the risk of acting in moral hypocrisy. In contrast, in an asymmetrical situation in which you are in a position of advantage, imagining yourself in the other's shoes has a higher probability of stimulating moral action, as was demonstrated in the experiment in which the other participant gets nothing of value. So, religious teachers, moral philosophers, and psychologists may be right that imagining yourself in the other's position stimulates moral action in agreement with one's own moral standards. However, as the aforementioned research suggests, this imagination is particularly effective in asymmetrical conditions.

Perspective-taking is basic to DST, particularly to the notion of the-other-in-the-self, which indicates the other as an external (extended) position in the self. This theory does not assume that actual others in one's social environment are automatically part of the extended self. Only individuals, groups, or aspects of nature that are appropriated by the self as having personal significance function as its external positions and evoke positive and/or negative emotions.[92] An important consequence is that, when the other is appropriated as part of the self and when there is an emotional involvement or attachment in the relationship with the other,

---

[89] Johnson (1993).   [90] Kohlberg (1976).   [91] Batson et al. (2003).   [92] James (1890).

there is a higher chance that the individual will be willing to place themselves in the position of the other. However, when the range (bandwidth) of external positions is rather limited (e.g. the self is attached only to a small circle of family members or friends), then it is more difficult to take the position of the other, particular when the other is unfamiliar or seen as a "stranger."[93] In order to correct this social myopia, it makes sense to look for theoretical and practical ways to expand the moral circle in the external domain of one's position repertoire beyond one's limited group of significant others. And to realize this purpose, DST presents a model of four levels of identity associated with increasing circles of inclusiveness: the individual, social, human, and ecological levels.[94] This model has the potential of correcting a bias in mainstream theories of morality. Social psychologists, biologists, and evolutionary scientists have documented numerous examples of selfless and empathic behaviors as relevant to the origins of human morality. However, the main focus of such work is on the topics of fairness, empathy, or altruism in face-to-face contacts, in situations where individuals typically know and depend on each other.[95] Therefore, in order to expand morality beyond the individual and group levels, I will in Chapter 6 outline an extended identity model in which moral considerations at the human and ecological identity levels are paramount.

Moral Multiplicity

A general moral guideline for reducing hypocrisy is *avoiding basing one's moral mandates on one superordinate or end position*. Utopic visions in particular tend to culminate in an idealized end position that excludes any critical counter-position and, moreover, leads to deceptive forms of hypocrisy. The Christian rule "love thy neighbor" has not protected numerous people from the Inquisition, religious wars, and the mass killing of "heretics." Communism, which originally was egalitarian, finally produced a society in which unwelcome dissidents were punished by sending them to penal camps in Siberia. At the time of writing this book, news is spreading that Russian lawmakers have drafted legislation that punishes "false information" about the Kremlin's war in Ukraine with up to fifteen years in prison. Such measures not only cause anxiety across the whole nation, but also stimulate people to pay lip service to authorities in hypocritical ways.

[93] Schellhammer (2019).   [94] Hermans (2022).   [95] Ellemers et al. (2019).

In order to reduce hypocrisy, it is helpful to consider another moral position that is deviant from one's spontaneous impulses before making a decision and going into action. If one feels the tendency to act on the basis of *one* moral position, it is recommended to act *after* placing oneself in an alternative or conflicting position in oneself or in another individual instead of taking that position as the only mandate for action. As soon as moral positions are involved in mutual dialogical relationships, over-positioning in the direction of one exclusive end position is thus prevented. In such cases, different positions can, at an early stage, complement, criticize, and correct each other so that alternative moral pathways are not excluded or do not fall outside one's vision as a result of the moral blindness of a mono-positional stance.

From the perspective of moral multiplicity, the moral middle ground is a special case, as it is morally ambiguous. The examples of white lies outlined earlier in this chapter demonstrate that in such cases it is not possible to avoid hypocrisy entirely. When telling a white lie, one is not totally honest and not entirely friendly, but instead is somewhere in the middle. Therefore, I assume that hypocrisy cannot be avoided entirely in every form of human communication. I suppose that, from a moral point of view, it is better to strive to *deal* with hypocrisy than to eradicate it. Self-awareness, self-dialogue, and dialogue with other persons have the potential of generating new thinking and of stimulating the exploration of areas where potential answers to hypocrisy can be found.

Summary

In this chapter, I discussed some of the main works of three authors as significant examples of visions that advocate a radical reversal from moral bad to moral good: Jean Genet, Marquis de Sade, and Anton LaVey. All three of them, most explicitly LaVey, accuse society of being morally hypocritical. Expanding on this characterization, I referred to empirical research vis-à-vis hypocrisy in the psychology of morality. This led to the presentation of a moral-pluralistic approach that allows us to see that we often find ourselves in situations in which different moral positions are prominent and can come into conflict with each other. Along these lines, I argued that moral pluralism is an essential characteristic of the moral middle ground. As a demonstration, I used white lies as an everyday example and referred to Max Weber's "ethic of responsibility" as a sociological concept that is particularly relevant to political leadership. Then, the mono-positionality of some utopian visions was criticized, as such visions are focused on one ideal end position that does not allow counter-positions or alternative points of view to be expressed, thereby preventing the emergence of meaningful moral dialogue and dialogical selves. As practical implications of this chapter, I offered three guidelines for dealing with hypocrisy: the roles of self-awareness, perspective-taking, and the stimulation of moral multiplicity.

CHAPTER 3

Rejecting Bad via Externalization

> Dictatorships start wars because they need external enemies to exert internal control over their own people.
>
> Richard Perle[1]

From February 24, 2022, onward, Ukrainian cities were hit by Russian missiles and destroyed by its army, resulting in mass civilian casualties and huge numbers of refugees fleeing across the border to Poland. Soon thereafter, Putin had to face accusations of following in the footsteps of Hitler, the reviled former leader of Germany. After Europe entered its biggest crisis since World War II (WWII), the hashtag #PutinHitler began trending on social media. In a Voice of America broadcast,[2] Jonathan Katz, a German Marshall Fund senior fellow and director of Democracy Initiatives, declared that Putin "is this century's equivalent to Hitler, and the threat he poses to Europe, U.S. and global security extends far beyond the current conflict in Ukraine." The same broadcast quotes Rabbi Abraham Cooper, Associate Dean of the Simon Wiesenthal Center, a Jewish human rights organization, who says: "Tragically, what the world is witnessing today invokes memories of the Nazi Blitzkrieg." "To be clear, no one is accusing Vladimir Putin of preparing death camps and gas chambers. But the brutality of the Russian military in invading a peaceful neighbor that includes indiscriminate targeting of civilians and decimating cities evokes memories of Nazi armies invading the USSR (Soviet Union) in 1941."[3]

I feel a strong need to bring Hitler and Putin together in one chapter for personal and historical reasons. I was born in the Netherlands before WWII and witnessed as a young child both the presence of the Nazis in my hometown and the celebration of its liberation by the American army. In the aftermath of WWII, I and many with me thought that we had

---

[1] Brainy Quote, November 29, 2022.   [2] Herman (2022).   [3] Ibid.

learned so much from this dehumanizing disaster that we did not believe that this could ever happen again.[4] Yet, in the same Europe, it happened again when Putin started his invasion in Ukraine and used a propaganda machine similar to that of Hitler. Now, having arrived in the final stage of my life, I reflect on the atrocities of the recent war. The shocking events – WWII and the Ukraine war – motivated me to pose the question to myself of what is going on in the minds of those leaders and also in the selves of all those citizens who are willing to support them. In particular, I wanted to know what are the deeper *commonalities* in the social construction of the identities of citizens who are more than eighty years removed from each other yet subjected to the same processes that led to destruction and war.[5]

Four commonalities that shape these identities will be distinguished: the ideal of purity, the process of dehumanization, the risky combination of internal unity and external division, and enemy image construction. I call them "the four dead ends" of identity construction, as they carry the seeds of aggression, violence, and genocide and obstruct any opportunity for dialogue. During this exploration, I will frequently create bridges between the four dead ends and findings in the psychology of morality in order to understand what is happening in the selves of individual people. Moreover, I will draw relationships between the four dead ends and Dialogical Self Theory (DST) and explore what this theory can learn from these phenomena and what it can contribute to their further understanding. From these insights I will draw some practical implications.

Hitler's Worldview

Adolf Hitler (1889–1945; Figure 3.1), *Der Führer* (The Leader), was an Austrian-born German politician who was the dictator of Germany from 1933 until his death in 1945. He rose to power as the leader of the Nazi Party and became the *Kanzler* (chancellor) of Germany in 1933. During his dictatorship, he initiated WWII in Europe by invading Poland on

---

[4] A nationwide survey in the USA released on January 25, 2023, revealed a "worrying lack of basic Holocaust knowledge" among adults under forty years of age, including over one in ten respondents who did not recall ever having heard the word "Holocaust" before. The survey, the first fifty-state survey of Holocaust knowledge among millennials and Generation Z, showed that many respondents were unclear about the basic facts of the genocide: www.nbcnews.com/news/world/survey-finds-shocking-lack-holocaust-knowledge-among-millennials-gen-z-n1240031.

[5] For a historical analysis of Hitler's Nazi Germany, see Goldhagen (1996).

Figure 3.1   Hitler with his *"Heil"* salute.
Source: Heinrich Hoffmann/Archive Photos/Getty Images.

September 1, 1939. He was the central figure in the Holocaust, the genocide of about six million Jews and millions of other victims, including gypsies and citizens from Slavic countries.

After his father (Alois Hitler) retired, Adolf spent most of his childhood in Linz in Upper Austria, which remained his favorite city throughout his life. He feared and disliked his father but was a devoted son to his beloved mother, who died in 1907 after suffering from breast cancer. Unsuccessful as a student, he never advanced beyond a secondary education. After leaving school, he visited Vienna and then returned to Linz, where he dreamed of becoming a painter. Although he had some artistic qualities, he twice failed to get accepted by the Academy of Fine Arts. For some years he lived a lonely and isolated life and earned a living by painting postcards and illustrations for advertisements. At that time, Hitler already showed some traits that characterized his later life: social isolation and secretiveness. Preferring a bohemian mode of life, he strongly disliked cosmopolitanism and the multinational character of Vienna.[6]

---

[6] Encyclopedia Britannica, www.britannica.com/biography/Adolf-Hitler, retrieved April 20, 2022.

Hitler's Experience of Germany's Capitulation

According to one of the leading scholars of Nazi Germany, Ian Kershaw,[7] Hitler's *Weltanschauung* was the rationalization of a deeper, more profound feeling that was buried inside him: a burning thirst for revenge against those who had destroyed all that he considered to be morally good. This feeling found its origin in the immense carnage of World War I (WWI; 1914–1918), in which he was involved as a committed and courageous soldier, fanatical about the German cause, an experience that had given him a strong purpose for the first time in his life. His mission was already expressed in one of the letters he wrote from the front, in 1915, in which he spoke of making a huge sacrifice in the service of producing a postwar homeland "purer and cleansed of alien influence."[8] The unexpected news of Germany's capitulation in November 1918 that reached him while he was in a hospital recovering from mustard gas poisoning appeared to be utterly traumatizing to him. This news hit him like a sledgehammer blow in a phase of his life in which he had identified his personal fate wholly with that of the German Reich. Those who had undermined Germany's national prestige and reduced it to shame would have to pay for it. This personal fire within him was never extinguished after that.

Driven by his personal fire and ambition, Hitler fanatically pursued two goals that were closely interlinked: restoring Germany's greatness after the shameful capitulation in 1918 and taking revenge on those responsible for the national humiliation that his nation had to suffer as a result of the Treaty of Versailles of 1919. As he repeatedly remarked, this humiliation could only be responded to "by the sword." In his view, those who were responsible for these most terrible crimes of all time, for the "stab in the back" of the capitulation, were the Jews. He despised them as the main carriers of capitalism in Wall Street and the City of London and also as the hidden forces behind Bolshevism, the communist form of government adopted in Russia following the Bolshevik revolution of 1917. Given his unshakable belief in the fiction of the "Jewish World Conspiracy," he saw them as his main enemies who would always block his path and frustrate his plans of restoring the worth of the German nation. Therefore, a persistent fight against international Jewry would be needed as a way to realize the final restoration of Germany's worth and pride.[9] Along these lines, Hitler arrived at a situation of toxic anti-positioning against Judaism, which he feared and despised as the ultimate evil.

---

[7] Kershaw (2008).   [8] Ibid. (p. 90).   [9] Ibid. (p. 91).

Young Hitler

As biographer Paul Ham notes in his book *Young Hitler*,[10] writing about him is notoriously difficult, because every word or phrase is conditioned by the horrible fact of the Holocaust. There are events in his early life that would humanize him, such as his love for his mother, his friendships with Jews in Vienna, and his respect for the Jewish doctor who treated his mother. However, such biographical details only seem unusual or surprising in the light of the events that followed. Ham wonders if one should attempt to humanize him, as for some individuals it would be morally obscene to try to imagine Hitler as a boy, a youth, a soldier. For them, he should always exclusively be marked as the monster of the Holocaust. However, the problematic side of this attitude is that we learn nothing from this kind of thinking. The deeply unsettling fact, Ham continues, is that, in many ways, Hitler was human – all too human. His thinking was influenced by the ways many people think, then and now. His worldview was a motley mixture of popular notions, partly contrived by himself and partly appropriated from others, as he himself admitted. He collected his early, distorted views on social Darwinism and pan-Germanism, including views on race and the Jews, from popular newspapers and Viennese politicians. And some of those politicians were as extreme in their expressions of anti-Semitism as Hitler would later become.

It is all too easy and lazy to brand Hitler as a monster, a psychotic killer, the incarnation of evil, and then walk away, Ham continues, as if we have understood his personal influence as the main cause of the war. The unsettling truth is that Hitler personified the attitudes of significant parts of the population and still does so in many parts of the world. The historical truth is that feelings of violent nationalism in combination with hatred for easily scapegoated minorities were so deeply ingrained in Germany after WWI that there was fertile soil for the rise of a politician who would later articulate and enact those feelings. Yet, his character was far from ordinary. He possessed an iron will, a formidable memory, a talent for mass manipulation, and a rare charisma as a public speaker. His ferociously anti-Semitic speeches reflected the feelings of many Germans after WWI, when national humiliation in combination with an acute economic crisis brought otherwise civilized people to support an individual who, in more peaceful and prosperous times, would have been rejected as a delusional crank.[11]

---

[10] Ham (2014).   [11] Ibid.

Hitler's Friendship

We can learn a bit more about the special character of young Hitler when we listen to the story of August Kubizek, a fifteen-year-old school dropout at that time, who met Hitler at the opera in Linz in 1904. Kubizek, nine months older than Hitler, became his only one teenage friend. They met by the colonnades at the back of a theatre, and he portrayed Hitler in this way: "He was a remarkably pale, skinny youth who was following the performance with glistening eyes. I surmised that he came from a better-class home, for he was always dressed with meticulous care and was very reserved."[12] Neither of the boys followed sport or showed much interest in girls. Although it has been suggested, they were not homosexual. They regularly attended the Linz performances and shared a love of opera, chiefly Wagner.

Kubizek's memoir, written in 1951,[13] is regarded as an authentic document about Hitler's youth, as Ian Kershaw and other historians have attested. Although it may be subjected to the judgment of hindsight and may contain errors of emphasis, it accurately portrays in well-edited prose their lopsided friendship. Hitler was running the show as the braggart, poseur, and man-about-town, while the modest Kubizek took the position of the self-effacing acolyte and patient listener. When they were walking together, Hitler delivered long speeches on any subject that fascinated him, and he did so with a verbal dexterity that astonished Kubizek. It may be revealing how young Hitler, portrayed by Kubizek, was already in his younger years dedicated to opinions that expressed strong convictions:

> These speeches, Kubizek recalled, usually delivered somewhere in the open, seemed to be like a volcano erupting. It was as though something quite apart from him was bursting out of him. Such rapture I had only witnessed so far in the theatre, when an actor had to express some violent emotions, and at first, confronted by such eruptions, I could only stand gaping and passive, forgetting to applaud. But soon I realised that this was not play-acting. No, this was not acting, not exaggeration, this was really felt, and I saw that he was in dead earnest ... Not what he said impressed me first, but how he said it. This to me was something new, magnificent. I had never imagined that a man could produce such an effect with mere words. All he wanted from me, however, was one thing – agreement.[14]

Ham adds that "[d]uring these interminable tirades Hitler showed no sense of humour or humility, a trait this deadly earnest youth would carry

---

[12] Ibid. (p. 13, Kindle edition).   [13] Ham (2014).   [14] Ibid. (p. 14).

into manhood."[15] This is what Hitler, and many dictators with him, lacked: a sense of humor and the ability to put things into perspective. Humor functions as a temporary break of any strong opinion, conviction, self-aggrandizement, and self-inflation. It facilitates stepping out from your favorite position into one that enables you to share a smile about what you said a moment ago. Humor takes you across the border of your usual position and stimulates looking at it from another perspective. Humor works as a stop signal that prevents continuing, in a linear way, on the road of over-positioning, resulting in blindness to alternative positions. It seems that Hitler, already by his adolescence, lacked this self-relativizing sense of humor in the monological speeches that he would use effectively later in his life to seduce his audience to moving into just one dominating political position only. Hitler's device seemed to be: Reject any multiplicity of positions and avoid any alternative routes.

Hitler's Models

To understand how the young Hitler developed into a fierce anti-Semite, we need to know who the main figures were who strongly influenced his developing political ideas or, in DST terms, who served as significant external positions in his extended self. Two Viennese politicians and radicals served as his touchstones: the pan-German leader, Georg Ritter von Schönerer, and Vienna's mayor, Dr. Karl Lueger. In *Mein Kampf,* Hitler would portray them as admirable failures, as he learned important lessons from them but, at the same time, was aware of their weaknesses. Paul Ham describes Schönerer, a once-popular leader of the pan-German movement, as anti-Catholic, anti-Habsburg, antiliberal, and a fierce anti-Semite. He propagated the elimination of the Jewish influence in all areas of public life. He anointed himself "*Führer*" and insisted on the "*Heil*" greeting, but he had a limited appeal beyond his immediate, dwindling circle. He received a humiliating twenty votes in the 1911 elections. Later, Hitler realized that Schönerer made two chief mistakes. He ignored the importance of mass appeal and he did not offer his followers a fixed outgroup on whom to focus their hatred. Later, as *Führer*, Hitler acted on these "lessons" by mobilizing a powerful propaganda machine and turning the full wrath of the Nazis on the Jews as his main target.[16]

Dr Lueger, Vienna's mayor from 1897 to 1910, the so-called Lord of Vienna, had a formidable, practical influence on young Hitler. As a fully-

[15] Ibid.   [16] Ham (2014).

fledged pan-German, he sought to preserve the city's Germanness in a sea of racial chaos. Hitler was greatly impressed by Lueger's extraordinary oratory, coupled with his simple slogans such as "Vienna is German and must remain German!" Or "Greater Vienna must not turn into Greater Jerusalem!"[17] He knew how to focus all his voters' frustrations on one powerful movement – anti-Semitism – in this way reducing everything that went wrong to one simple formula: The Jew is to blame. He pretended to defend Christianity against "a new Palestine," appealing to the ancient Catholic hatred of these "Christ killers," and he rallied his voters against the "press Jews," "stock exchange Jews," "ink Jews" (intellectuals), and "beggar Jews" (eastern immigrants). Lueger exploited the Jews as a kind of political glue to unite citizens from different circles in a classless social movement. Ham shows that, through Lueger, the young Hitler received an absorbing tutorial in the art of political persuasion and, in particular, the power of oratory and propaganda. However, Lueger never went to the extreme. He had powerful Jewish friends and never thwarted Jewish businesses. Therefore, Hitler would later take a more radical position and ominously dismissed Lueger's anti-Semitism as a half-hearted sham.[18]

Ham concludes that these public figures influenced Hitler's early thinking, but they did not entirely dominate it, and they did not serve as pure role models for him. He was nobody's disciple. Although he admired them, he neither joined their parties nor agreed with everything they said. Rather, he extracted the elements that appealed to him and further confirmed his emerging prejudices. Hitler later claimed his Vienna years as having formed the "granite foundation" of his political struggle against world Jewry and Marxism. In *Mein Kampf*, he validated retrospectively his life as a heroic path from an impoverished artist to political thinker, culminating in his position as a revolutionary leader.

The emergence of a figurehead such as Hitler and his dramatic role in history cannot be adequately understood on the basis of any personality characteristic, personality dysfunction, or psychiatric disease alone. At least such explanations should be complemented with an analysis of influential examples or models that served as powerful sources of inspiration for Hitler in his rise to dictatorship. Politicians such as Schönerer and Lueger were not simply relevant "sources of information" to him. Rather, they were incorporated as ambivalent external positions in his developing self. He identified with them and, at the same time, criticized

---

[17] Ibid. (p. 29, Kindle edition).   [18] Ibid.

them because they did not go far enough. He wanted to become a "better Schönerer" and a "better Lueger." They showed him the right direction, but he had to go his own way on the road to over-positioning, finally ending up hiding in a bunker under his headquarters in Berlin, where he committed suicide by swallowing a cyanide capsule and shooting himself in the head on April 30, 1945.

In his book *Het Dictator Virus: Slecht Voorbeeld Doet Slecht Volgen* (*The Dictator Virus: Bad Example Makes Bad Following*),[19] the Dutch independent consultant Frank Schaper provides an extensive list of dictators across history ranging from Alexander the Great (Macedonia, fourth century BCE) to contemporary dictators such as Bashar al-Assad (Syria), Viktor Orbán (Hungary), Recep Tayyip Erdoğan (Turkey), Vladimir Putin (Russia), Xi Jinping (China), and others. He draws "evolution lines" along which the dictator virus spreads across history. For example, Alexander the Great was a model for Napoleon, who, in turn, influenced, among others, Vladimir Putin, who figured as an example for Viktor Orbán. He summarized such influences in terms of a "role model effect": Dictators mirror the aspirations of preceding autocratic leaders as shining examples and imitate or elaborate on their political ideals and leadership styles. Moreover, Schaper observes that many such "strong leaders" evade term limits and extend their hold on power as long as possible by suspending elections and reducing civil liberties. In DST terms, such leaders don't allow space for the development of counter-positions (with views *different* from their own), permitting themselves to continue on the road of over-positioning in the direction of an idealized end position (see Chapter 2).

In the next part of this chapter, I want to explore more extensively Hitler's worldview by referring to some parts in *Mein Kampf*, focusing on four themes that pop up in his document: purification, dehumanization, internal unity/external division, and enemy image construction. In order to provide a broader perspective on dictatorship, I will link Hitler's role in the previous century with the political aspirations of Putin in the present century. I will show that the same four themes also underlie the speeches of Putin, as discussed in the writings of authors who comment on his political position. I then present some theoretical and empirical work on the same themes in the psychology of morality. Along these lines, my wish is to create linkages between the political views of major figures, such as Hitler and Putin, with the moral inclinations of "normal" individuals as they are studied in social scientific research.

[19] Schaper (2015).

Purification

The purity of a first love can elevate us to heaven, we are touched by the innocence of a child, and we are deeply impressed by the purity of a natural scene. Personally, I experience pure joy when I listen to Bach's Badinerie as part of his Suite no. 2. However, purity as the aim of a political ideology can bring us to the deepest layers of hell. Let's have a look at the example of Hitler.

In his book *Mein Kampf,* Hitler looks for the fundament of racial purity in nature. In his view, nature takes certain measures to correct the obnoxious effect of racial mixture, and he makes sure that nature is not in favor of the mongrel. He predicts that "[t]he later products of cross-breeding have to suffer bitterly, especially the third, fourth and fifth generations. Not only are they deprived of the higher qualities that belonged to the parents who participated in the first mixture, but they also lack definite will-power and vigorous vital energies owing to the lack of harmony in the quality of their blood."[20] And he adds that people of mixed blood are not only relatively inferior to people of pure blood, but also doomed to become extinct more rapidly. He expects that when no new blood from the superior race enters the racial stream of the "mongrels" and when those mongrels continue to cross-breed among themselves, these cross-breeds will die out because they have insufficient powers of resistance. And, over the course of many thousands of years, a new mongrel race will be produced in which the original elements of the pure race will become so wholly mixed that traces of the original elements will be no longer detectable. These mongrel races would lack the flexibility and constructive capacity of the pure race with its homogeneous blood making it mentally and culturally superior. Along these lines, Hitler formulates the following principle that he evaluates as valid: "... every racial mixture leads, of necessity, sooner or later to the downfall of the mongrel product, provided the higher racial strata of this cross-breed has not retained within itself some sort of racial homogeneity."[21] In his view, history is full of instances that prove this law: "It shows, with a startling clarity, that whenever Aryans have mingled their blood with that of an inferior race the result has been the downfall of the people who were the standard-bearers of a higher culture."[22]

In support of his megalomanic utopic vision, Hitler refers to history as justifying his conclusion that it was the Aryan alone who founded a

[20] Hitler (1939, p. 311).   [21] Ibid. (p. 312).   [22] Ibid. (p. 223).

superior type of humanity. He elevates the Aryan as the "Prometheus of mankind, from whose shining brow the divine spark of genius has at all times flashed forth, always kindling anew that fire which, in the form of knowledge, illuminated the dark night by drawing aside the veil of mystery and thus showing man how to rise and become master over all the other beings on the earth." And he contrasts this shining future with a dystopic warning: "Should he be forced to disappear, a profound darkness will descend on the earth; within a few thousand years human culture will vanish and the world will become a desert."[23]

Dehumanization

Hitler dehumanized the Jews by reducing them to nonhuman entities. He feared them as dangerous and despised them at the same time. From a historical perspective, he observes that: "In times of distress a wave of public anger has usually arisen against the Jew; the masses have taken the law into their own hands; they have seized Jewish property and ruined the Jew in their urge to protect themselves against what they consider to be a scourge of God."[24] He adds that "in times of distress they looked upon his [the Jew's] presence among them as a public danger comparable only to the plague."[25] And he sees them as a threat to women of the noble Aryan race: "Systematically these negroid parasites in our national body corrupt our innocent fair-haired girls and thus destroy something which can no longer be replaced in this world."[26]

Hitler's radical rejection of ideologies different from his own was expressed in the way he dehumanized representatives of Marxism. Writing about Marxist teachings, he considered two alternatives: "Did the founders foresee the effects of their work in the form which those effects have shown themselves to-day, or were the founders themselves the victims of an error?" If the second question would be answered affirmatively, "then it was the duty of every thinking person to oppose this sinister movement with a view to preventing it from producing its worst results."[27] However, if the first question would lead to an affirmative answer, "then it must be admitted that the original authors of this evil which has infected the nations were devils incarnate. For only in the brain of a monster, and not that of a man, could the plan of this organization take shape whose

[23] Ibid. (p. 226).   [24] Ibid. (p. 15).   [25] Ibid.   [26] Ibid. (p. 429).   [27] Ibid. (p. 60).

workings must finally bring about the collapse of human civilization and turn this world into a desert waste."[28]

Internal Unity/External Division

We may admire a soccer team that functions as a perfect unit, we feel united with our family members at a birthday celebration, and we act together in support of the victims of a disaster. However, political unification that suppresses ingroup diversity and, at the same time, creates rigid boundaries with outgroups is a recipe for war.

Hitler's political ideals can only be understood if we recognize that his striving for national unity coincided with the simultaneous tendency to create separation from groups or countries that do not belong to that unity. From a historical perspective, we should keep in mind that after the fall of the French conqueror Napoleon, a movement started that aimed at the reunion of the German states in one great Reich. A first decisive step toward that purpose was the foundation of a German Empire in 1871, which emerged after the Franco-Prussian War. However, this Empire did not include the lands known as German Austria, which remained under the Habsburg Crown. It was the dream of Otto von Bismarck, founder and first chancellor (1871–1890) of the German Empire, to unite German Austria with the German Empire. However, this remained only a dream until Hitler turned it into a reality in 1938. This dream of bringing together all the German states under one united Reich, as an expression of German patriotism and statesmanship, had been one of Hitler's main ideals since he was young.[29]

For Hitler, the ideal of German unity was closely related to racial purity: "A people that fails to preserve the purity of its racial blood thereby destroys the unity of the soul of the nation in all its manifestations. A disintegrated national character is the inevitable consequence of a process of disintegration in the blood."[30] In his endeavor for racial unity, he went so far as to expect that one should sacrifice one's life in the service of the nation: "Here the instinct for self-preservation has reached its noblest form; for the Aryan willingly subordinates his own ego to the common weal and when necessity calls he will even sacrifice his own life for the community."[31]

---

[28] Ibid. (p. 60).   [29] Ibid. (p. 12, introduction by James Murphy).   [30] Ibid. (p. 265).
[31] Ibid. (p. 232).

Hitler was aware that the unification of the German nation would be more successful if it was associated with a sharp division from a common outside adversary. His formula for success was internal unification and external division. Motivated by these thoughts, he criticized the earlier pan-German movement that was directed toward the political unification of all people speaking German or a Germanic language. According to Hitler, this movement failed because it did not get the support of the broader population. The movement would never had made this mistake if it had properly understood the psyche of the broader masses that can be activated when they see a common single adversary: "If the leaders had known that, for psychological reasons alone, it is not expedient to place two or more sets of adversaries before the masses – since that leads to a complete splitting up of their fighting strength – they would have concentrated the full and undivided force of their attack against a single adversary."[32] Hitler's single enemy that was the target of his exceptional rhetorical capacities was the Jew.

Enemy Image Construction

In the English translation of *Mein Kampf* cited in this book, I counted the words "enemy" or "enemies" 178 times, while the words "friend," "friends," "friendship," and "friendly" were used only thirty-six times. The frequent use of the former words reflected Hitler's need to fight against a common enemy in order to unite the masses and concentrate their full anger and frustration on a favorite scapegoat. He demonized his main enemy, the Jew, in this way: "He will stop at nothing. His utterly low-down conduct is so appalling that one really cannot be surprised if in the imagination of our people the Jew is pictured as the incarnation of Satan and the symbol of evil."[33] By describing the Jews in satanic terms, Hitler placed the moral bad completely outside; that is, outside his nation, outside the German-speaking people, and outside himself.

Thinking of ways to solve the problem of the "Jewish peril," he arrived at a conclusion that reflected the most extreme form of dealing with one's enemy: "The nationalization of the masses can be successfully achieved only if, in the positive struggle to win the soul of the people, those who spread the international poison among them are exterminated."[34] And, ominously, he proposed a fantasy that foreshadowed the Holocaust: "At the beginning of the War [WWI], or even during the War, if twelve or

---

[32] Ibid. (pp. 101–102).   [33] Ibid. (p. 15).   [34] Ibid. (p. 265).

Figure 3.2   Russian President Vladimir Putin (left) meets with French President
Emmanuel Macron in Moscow on February 7, 2022.
Source: SPUTNIK/AFP/Getty Images.

fifteen thousand of these Jews who were corrupting the nation had been
forced to submit to poison-gas, just as hundreds of thousands of our best
German workers from every social stratum and from every trade and
calling had to face it in the field, then the millions of sacrifices made at
the front would not have been in vain."[35] In this way, a most radical
national unification created an energy that could, finally, be transferred to
the most awful atrocities of the "final solution."

Putin's Worldview

Vladimir Vladimirovich Putin (born October 7, 1952; Figure 3.2) is a
Russian politician and former intelligence officer of the KGB[36] and has
been the president of Russia since 2012 and previously from 2000 until
2008. He was also the prime minister from 1999 to 2000, and again from
2008 to 2012. He is currently the second longest-serving European
president after Alexander Lukashenko of Belarus. When, in 1999, Boris

---

[35] Ibid. (p. 518).
[36] The KGB was the main security and intelligence agency for the Soviet Union from 1954 until the
collapse of the nation in 1991.

Yeltsin stepped down as president of Russia, he proposed Putin as his successor. Some months later, Putin achieved a remarkable electoral victory after his success in the battle to keep Chechnya from seceding. In his first term, he gained central control over Russia's eighty-nine regions and republics and gained national support by reducing the power of Russia's unpopular financiers and media tycoons. He easily won reelection in 2004 and continued his success in 2012, when he won a third term as president. In 2014, he initiated the occupation and annexation of the Ukrainian autonomous republic of Crimea. In February 2021, he recognized the independence of the self-proclaimed people's republics of Donetsk and Luhansk. On February 24, 2022, he announced the beginning of a "special military operation" in Ukraine. President Volodymyr Zelensky of Ukraine made clear that his country would defend itself, and Western leaders condemned Putin's unprovoked attack and promised swift and severe sanctions against Russia.[37]

Putin's father, Vladimir Spiridonovich (1911–1999), worked as a toolmaker in a plant making railway carriages and is described as a model supporter of communism, genuinely believing in its ideals and trying to put them into practice in his own life. He became the secretary of the local Party cell in 1947 and later joined the factory's Party bureau. Vladimir's mother, Maria Ivanovna (1911–1998), was a devoted Orthodox Catholic believer and regularly slipped off to church, which was not usual in those days of official atheism and persecution. Secretly, baby Vladimir was christened, and his mother took him regularly to religious services. His communist father knew about his wife's churchgoing but turned a blind eye. Later, Putin stated that on the eve of a visit to Israel, his mother, as a devoted believer, gave him a baptismal cross to have blessed: "I did as she said and then put the cross around my neck. I have never taken it off since."[38]

When Vladimir Putin was born in 1952, his parents could look back upon hard times they had been through. For the close-knit family, his birth symbolized the end of the sufferings of the past and the privations of WWII. Putin's father and mother met as adolescents and married at the age of seventeen in 1928. Their first son, Oleg, died before reaching his first birthday. In 1932, the couple moved to Leningrad, where they witnessed the onset of WWII, known in Russia as the "Great Patriotic

War." Their second son, Victor, died of diphtheria aged five in the first year of the blockade and was buried in a communal grave. When, just before Leningrad was surrounded by the Germans, Putin's mother Maria had the chance to leave, she decided to stay with her husband, who was fighting to defend the city. A lack of food left her so weak that she could barely move, and only her husband's soldier's rations saved her life. The fighting left Putin's father with a limp until the end of his life. When the blockade of Leningrad ended, over 1.5 million of the 3 million inhabitants had died of hunger and illness, and 200,000 had died from bombs and shells. Among the survivors of the siege were Vladimir Senior and Maria.[39]

Putin's First Fight

In their book *Mr. Putin: Operative in the Kremlin*, Fiona Hill and Clifford Gaddy[40] mention that Vladimir Putin frequently tells personal stories that exemplify how he learned, while growing up in Leningrad, to rely on his own resources. He describes these stories as shaping his general approach as Russian prime minister and president. In this context, he refers to his early childhood in Leningrad's backstreets and courtyards. In one of these stories, he recounted that he was, at the age of seven, a rebellious kid in school from a tough neighborhood. Because of this social background, he claims, he was rejected by the Young Pioneers, a Soviet organization for children. He found his way by joining boys in his neighborhood, who ran around in packs, or gangs, and frequently got into fights. With pride he enumerates the lessons he learned from his first fight with an adversary:

> The first time I got beat up, it was a disgrace . . . That incident was my first serious street "university." . . . I drew four conclusions. Number one. I was wrong. I don't remember the exact details of the conflict, but . . . [b]asically I insulted him for no good reason. So he immediately beat me up, and I deserved it . . . Conclusion number two . . . I understood that you shouldn't act like that to anybody, that you need to respect everybody. That was a nice "hands-on" lesson! Number three. I realized that in every situation – whether I was right or wrong – I had to be strong. I had to be able to answer back . . . And number four. I learned that I always had to be ready to instantly respond to an offense or insult. Instantly! . . . I just understood that if you want to win, then you have to fight to the finish

---

[39] Ibid.
[40] Hill and Gaddy (2013). The authors are members of the Brookings Institution, a nonprofit public policy organization based in Washington, DC, that has the mission of conducting in-depth research leading to new ideas for solving problems facing society at the local, national, and global level.

in every fight, as if it was the last and decisive battle . . . you need to assume that there is no retreat and that you'll have to fight to the end. In principle, that's a well-known rule that they later taught me in the KGB, but I learned it much earlier – in those fights as a kid.[41]

Later, Putin's fighting spirit took him off the streets when he was around ten or eleven years old. First, he practiced boxing, judo, and sambo, which is a combination of judo and wrestling. From his experiences in sports, he learned to respect his opponents, to build inner strength, and to prepare himself for competition. In his later political career, Putin faced many challenges that enabled him to apply all these lessons, such as in the second war in Chechnya that marked his entry into official office in 1999–2000.[42] Perhaps his greatest (and final?) challenge was his invasion of Ukraine, where he manifested himself as a ferocious warrior who never gives up.

Putin as a Masculine Hero

In her analysis of Putin's political position, historian Elizabeth Wood[43] noticed that Putin made WWII a personal and even sacred event (compare the meaning of WWI for Hitler). He has created a myth and a ritual that elevates him as the man who takes Russia's unification as his personal mission, at the same time presenting himself as the "natural hero-leader," "the warrior" who is personally dedicated to defending his Motherland. A series of actions illustrate his personal engagement: his narration of his own family's suffering at the time of the Leningrad blockade, his meetings with veterans, his visits to churches that have associations with war situations, the creation of new uniforms, his participation in parades, and his establishment of schools where girls receive a military education.[44] A commonality of these settings is that Putin is personally connected to WWII and to Russia's greatness as a legitimate and dutiful son of Leningrad and as a father to a new generation of youngsters associated with the military. "Each setting helps to reinforce a masculine image of Putin as a ruler who is both autocrat and a man of the people"[45] (see Figure 3.3).

Furthermore, Wood observes that historians and observers of Russia have wondered whether Putin and his advisers have tried to create a new

---

[41] Ibid. (pp. 93–94).   [42] Ibid. (p. 94).   [43] Wood (2011).
[44] Masculinity formed also part of the idealized identity that the Nazis tried to instill in the youth, resulting in the militarization of the Hitler Youth (Lepage, 2009).
[45] Wood (2011, p. 172).

Figure 3.3   Vladimir Putin in his masculine position.
Source: Alexsey Druginyn/AFP/Getty Images.

cult around his personality. Focusing on the close connection between Putin and WWII, an image has been created that aligns him personally with the history and fate of the country. As a person and leader, he is identified with the ongoing commemoration of WWII, with the suffering of the people, and with the redemption of the nation. The frequent invocation of WWII as the "Great Patriotic War" culminates in the celebration of May 9 as Victory Day, the holiday that commemorates the victory over Nazi Germany in 1945. This celebration has increasingly taken on a personal quality aimed at associating Putin directly with the holiday and victory in the war.

The event of Russia's victory in WWII is so vividly memorialized that it seems to be May 9 "every day." From 2014, at least one war film has been released per month in Russia, and 75 percent of those movies are about WWII. Given the exposure to this broad film menu in which WWII and the ultimate victory over Nazi Germany are memorialized and celebrated, it is perhaps unsurprising that there is no widespread resistance in the Russian population against the invasion of Ukraine under the banner of the denazification of the country.[46]

The Putin Phenomenon as a Leadership Cult

In a paper entitled "The Putin Phenomenon," political scientists Stephen White (University of Glasgow) and Ian McAllister (University of Canberra)[47] showed that the Putin presidency in Russia, as it progressed in the first decade of its existence, became increasingly popular and that a leadership cult developed around the president himself. There was general satisfaction with this leadership, and he was regarded as increasingly successful in all fields of policy, particularly in the international affairs of that time. The authors provided a series of examples of this leadership cult that may look amusing to the eyes of Western readers but demonstrate how Putin's popularity was ingrained in the everyday lives of Russian citizens.

There were popular sayings in Russia, such as "When Putin smiles, a child is born. If the smile is wider than usual, expect twins," or "A fork that Putin ate from can kill a vampire with a single stab." In Magnitogorsk, the overalls Putin had worn during a visit were displayed in the city museum. Elsewhere in the town, a "Putin Bar" opened, selling "Vertical Power" kebabs and milkshakes named "When Vova [Putin's nickname] Was Little." An all-female Russian band wrote a song called "Someone Like Putin" (someone who "doesn't drink" and "won't run away"). At Putin's fiftieth birthday in September 2002, readers of the newspaper *Argumenty i fakty* (*Arguments and Facts*) wanted to present their president with a samurai sword so that he could wipe out whoever he wanted. In a town in the Pskov region where the presidential motorcade had made a stop in August 2000, visitors were offered a tour "in Putin's footsteps" that went to the places "where Putin bought a cucumber," "where Putin took off his jacket and tried water from a spring," and "where Putin touched a tree and made a wish."[48]

[46] de Bruijn (2022).　　[47] White and McAllister (2008).　　[48] Ibid.

Perhaps also surprising to Western readers is that the president, who is used to presenting himself as very masculine, appeared to enjoy particularly high levels of support among women. White and McAllister mentioned that there was a "new category of patients – women who are madly in love with President Vladimir Putin." They mention the case of Lyudmila, a woman in her late thirties who had started to collect newspaper articles about the president, which she kept in a cabinet next to her bed. She asked her husband to turn down the television when Putin was speaking on the radio. Once, the couple had such a fight that they stopped speaking to each other for three days. After retreating to the children's room, she hung a portrait of the president above the bed. However, her husband came in and threw everything on the floor. Lyudmila dissolved in tears and, finally, had to consult a private psychiatrist. This specialist explained that Lyudmila's case was "not unique." He had noticed that many women saw Putin as a "superhusband, the ideal partner," someone who would "never betray them, and never get dead drunk."[49]

The date (2008) of the mentioned paper raises the question as to whether Putin's approval ratings have changed after he started the invasion of Ukraine. This is clearly not the case. Whereas in March 2008 he received, as president of Russia, an approval rating of 85 percent, this rating was at the level of 83 percent in March 2022. The disapproval rating of his presidency was 13 percent in 2008 and 15 percent in March 2022.[50] As these numbers suggest, Putin's popularity has not changed significantly, although it has shown considerable fluctuations during his presidency. These numbers are based on the question "Do you approve of the activities of Vladimir Putin as the president (prime minister) of Russia?" It is not clear to what extent the answers reflect the personal opinions of the respondents or are dictated from above.

Tsar Peter the Great as Putin's Model

Just as Hitler found his role models in the radical pan-German leader Georg Ritter von Schönerer and in Vienna's mayor Dr. Karl Lueger, Putin is assumed to have found his main idealized predecessor in Peter the Great (1672–1725). This historical icon modernized Russia, which, at the start of his rule, was far behind the powerful and more economically advanced Western countries. His purpose was to transform his country into a major power, and he did so through numerous reforms that enabled Russia to

---

[49] Ibid. (p. 608).   [50] www.statista.com/statistics/896181/putin-approval-rating-russia/.

make incredible progress in the development of its economy, education, science, culture, and foreign policy.[51]

As historian Niall Ferguson[52] notes, it is a common assertion that Putin is hell-bent on the resurrection of the Soviet Union, and it is well-known that he considers the collapse of the Soviet Empire "the greatest geopolitical catastrophe of the century." But in fact he is trying to bring back the tsarist Russian Empire, with Peter the Great as his hero, even more than the Soviet Empire of Stalin, his other role model. Putin made his admiration for the tsar very clear in an interview with Lionel Barber, then editor of the *Financial Times*, in 2019. During this interview, in the presence of a towering bronze statue of the visionary tsar that loomed over his ceremonial desk in the cabinet room, Putin mentioned Tsar Peter as his favorite leader:

BARBER: "You have seen many world leaders. Who do you most admire?"
PUTIN: "Peter the Great."
BARBER: "But he is dead."
PUTIN: "He will live as long as his cause is alive just as the cause of each of us.
         (Laughter). We will live until our cause is alive."[53]

What was Peter's cause? As Ferguson assumes, the cause was to make Russia a great European power, capable of matching Austria, Prussia, Britain, and France in military might and in its economic and bureaucratic foundations. Historians would not dispute that he achieved that purpose, as exemplified by the Battle of Poltava on July 8, 1709, when Tsar Peter won the most important victory of his reign by defeating the army of Charles XII of Sweden, one of the great powers during the seventeenth century. Putin wants more than to reverse the decline of the Soviet Union. It is the tsarist Russian Empire that Putin is trying to bring back, with Peter the Great, more than Stalin, as his hero.[54]

Peter the Great and Stalin are, in terms of DST, external positions in Putin's self, and they make us understand that the deeds or misdeeds of political leaders do not simply reduce to characteristics of their personality only. Via their external positions, self and society are intimately interconnected, and via them we can see that a "dictator virus" can infect leaders even if they live in different centuries and are geographically far removed

[51] Encyclopedia Britannica, www.britannica.com/biography/Peter-the-Great, retrieved May 5, 2022.
[52] Ferguson (2022).
[53] Russian President Vladimir Putin's interview (June 27, 2019) with *Financial Times* editor Lionel Barber and *Moscow Bureau* chief Henry Foy on the eve of the G20 Summit in Osaka, Japan.
[54] Ferguson (2022).

Table 3.1 *The four dead ends of social construction by Hitler and Putin.*

	Hitler	Putin
Purification	Aryan race	Denazification of Ukraine
Dehumanization	Jews as rats	Dissidents as gnats
Internal unity/external division	Pan-Germanism vs. communism	Russian Empire vs. the West
Enemy image construction	Anti-Semitism	Anti-West

from each other. In DST, the self figures as a "society of mind" populated not only by internal positions (I as . . .), but also by external positions (perceived, remembered, or imagined others) phrased, for example, as "my hero" or "our hero." In their mutual dynamic relationships, internal and external positions construct and reconstruct each other in reciprocal ways. In fact, external positions are not outside objective realities but *constructions* of the other as part of the self, as they mediate between internal positions and the actual others as objective realities in the outside world. As we see, in both Hitler's and Putin's cases, external positions as extensions of the self may help us to understand that the selves of these leaders do not function as "self-contained identities" but as figures with purposes and ideals that are embedded in history and culture. Now the question arises as to whether we can find in Putin's worldview the same moral categories that we already detected in Hitler's case (see Table 3.1).

Purification

The purity of the Russian Empire as expressed by Putin's ideological ideals requires citizens to pledge unwavering loyalty to the "*vozhd*" (leader, guide), speak fluent Russian, follow Orthodox culture, and join, without hesitation, any war to which the Empire calls them. At the same time, this "new man" is expected to reject the degenerate West as infected by the "diseases" of LGBTQ+ persons, who contaminate the purity of the Russian nation.[55]

According to social scientist James Wertsch,[56] the idea that Russia is an innocent and pure nation that has been frequently victimized by military invasions and unwelcome infiltration of alien ideas is deeply engrained in its national narrative. In this context, Putin regularly quotes the Russian

[55] Kamusella (2022).   [56] James Wertsch, interviewd by Savat (2022).

philosopher Ivan Ilyin (1883–1954), who has provided him with the metaphysical and moral justification for establishing an authoritarian state and a purified nation.

The almost forgotten philosopher Ivan Ilyin, now revived and celebrated by Putin, provided him with a metaphysical and moral justification for political totalitarianism in the form of a fascist state. Ilyin proposed that in the beginning was the Word, purity and perfection, and the Word was God. However, God made a youthful mistake. He created the world with the intention to complete himself, but instead besmirched himself by making a disordered and imperfect world. So, not Adam but God was guilty of the original sin leading to the increasing hold of Satan on the world. Therefore, Ilyin understood history as a disgrace and despised the world as a meaningless farrago of fragments. The pluralism of modern society deepened the flaws of the world and kept God in the prison of his exile. He had only one hope: That a righteous and pure nation would follow a great Leader able to establish a political totality so that the world could be repaired and the divine redeemed. Any means that might bring about the return to this pure community, in the form of a Russian Christian fascist state, were justified.[57]

The idea of the reparation of original purity and unity provided Putin with an ideological basis for the "denazification" of Ukraine. In his own country he used it as a legitimation for blocking access to Facebook and major foreign news outlets, and it justified enacting a law to punish with up to fifteen years in prison anyone who would spread "false information" about the Ukraine invasion. He effectively criminalized any public opposition that would speak of a "war" instead of what the Kremlin announced as a "special military operation." The fact that the lower house of Parliament, the State Duma, passed a law criminalizing "false information" on March 3, 2022, by a unanimous vote can be understood, from a democratic point of view, as an alarming signal of the apparent lack of any effective opposition in present-day Russia.[58]

The ideal of a totalitarian state supported by a purified nation fosters and even pushes the creation of a "we-position" led and guided by a strong leader who is accepted as a structurally dominant I-position in the extended self of his followers. If successful, this strategy reduces the multiplicity of I-positions and their diversity and fosters a politically monological self. Also, the uniqueness of these positions is reduced, with

[57] Snyder (2018).   [58] Troianovski (2022).

the consequence that dissidents are not allowed to speak from their own, original points of view. This fascist ideology forces or seduces people to speak with *one* voice only, at the cost of the democratic organization of self and society.[59]

Dehumanization

On March 19, 2022, Putin unleashed a venomous tirade at those who oppose his course and likened them to insects: "The Russian people will always be able to distinguish true patriots from scum and traitors and will simply spit them out like a gnat that accidentally flew into their mouths – spit them out on the pavement." And he added: "I am convinced that such a natural and necessary self-purification of society will only strengthen our country, our solidarity, cohesion and readiness to respond to any challenges."[60]

Reducing opponents or scapegoats to subhuman beings reminds us of Hitler's propaganda machinery in which Jews were likened to "rats." In WWII, the Nazi German Ministry of Propaganda created a film called *Der Ewige Jude* (*The Eternal Jew*) that depicted Jews as unclean and disease-ridden by comparing them to teeming swarms of rats, and it characterized Jewish ritual practices as disgusting, foreign, and dangerous. The film ends with a speech by Hitler proposing "the annihilation of the Jewish race in Europe."[61]

In 2022, several months after the invasion of Ukraine by Russian troops, there appeared reports of mass civilian graves in Manhush near Mariupol and in the streets of Bucha, where executed and mutilated bodies were found after the retreat of the Russian army. In Makariv, bodies were found lying face down on the ground, shot in the back of their head. This method for the mass killing of civilians was also for the Nazis in WWII a way to disable the normal revulsion that most people feel for civilian executions. In his book *Making Monsters: The Uncanny Power of Dehumanization*, David Livingstone Smith wrote that "[t]he human face is by far the richest source of social information and the most intimate channel of connection between people. . . . When we gaze into a person's eyes, we cannot help responding to that person as a human being. We cannot help but see them as human – to automatically regard the

---

[59] Hermans (2018).   [60] Huffington Post (2022).
[61] Philadelphia Holocaust Remembrance Foundation: Antisemitism explained, www .philaholocaustmemorial.org/antisemitism-explained, retrieved May 9, 2022.

face's bearer as one of our own kind."[62] This explains the blindfolding of victims of mass shootings by the German Einsatzgruppen during the WWII years. Apparently, for many the killing experience is psychologically devastating, and therefore a direct confrontation with the face of the victim had to be avoided.[63]

The advance of military technology facilitates the dehumanization of war victims. The use of long-range weapons and drones makes the purposeful killing of civilians easier. Putin's army has attacked hospitals and other buildings where civilians take shelter and has blasted the whole city of Mariupol to ruins. It has obstructed ways out from the war zones and prevented the provision of relief supplies for injured and starving people. Some extreme Russian nationalists legitimized these actions by dehumanizing the whole Ukrainian identity. A representative of one neofascist Russian party said: "We are fighting not against people but against enemies, not against people but against Ukrainians."[64] This leads to a situation in which Putin and his followers see Ukraine as part of a large Slavic empire while at the same time dehumanizing the specific identity of the Ukrainians by devaluating them as "Nazis." How is it possible to assert Slavic brotherhood while murdering many thousands of one's Slavic neighbors?

Maybe Dmitri Medvedev, Vice-Chairman of the Security Council of the Russian Federation and Russia's past president, made an attempt to "solve" the contradiction between inclusion and rejection of the Ukrainians in a post on his Telegram channel (April 5, 2022) entitled "On Fakes and True History." In this text, he declared that the task of the "demilitarisation" and "denazification" of Ukraine will be carried out not only on the battlefield. The most important objective is to change the consciousness of some Ukrainians, which is "bloody and full of false myths." This aim would serve to "ensure peace for future generations of Ukrainians and build an open Eurasia – from Lisbon to Vladivostok."[65] So, if I understand these statements well, the Ukrainians can be humanized again after they have lost their "false consciousness" so that they, and other nations, can be included in a large Eurasia.

In terms of DST, the process of dehumanization touches upon the notion of the I-position (and the we-position as its extension). As I have argued in a previous publication,[66] I-positions may strongly differ in the experience of "I-ness." This refers to the experience and awareness that a particular thought, emotion, or action originating from myself or from

---

[62] Livingstone Smith (2021, p. 221), quoted by Gerson (2022).   [63] Gerson (2022).   [64] Ibid.
[65] Domańska (2022).   [66] Hermans (2022).

another person is belonging to me, is close to me, and is experienced as inseparable from my awareness as a subject. This concept is close to William James's[67] capacity of the I as "appropriating" a particular thought and to psychotherapist Carl Rogers'[68] notion of "ownership of experience." When, in contrast, I position myself, or I am positioned by others, in a way that I experience as "strange," "alien to me," "weird," or even "absurd," the I-ness of this position is hardly discernable or even absent. In such cases, I experience that as "I'm not myself," "I lost myself," or "I'm a stranger to myself." Not only internal positions but also external ones may differ strongly in the degree of I-ness. People who are close to me, belong to me, and with whom I can easily identify represent external I-positions with a high degree of I-ness (or we-ness in the case of other groups). Persons or groups that I experience as "far from my bed" or with whom I strongly disagree or whom I dislike are experienced as having a low degree of I-ness. During the process of dehumanization, certainly in situations where others are reduced to subhuman entities, the I-ness or we-ness of other people as members of the extended self is seriously reduced. Dehumanization transforms I-positions into it-positions, devoid of their first-person qualities and unique perspectives.[69] The reduction of the self of the other to an it-position is well illustrated by the concept of the "male gaze" that presents women as sexual objects.[70]

Internal Unity/External Division

A telling example of the combination of internal unity and external division is Putin's[71] essay "On the Historical Unity of Russians and Ukrainians." Putin argues that Russians and Ukrainians, along with Belarusians, are one people, belonging together as a triune Russian nation. In support of this claim, he describes in length his views on the history of Russia and Ukraine, leading to the conclusion that Russians and Ukrainians share a common heritage and destiny.

Putin argues that Russians, Ukrainians, and Belarusians are all descendants of "Ancient Rus," also called Kievan Rus, a loose federation of principalities in Eastern Europe and Northern Europe that existed from the late 9th to the mid-13th centuries. However, his emphasis on the historical unity of Ancient Rus coexists with a strong opposition to those who threaten this precious unity. Ironically, he accuses his opponents for

---

[67] James (1890).   [68] Rogers (1951).   [69] Hermans (2022).   [70] Mulvey (1975).
[71] Putin (2022).

the same reasons he and his oligarchs are often reproached for: "Radicals and neo-Nazis were open and more and more insolent about their ambitions. They were indulged by both the official authorities and local oligarchs, who robbed the people of Ukraine and kept their stolen money in western banks, ready to sell their motherland for the sake of preserving their capital."[72]

He ends his essay with a clear warning: "All the subterfuges associated with the anti-Russia project are clear to us. And we will never allow our historical territories and people close to us living there to be used against Russia. And to those who will undertake such an attempt, I would like to say that this way they will destroy their own country."[73] The Nazis as the external threat to Russia's unity parallels Hitler's mobilization of a powerful propaganda machine that turned his full wrath on the Jews as his main target.

The dubious combination of internal unity and external division is in flagrant contrast to the conceptual basis of DST. In the notion of the I-position, multiplicity and unity are combined in one and the same composite term. Unity is expressed by attributing an "I," "me," or "mine" imprinted to different and even contradictory positions in the self, indicating that these positions are felt as belonging to the self (e.g. "I as ambitious," "my father as an optimist," "my beloved children," "my irritating colleagues"). In a similar way, we-positions reflect both unity and multiplicity at the same time (e.g. we as citizens, our neighbors, our opponents). As differentially positioned in time and space, self and society represent unity-in-multiplicity and multiplicity-in-unity. This implies that unity can exist *in the midst of multiplicity.* Instead of external division, an internal unity can coexist with and become fed by internal multiplicity, which allows agreement, disagreement, contradiction, and opposition as part of and belonging to an encompassing unity.[74]

Enemy Image Construction

In an article entitled "Instrument of Putin or Blower," the Dutch journalist Mark Duursma[75] writes about the close connection between Putin and Patriarch Kirill (Figure 3.4), the Primate of the Russian Orthodox Church. In his speech in the Cathedral of Christ the Savior in Moscow on March 6,

---

[72] Ibid.   [73] Ibid.   [74] Hermans (2022); Hermans and Hermans-Konopka (2010).
[75] Duursma (2022), translated by HH.

Figure 3.4   Moscow's Patriarch Kirill.
Source: Sefa Karacan/Anadolu Agency/Getty Images.

2022, the patriarch expressed his "concern" about the people of the Donbas region in Ukraine. He said:

> For eight years there have been attempts to destroy what exists in the Donbass. And in the Donbass there is rejection, a fundamental rejection of the so-called values that are offered today by those who claim world power. Today there is a test for the loyalty to this new world order, a kind of pass to that "happy" world, the world of excess consumption, the world of false "freedom." Do you know what this test is? The test is very simple and at the same time terrible – it is the Gay Pride parade . . .[76]

The patriarch, as a church leader, positions himself clearly as an ally to Putin's political position. The close connection between church and state in present-day Russia is expressed by Kirill's rhetorical question: "Who is attacking Ukraine today, where the suppression and extermination of people in the Donbass has been going on for eight years? Eight years of suffering and the whole world is silent: what does that mean? But we know that our brothers and sisters are really suffering; moreover, they may suffer for their loyalty to our Church."[77]

[76] Bitter Winter (2022, n.p.).   [77] Ibid.

Kirill, the highest spiritual leader of the Russian Orthodox Church, is included in the European Union's sanction list. As such, he finds his name amongst tens of military members who played an active role in the Bucha massacre and the siege of Mariupol. Also, his fortune is a problem for his reputation. In 2012, there was a scandal regarding his Breguet watch, which was priced at 28,000 euros. In December 2019, *Novaya Gazeta* drew attention to Patriarch Kirill's involvement in automotive, oil, jewelry, and fishing businesses. The newspaper cited reports claiming that the patriarch's estimated net worth is $4–8 billion, but these figures can't be verified, as Kirill keeps his savings in banks in Switzerland, Italy, and Austria.[78]

Both men, Putin and Kirill, create a coalition between state and church. They find each other in their rejection of sexual liberties, gender liberties, gay marriages, and Western democracy. Their common worldview is a mix of nationalism, a nostalgic longing for the past, and a rejection of Western democracy, all reasons for them to consider Ukrainian democracy as a threat. The state–church coalition, embodied by these two powerful men, provides Putin with a legitimation of his geopolitical ambitions. They confirm each other in the conviction that an ideological conflict is going on between East and West, a conflict that is, at the same time, a clash between good and evil. The state–church alliance allows Putin to call his invasion in Ukraine and, more generally, his enmity to the West a *moral* enterprise.[79]

The attack on Ukraine was again dressed up as a moral enterprise on September 30, 2022, when, at the occasion of the annexation of a part of Ukraine into the Russian Federation, Putin presented the invasion in Ukraine as a fight against satanism, which he perceived as an inspiring source of both the Ukrainian and Western governments. In this speech, Putin said that countries opposing Russia have now renounced "traditional faiths and values" and are dominated by "a religion on the contrary – outright Satanism."[80]

In DST, the concept of "coalition" is a central one, referring to situations in which two or more I-positions or we-positions strengthen each other so that the whole is stronger than the parts in their isolation. The question may arise as to which position, in the case of a state and church

---

[78] https://meduza.io/en/feature/2020/10/28/new-proekt-investigation-uncovers-millions-of-dollars-in-real-estate-belonging-to-patriarch-kirill-and-his-family-members.
[79] Duursma (2022).   [80] Introvigne (2022).

coalition, is the dominant one of the two. Referring to the cooperation between Putin and Kirill, Pope Francis, the head of the Catholic Church, gave a remarkable answer to this question. In a meeting on the media platform Zoom with the leader of the Russian Orthodox Church, he warned him not to be "Putin's altar boy" and not to justify the Russian president's invasion of Ukraine. In his later reflections on the conversation, Francis said that Kirill had been listing off all the justifications for the war from a sheet of paper. The pope had listened to him and then told him: "I don't understand anything about this. Brother, we are not state clerics, we cannot use the language of politics but that of Jesus. We are pastors of the same holy people of God. Because of this, we must seek avenues of peace, to put an end to the firing of weapons."[81] Translated into DST terms, the pope suggested that in the coalition between the positions of Putin and Kirill, the position of the former was dominant and the position of the latter subservient. Even more importantly, this coalition was, in the pope's view, undesirable altogether, as the two positions should be relatively autonomous, each with their own goals and specific moral values.

In all this information on the worldviews of Hitler and Putin, I don't want to adhere to any theory that states that one influential figure determines the fate of a whole nation. No matter how influential political leaders might seem to be, they are certainly not the only causes of a war, nor are they the only sources of the identity formation of their followers. There are always other factors over which these leaders have not much influence, like economic power, geographical factors, international relations, and historical precursors.[82] In the preceding sections, I only wanted to refer to a variety of common factors in the worldviews of two dictatorial leaders and their implications for the identity construction of their followers.

Moral Psychology

In the second half of this chapter, I want to examine what are the moral implications of Hitler's and Putin's worldviews by relating them to recent developments in the psychology of morality. Therefore, I will continue to take the four dead ends of identity construction as a basic structure of this chapter and stipulate in detail what are their moral implications. I hope that educational specialists and teachers recognize this and come to understand that what we usually call "good" also contains the seed of "bad."

---

[81] Bella and Westfall (2022).   [82] Kershaw (2022).

Purification

From the literature in moral psychology, we learn that purity has an intrinsic moral value.[83] Originally, purity was related to the evolutionary needs of avoiding the absorption of toxins, parasites, or bacteria. However, the original concerns over purity and contamination of one's body subsequently extended to concerns over the purity of one's social conduct and belief system. Demands on purity are based on the belief that people ought to be, both in their bodies and minds, clean, chaste, and spiritually pure. From this point of view, it is virtuous to cleanse the soul, to act within the "natural order," and to reject contaminating influences. It is immoral to behave in a way that is self-polluting, filthy, and animal-like.[84]

In traditional cultures, fear of contagion from the "impure" lies at the heart of their social structures. India's caste system is one of the most cited cases.[85] One of the main defining aspects of a caste member's identity is their purity. Brahmans are considered as the purest and are afforded the highest position in society. In contrast, Dalits, the "untouchables," are considered as physically dirty and morally unclean. They are not permitted to marry someone from a higher caste, to participate in religious rituals, or to be in physical proximity with somebody from the upper classes. Although to a lesser extent and in a very different social context, fear of contagion can also be observed in the history of racial tensions between whites and blacks in the United States. "Whites only" devices and separate seating areas illustrate the illusory fear that blacks would pollute communal property (Figure 3.5). Such fears also exist in the sexual domain. An extreme example is North Carolina pastor Charles L. Worley, who ranted that all "queers and homosexuals" should be quarantined inside an electric fence.[86] Apparently, fear of contagion originating from interaction with the physical world can spill over into discrimination and social segregation.

Dehumanization

In a review of the phenomenon of dehumanization, morality researchers[87] have demonstrated that the category mistake of perceiving certain human beings as less than human is remarkably tenacious and widespread. They give some examples. Immigrants are likened to infectious diseases or

---

[83] Haidt and Graham (2007); Horberg et al. (2009).   [84] Ibid.   [85] Zhong and House (2014).
[86] Ibid. For Charles Worley's statements, see also *Huffington Post* (May 21, 2012).
[87] Haslam and Loughnan (2014).

Figure 3.5   Men drinking from segregated water fountains in the American South.
Undated photograph.
Source: Bettmann/Getty Images.

invasive pests. African sportsmen are greeted with monkey noises in some European football stadiums. Indigenous people are stereotyped as brute savages. Victims of genocide are labeled as vermin by their perpetrators. Sex magazines portray women as mindless, pneumatic objects. Tourists look at homeless people as if they are transparent obstacles. Tired doctors view their patients as inert bodies, whereas patients feel their personal identities are stripped away by a depersonalizing medical machine.

In the field of moral psychology, many researchers refer to the classical insights of Albert Bandura.[88] In his theory, the concept of "self-sanction" plays a central role in the regulation of inhumane conduct. As part of the socialization process, adopted moral standards serve as guides and deterrents to one's conduct. Behaving in agreement with internal standards gives self-satisfaction and a sense of self-worth. However, if we violate our moral standards, such behavior would bring self-condemnation. But these moral standards do not function as fixed or automatic internal regulators of conduct. They work only if they are activated. There are situations in

[88]   Bandura (1990).

which self-sanctions are deactivated so that inhumane conduct can occur. Given the same moral standards, selective activation or disengagement of moral standards permits dehumanization. This enables otherwise-conscientious people to perform self-serving activities that have detrimental social effects. In this process, detrimental conduct is made personally and socially acceptable by paying lip service to moral purposes. To understand aggressive conduct not only by leaders such as Hitler and Putin but also by their supporters, this quotation by Bandura seems to be particularly relevant:

> Radical shifts in destructive behavior through moral justification are most strikingly revealed in military conduct. People who have been socialized to deplore killing as morally condemnable can be rapidly transformed into skilled combatants, who may feel little compunction and even a sense of pride in taking human life in combat. The conversion of socialized people into dedicated fighters is achieved not by altering their personality structures, aggressive drives, or moral standards. Rather, it is accomplished by cognitively restructuring the moral value of killing, so that it can be done free from self-censuring restraints ... Through moral sanction of violent means, people see themselves as fighting ruthless oppressors who have an unquenchable appetite for conquest, or protecting their cherished values and way of life, preserving world peace, saving humanity from subjugation to an evil ideology, or honoring their country's international commitments. The task of making violence morally defensible is facilitated when nonviolent options are judged to have been ineffective, and utilitarian justifications portray the suffering caused by violent counterattacks as greatly outweighed by the human suffering inflicted by the foe.[89]

In this context, Bandura makes clear that the activation of moral standards partly depends on how the perpetrators perceive the people toward whom the behavior is directed. When others are seen as human, empathetic or vicarious emotional reactions through perceived similarity are activated. The pleasure and suffering of similar persons are more vicariously arousing than those of strangers who are perceived as devoid of human qualities. When victims are perceived as insensitive or unfeeling, distress to their suffering is weakened and empathy is not aroused. This lack of empathy is prevalent in situations of rape, in which women are entirely dehumanized and subjected to a most extreme form of aggression common during the Holocaust, the invasion of the Russians in Ukraine, and in all situations where women, men, and children are being raped in countries where tribal wars are taking place.

---

[89] Ibid. (p. 29).

Figure 3.6   Picture referring to the Abu Ghraib torture and prisoner abuse.
Source: RAMZI HAIDAR/AFP via Getty Images.

At this point, it makes sense to refer to the toxic masculinity systematically expressed by both Hitler and Putin. Bandura refers to cross-cultural studies revealing that aggressive sexuality is an expression of the ideology of male dominance. In societies and cultures where violence is a way of life, male supremacy reigns, rape occurs frequently, aggressive sexuality is seen as a sign of manliness, and women are treated as property. In contrast, rape is rare in societies that reject interpersonal aggression, endorse equality in sexual relationships, and treat women with respect. When prestige is attributed to male dominance and aggressive sexuality, self-censure for the sexual abuse of women is apparently weakened.[90]

Dehumanization practices are also stimulated by coalitions between aggression and a positively experienced I-position, "making fun." In his book *The Lucifer Effect: Understanding How Good People Turn Evil*, Philip Zimbardo[91] reflected on his famous and controversial Stanford prison experiment during the 1970s and compared it with the horrendous abuse and torture of prisoners by the US Military Police at the Abu Ghraib prison in Iraq (Figure 3.6). Zimbardo rejects the allegation that these

[90] Ibid. (p. 38).   [91] Zimbardo (2007).

immoral deeds were the sadistic work of just a few rogue soldiers, so-called bad apples, and, moreover, he does not believe that this behavior can be reduced to some questionable personality characteristics of the perpetrators. Instead, he argues that situational forces are at work similar to those in the Stanford prison experiment. In particular, he was interested in the abusive behaviors that are depicted in the revolting set of "trophy photos" in the Abu Ghraib prison taken by the soldiers while engaging in the torture of their prisoners. These photos remind one of pictures taken by big-game hunters in Africa who proudly displayed themselves posing with the animals they had killed. The Abu Ghraib photos (Figure 3.6) showed men and women in the act of abusing their "lowly animal creatures." In the images one sees guards punching, slapping, and kicking detainees; arranging naked, hooded prisoners into piles and pyramids; forcing naked prisoners to wear women's underwear over their heads; forcing prisoners to masturbate or simulate fellatio; hanging prisoners from cell rafters; and dragging a prisoner around with a leash tied around his neck.[92] As these atrocious images demonstrate, there was a coalition at work between abuse and amusement, with the energy of fun transferred, via a process of transpositioning, to the degrading of the prisoners.

Internal Unity/External Division

In their review article on social unity and other moral motives, social psychologists Tage Rai and Alan Fiske state that the striving for unity is "directed toward caring for and supporting the integrity of ingroups through a sense of collective responsibility and common fate."[93] When participating in a united group, people are expected to protect each other and provide support for group members if they need it. If someone is harmed by an outgroup member, the other members feel transgressed, and they feel the need to respond. On the other hand, if an ingroup member commits a violation of the moral norms of the group or contaminates its integrity, the entire group bears responsibility and feels polluted and shamed and, as a reaction, wants to cleanse itself. When the group or one of its members feels threatened, this is felt to be an intimidation of all of them.

Ingroup members are motivated to unite against any outsiders who are perceived as threatening the cohesion of the ingroup. The protection of unity and coherence can be a source of ethnic violence and genocide, particularly in situations where outgroups are perceived as disgusting

---

[92] Ibid. [93] Rai and Fiske (2011, p. 61).

threats of contamination. Such threats can only be responded to by protection measures or counter-aggression in order to preserve the integrity of the ingroup. Earlier in this chapter, I have sketched examples of these responses in Hitler's hatred of Jews and Putin's striving for the denazification of Ukraine. Also, the 1994 genocide in Rwanda, where members of the Hutu ethnic majority murdered as many as 800,000 people, mostly of the Tutsi minority, illustrates this threat and subsequent aggression:

> The Hutu, wherever they are, must have unity and solidarity and be concerned with the fate of their Hutu brothers. The Hutu inside and outside Rwanda must constantly look for friends and allies for the Hutu cause, starting with their Hutu brothers. They must constantly counteract Tutsi propaganda. The Hutu must be firm and vigilant against their common Tutsi enemy. [Excerpt from the Hutu Ten Commandments, propaganda used to spur anti-Tutsi sentiment prior to the Rwandan genocide.][94]

Apparently, ingroup unity is protected by constructing a moral circle that includes those who belong to the community with the simultaneous exclusion of those who are perceived as a threat to or moral contagion of the ingroup. The coexistence of inclusion and exclusion creates razor-sharp boundaries between the "good people" located within the moral circle and the "bad people" outside this circle. Only those who are included in the circle of close allies are within the scope of moral concern.[95]

When coupled with social unity, hierarchy stimulates the ranking of groups, with the ingroup at the top and the outgroup at the bottom. For example, in Nazi Germany during the 1930s, a set of animal rights laws was passed that ranked both humans and animals in a hierarchical scale. Aryans, wolves, and eagles were at the top of the scale, whereas Jews and rats were at the bottom. The Nazis could use this scale as "legitimation" of their experimentation on Jews.[96] On a similar basis, Hitler could formulate his cherished thesis in *Mein Kampf*, mentioned earlier in this chapter, as follows: "... every racial mixture leads, of necessity, sooner or later to the downfall of the mongrel product, provided the higher racial strata of this cross-breed has not retained within itself some sort of racial homogeneity."[97]

The combination of hierarchy and internal unity versus external division creates the poisonous coalition of "we as united" and "I as obedient." Subordinates are motivated to respect, obey, and pay deference to the will

---

[94] Berry and Berry (1999), quoted by Rai and Fiske (2011, p. 61).   [95] Rai and Fiske (2011).
[96] Ibid.   [97] Hitler (1939, p. 312).

of superiors at the top of the hierarchy, while at the same time feeling united within safe boundaries provided by leaders, ancestors, or gods. Those superiors are granted the right to punish those who disobey or disrespect them. Subordinates may morally legitimize their actions as they would see it as their duty to act in accordance with the authority. A dramatic example of this united and obedient coalition is the My Lai massacre. On March 16, 1968, companies of US soldiers, led by Lt. William Calley, entered the village of My Lai, Vietnam, and murdered approximately 500 civilians, primarily women and children. At his trial, Calley stated that he killed the villagers because he was following the orders of his superiors and respected their authority. Unfortunately, such incidents are common in wartime. Nazi officers and officials made similar arguments to explain their acts of genocide during WWII, as notoriously exemplified by the case of Adolf Eichmann, the German-Austrian SS-Obersturmbannführer who was one of the major organizers of the Holocaust.[98] The guards in the Abu Ghraib prisoner abuse scandal also took refuge in this argument.[99] And the Russian soldiers indulging in the atrocities in Bucha and Mariupol during the Ukraine war could pass on their personal responsibility to their superiors, claiming to be just cogs in the machinery of a unified and hierarchically organized political and military system.

Enemy Image Construction

In my search for useful models explaining the construction of enemy images, I found Stephen Reicher and colleagues' proposal[100] the most viable. As a highly dynamic model, it fits very well with DST, which is equally dynamic through concepts such as positioning, counter-positioning, anti-positioning, and repositioning. As we will see later in this chapter, DST adds a significant dimension to Reicher's model by taking the position of the other (the enemy) into account as part of the extended self.

At the outset of their argument, Reicher et al. make one basic point. For far too long, they reason, research on the human capacity for evil has been obstructed by asking the wrong questions. If we want to move forward, they write, we need to change the questions we ask. Instead of wondering why people are doing evil things or how people can ignore their evil

---

[98] See also the Eichmann tapes with his own confessions (Kershner, 2022).
[99] Rai and Fiske (2011).   [100] Reicher et al. (2008).

doings, research needs to explain how people can come to celebrate inhumane acts as expressions of virtue. In other words, how can bad conduct find its origin in the striving for moral good?

How could it happen that Nazi staff members, devoted to the Holocaust, were notable for their initiative and for their ideological zeal? Officials like Eichmann believed that they were doing the right thing, and they were stubborn in their conviction in the full knowledge of the genocide that was taking place. How can we understand that not only the Eichmanns but also "ordinary people" could believe that killing was the right thing to do?

To answer this question, Reicher and colleagues identify five steps in the definition of social identities that help to explain acts of extreme inhumanity. These are: (1) the creation of a *cohesive* ingroup through shared social identification; (2) the *exclusion* of specific populations from the ingroup; (3) constituting the outgroup as a *danger* to the existence of the ingroup; (4) the representation of the ingroup as uniquely *virtuous*; and (e) the celebration of outgroup *annihilation* as the defense of ingroup virtue. I will summarize these five steps here and complement them by including some references to Hitler's and Putin's purposes and actions.

Step 1:   Identification: Creating a Cohesive Ingroup
In general, research shows that people are able to act purposively, meaningfully, and collectively when they assume a common social identity (e.g. Catholics, socialists, Jews, Palestinians, Germans, Russians, Dutch). Collective experiences are positive and beneficial for our well-being and protect us against negative influences of stressors. When we feel supported and accepted by others and when our views are validated by others, these are positive experiences in and of themselves. Moreover, the coordination of action on the basis of shared social identification makes it an important source of empowerment. It stimulates group members to pull together in order to overcome obstacles and to achieve collective goals.

Step 2:   Exclusion: Placing Targets Outside the Ingroup
When people such as minority groups or those considered to be "deviant" are excluded from group memberships, it deprives them of the associated personal and interpersonal entitlements. When defined as "outsiders," they are excluded from both political and civil society and they are seen as less able to represent community organizations. When they are deprived of the positive favors accorded to ingroup members, outgroup members have a higher chance of being discriminated against.

Reicher and colleagues emphasize that, particularly in the case of national groups, the definition of category boundaries is absolutely critical. The same people are treated very differently as a function of whether they are included within the national boundary definition or not. As an example, the researchers refer to the appeal of Nazism as a moral project in a world of misery, chaos, and decay. As Goebbels, chief propagandist for the Nazi Party, put it: "What is the first Commandment of every National Socialist? ... Love Germany above all else and your ethnic comrade [*Volksgenosse*] as your self."[101]

Just as Hitler envisioned in the 1930s a "Greater Germanic Reich" (*Großgermanisches Reich*) through plans to annex such territories as Austria, western Poland, and Bohemia, so Putin is dreaming of a "Greater Russia." Repeatedly, he has used memes such as "the triune Russian people," which includes the East Slavic people as part of Russia. Similarly, he has referred to the "all-Russian nation" and the "*Russkiy Mir*" (Russian World) throughout his tenure as president and prime minister since 2000. At the same time, he has employed these concepts to deny Belarusians and Ukrainians from having a national identity of their own that is separate from the Russian imperial project.[102] Reicher and colleagues make clear that, although category exclusion is a necessary step toward hatred and genocide, it is not a sufficient condition. Further steps are necessary.

Step 3: Danger: The Outgroup as Threatening Ingroup Identity
There are many groups that are not "belonging to us," but they are not necessarily "against us." For example, in some cases, the influx of immigrants evokes little negative comment and may even attract positive comment when incomers are welcomed as complementing or enriching one's own country. Opposition or even animosity arises when particular groups are seen as constituting a problem for their hosts. Typically, this occurs when problems are regarded as deriving from inherent characteristics of the incomers: their backwardness, their aggression, the threat of rape of women. Ideologies such as racism are based on the deceitful assumption that immigrant groups are *inherently* of a bad or dangerous kind and endanger "our values," "our culture," and "our way of life."

Often "nature" is invoked in order to claim that outgroups are a threat to their hosts, which explains, according to Reicher and colleagues, two widely found forms of hate discourse. One is an obsession with sex and

[101] Koonz (2003), quoted by Reicher et al. (2008, p. 1330).   [102] McIlhagga (2022).

sexuality. Outgroup members, such as black people, Jews, or Indians, are often portrayed as driven by sexual desires, their men as lecherous and with strong sexual potency, the women as seductresses. Given their undisciplined desires, "we" as ingroup are at risk at both the individual and collective level. Typically, rape is the ultimate metaphor for the corruption and defilement of "we" as the innocent and clean ingroup.

Another form of hate discourse is the use of animal images and metaphors, which was already described in this chapter. Recall the Nazi film *Der Ewige Jude* (*The Eternal Jew*), which depicted Jews as unclean and disease-ridden by comparing them to teeming swarms of rats. And Putin unleashed a venomous tirade at dissidents who opposed his course of action and likened them to insects. So, the outgroup is not simply different but subhuman, comparable to insects or other animals that are harmful and dangerous, with the result that outgroup members are stripped of their human identity and should be "removed."

Step 4: Virtue: Representing the Ingroup as (Uniquely) Good
In an insightful way, Reicher and colleagues observe that those involved in enacting the greatest brutality are often those who make great efforts to extol ingroup virtue. The more the ingroup is held to be virtuous and clean, the more serious the outgroup threat becomes. If this occurs, it becomes acceptable, even necessary, to "defend ourselves" by eliminating this outgroup threat or, if it is seen as necessary, by eliminating the outgroup itself.

In the 1930s, Hitler invested great efforts in extolling the distinctive virtues of ethnic Germans. The German *Volk*, he argued, were moral, pure, selfless, and loyal. Recall his remark on the inferiority of mongrels mentioned earlier in this chapter: ". . . they also lack definite will-power and vigorous vital energies owing to the lack of harmony in the quality of their blood."[103] He saw it as his call to defend these qualities and create a society in which they could flourish. Recall also the idea of the reparation of original purity and unity proposed by the philosopher Ivan Ilyin, which provided Putin with an ideological basis for blocking access to social media sites such as Facebook and major foreign news outlets.

Step 5: Annihilation: Praising Inhumanity as the Defense of Virtue
On the basis of this dynamic model, we can see how genocide can be welcomed as something to celebrate. As Reicher and colleagues observe:

[103] Hitler (1939, p. 311).

"Where 'they' are defined as not being of 'us' and as being against 'us' and where, in addition, we create a Manichaean view of the world in which we represent good and they represent evil, then their defeat – if necessary, their destruction – becomes a matter of preserving virtue."[104]

In the imagination of the Nazis, the Jews, portrayed as sewer rats, needed to be exterminated. But not everybody was selfless and noble enough to accomplish this unpleasant task. The coexistence of annihilation and decency was clearly expressed in a speech by Himmler,[105] when he addressed an audience in Poznan (a city in Poland) mainly composed of the SS: "Most of you must know what it means when one hundred corpses are lying side by side, or five hundred or a thousand. To have stuck it out and at the same time . . . to have remained decent fellows. This is a page of glory in our history."[106]

As we have seen earlier in this chapter, Putin also places himself on the side of the moral good, justified by the coalition between state and church in Russia. He and Patriarch Kirill found each other in their rejection of sexual freedom, gender liberties, homosexual marriage, and Western democracy. They shared the conviction that an ideological conflict exists between East and West, a conflict that, at the same time, coincides with a clash between good and evil. The state–church alliance confirmed Putin's conviction that his invasion of Ukraine and, more generally, his hostility to the West are moral enterprises. It's a noble task to remove immorality and degeneration.[107]

From their five-step model Reicher and colleagues derive several conclusions. They see one of them as important enough to bear repeating: ". . . the way we define ourselves may often be more relevant to genocide than the way we define others."[108] In our thinking of racism, discrimination, and hatred, they argue, our gaze is so firmly focused on our perception of the outgroup and on negative outgroup perceptions in particular that we almost entirely ignore the fact that *our* definition of ingroup virtue is necessary to outgroup destruction. Therefore, the researchers conclude that it is "important for psychologists and anti-racists to redirect their gaze and understand the centrality of *self-understandings* to the treatment of

---

[104] Reicher et al. (2008, p. 1336).
[105] Heinrich Himmler was a leading member of the Nazi Party of Germany and a main architect of the Holocaust.
[106] Rees (2005), quoted by Reicher et al. (2008, p. 1337).
[107] See also David Livingstone Smith's (2011) book *Less than human: Why We Demean, Enslave, and Exterminate Others*.
[108] Reicher et al. (2008, p. 1338).

others."[109] This statement is crucial for the question of how we can understand the intimate relationship between moral good and bad from the perspective of DST.

The kind of language we use positions us in relation to others. When we are threatened by others in situations of physical or sexual abuse, we position ourselves as "unsafe" or "threatened" and take appropriate action to protect ourselves via legal procedures or authoritative intervention. However, when we tend to position ourselves as "unsafe" in response to an increasingly broad range of behavior of the other (e.g. inappropriate comments, social or political conflicts, labor disputes), then it becomes increasingly difficult to solve such problems via dialogical interchange. The term "unsafe" motivates participants to protect themselves by closing the boundaries of their positions in relation to the "threatening other." This way of positioning the other, in a generalizing way, as a threat or enemy, opens the door to escalation and affective polarization instead of confronting the other with their actual or suspected misconduct in an open dissonant dialogue, an interchange in which not only agreement but also, even more significantly, disagreement play central roles.[110] In other words, when the term "unsafe" generalizes through a larger diversity of relationships regarded as problematic or unacceptable, it is used as a "container concept" that has the consequence of reducing the possibility of solving conflicts via dialogical confrontations.

Dialogical Self Theory and the Four Dead Ends

This chapter has focused on the four dead ends of identity construction: purification, dehumanization, internal unity/external division, and enemy image construction. We should consider the notion of "dead end" as a double entendre in this context. It not only means the end of a road or passage from which no exit is possible; in the present chapter, it also refers to *processes* that end in the deaths – many deaths – of victims of war and genocide. Purification, dehumanization, internal unity/external division, and enemy image construction are interwoven processes that often start with inspiring ideals or promising utopias but, over the course of time, inevitably create sharp boundaries with outgroups and, in their final consequences, culminate in destruction. How can these dead ends be understood from the perspective of DST and what is the potential of this theory for giving a productive response to them?

---

[109] Ibid. (emphasis added).   [110] For the concept of dissonant dialogue, see Chapters 5 and 6.

DST is constructed as an open, bridging theory that is designed to learn from other theories and insights and aims to contribute to them from its own original point of view. One central characteristic of DST is its *dynamic* nature, expressed in concepts such as positioning, counter-positioning, anti-positioning, repositioning, transpositioning, and over-positioning. Is it possible to use these processes to create more understanding of what is happening in the four dead ends? If this understanding is possible, an additional advantage would be that the processes and phenomena described in different scientific articles and books find a *meeting place* in such a bridging theory. Such meeting places are fertile grounds for reflection, thinking, and, not in the least, dialogue (see Chapter 5). And they will be helpful for exploring the moral middle ground (see Chapter 4) as the main theme of this book.

To summarize, the dialogical self can be conceptualized as a dynamic multiplicity of relatively autonomous I-positions in the self as a society of mind with the possibility of dialogical relationships among them (Chapter 1). Conceiving the self metaphorically as a "society" has the theoretical advantage that the self can be conceptually linked to the society at large so that their mutual influences and dynamics can be investigated. In this theory, the self does not function in social isolation and cannot be meaningfully studied and defined as "an entity in itself." Instead, the theory assumes that the self is *extended* to society, which implies that society is working *in* the self and influences and organizes it in its deepest layers.[111] Therefore, DST assumes the existence of not only I-positions, but also we-positions, on the assumption that collective ideas, ideals, and ideologies precede the individual self and organize it from the onset. The implication is that we-positions, if influential enough, determine which I-positions are dominant in the organization of the self and which I-positions are marginalized, suppressed, or neglected in the household of the self. And vice versa, selves have the possibility to confirm, change, damage, or innovate the society at large.[112]

Purification

The ideal of purification as outlined in this chapter lacks any multiplicity of we-positions of a particular nation, ethnicity, or racial group, and, by its implication, it organizes the I-positions of the individuals who belong to this group in an overly unifying way. A leader, nation, or social group that

---

[111] Hermans (2018).   [112] For the self as innovating the society, see Mead (1934).

aims at purification speaks with *one voice only* and is intolerant of opposition and disagreement as they are considered to be violations of the structurally dominant voice as the only valuable guideline for the future of the nation or social group. Therefore, purification is, by its nature, a monological instead of a dialogical process. The ideal of purification is very similar to a dualistic Manichaean worldview[113] that holds that the good power of God, mighty but not omnipotent, is opposed by the eternal evil power of the Devil, with the human person seen as a battleground for these powers. In a previous publication[114] I have summarized how DST is opposed to any kind of dualism:

> In DST, the good and the bad are not separated by any dualism or considered to be essentially different. Instead, they belong to each other as dialectical opposites and are intrinsically interwoven as the good covers in itself the germ of the bad and, vice versa, the bad, as a reality in oneself and others, implicates the potential of striving to the good. The problem of Manichean dualism is that people are seduced to locate themselves at the "good side" and perceive outsiders, exclusively and in an overgeneralizing way, as belonging to the "bad side." As history overwhelmingly demonstrates, "bad people" are perceived as enemies and have to be attacked or even exterminated as "villains" so that the "good people," glorifying themselves on their way to an utopic future, can continue their lives with the unnoticed blindness for the bad in themselves and the potential goodness in the rejected outgroup.[115]

As we have seen in the cases of Hitler and Putin, the ideal of pure race or a pure empire is morally dualistic, so that people who are not following the purist ideal are rejected as dangerous or as morally repulsive outsiders. The implication is that counter-positions that represent views that are *different* from the dominant one are not allowed, and their representatives have to be rejected and, in the ultimate case, even exterminated. Moreover, any repositioning of the original (pure) position in the direction of a different voice does not take place.

Dehumanization

For understanding the process of dehumanization from a DST perspective, a description of the nature of I-positioning is required. An I-position is a spatiotemporal act in the context of other I-positions in the self. It is the

---

[113] The philosophy of Manichaeanism is a dualistic religious system originating in Persia in the third century CE.
[114] Hermans (2022).   [115] Ibid. (p. 40).

sediment of processes of positioning, counter-positioning (space), and repositioning (time). In its different variants, positioning means placing oneself vis-à-vis somebody or something else and, at the same time, toward oneself in the metaphorical space of the self. As a relational-dialogical act, it represents a stance toward the other, physically or virtually, and it addresses the other and oneself via verbal or nonverbal orientations and communications. The I in the I-position reflects the personal, subjective, and unique nature of the self and its constituents.

The functioning of the self is not limited to processes that happen "within the skin." Other people, animals, nature, and even physical objects can become part of the extended self. As suggested by James,[116] they are felt as "mine," such as my colleague, my child, my puppy, my house, my neighborhood, the nature to which I belong. DST elaborates on this view by seeing the other as another I with their own subjectivity and unique perspective on the world. When, however, the other is reduced to a mere object that can be freely manipulated by the self on the basis of its own needs and wishes, the other is then reduced to an it-position and is no longer addressed in its subjectivity and unique perspective.

This reduction from "I to it" is discussed by Martin Buber,[117] who considered the term "I" not as a single word but rather as part of the word pair I–You. This pair should be distinguished from another word pair, I–It, which refers to a completely different attitude toward the world. Only the I–You relation facilitates the involvement in what he calls an "encounter." The You, encountered and respected as a *different* other, is addressed as a participant in a dialogical relationship. The I and the You may be highly continuous over time, but they manifest themselves in different qualities, comparable to I-positions in DST, in each new encounter. In Buber's view, the person speaks in many tongues – tongues of language, of art, of action. In contrast, the I as part of the I–It relation is an objectifying I and is monological rather than dialogical. The term "It" refers to an object of observation, classification, thinking, using, or abusing, but it is never approached as an addressable other with their own subjectivity and specific points of view. In contrast to the objectifying and utilizing I–It relation, the relational aspect of the dialogical I–You relation is characterized by Buber with the metaphors of "speech" and "breathing."

---

[116] James (1890).
[117] Buber (1970). Martin Buber (1878–1965) was a prominent philosopher, religious thinker, educator, and political activist known for his philosophy of dialogue.

In line with Buber, we might assume that in the process of dehumanization, other people are stripped of their status as external I-positions or others-in-the-self each with their subjective and unique perspective and instead are reduced to it-positions, entirely in the service of the self that strives for full control of the situation. At this point, we discern a coexistence of purification and dehumanization. When opponents or dissidents are seen and treated as impure, unclean, and filthy, then they deserve to be discarded or removed as undesirable or dangerous objects. When we conceive of positions, akin to Buber, as pairs rather than as isolated entities, then the others as filthy and unclean correspond with we as clean, we as pure, we as uninfected. The way we perceive others is intimately related to the way we view ourselves. At this point, it is essential to recall the model presented by Reicher and colleagues, who wrote that in our thinking of racism, discrimination, and hatred our gaze is so firmly focused on negative outgroup perceptions that we almost entirely ignore the fact that our definition of ingroup virtue can function as a preliminary stage of outgroup destruction. Thus, they emphasized that it is crucial to redirect our gaze and understand the centrality of self-understandings to the treatment of others. This self-understanding would be stimulated by posing the question of what is happening in our selves when we see other people as less human or, as is exemplified by Hitler's and Putin's worldviews, as inhuman or subhuman.

Internal Unity/External Division

There is no objection against unification of a group or community per se. When two or more people want to make something happen that they cannot achieve on their own, a certain degree of unity is required in the service of reaching a common goal. There are numerous quotations that express appreciation of unity among people, such as "We are only as strong as we are united, as weak as we are divided" (ascribed to J. K. Rowling), "There is beauty and power in unity. We must be united in heart and mind. One world, one people" (attributed to Lailah Gifty Akita), and "When spiders unite, they can tie down a lion" (unknown).[118]

However, the more the ingroup unifies and the more division is created with outgroups, the sharper are the boundaries among them, until it reaches a point at which dialogue become seriously hampered. The notion of boundary is central to DST, which distinguishes several types and

---

[118] https://kidadl.com/quotes/inspiring-unity-quotes-perfect-for-bringing-people-together.

dynamics: open boundaries that cannot close become soft; closed boundaries that cannot open become rigid. The combination of unification and
division results in sharp boundaries that become rigid so that communication between ingroups and outgroups is disrupted. Ideally, boundaries
between groups, like boundaries between selves, are flexible. And flexibility
implies that, depending on the position that is salient in a particular
situation, boundaries are open (e.g. I as empathic, I as interested) or closed
(e.g. I as defending myself, I as angry). This flexibility becomes seriously
weakened when, on a structural basis, internal unity is emphasized and
external division is sharpened. The risk of homogenization, necessarily
associated with internal unification, is that constructive disagreement and
critical self-reflection are reduced and self-correction and repositioning do
not occur.[119]

Internal unification in combination with external division is a fertile
source of escalation. When the ingroup unifies itself and fortifies its
boundaries, the outgroup may feel threatened by the unified force on the
other side and, in turn, become involved in the *same* process. On the
international and global level, we can see this process of escalating unification when the Russian invasion in Ukraine, motivated by Putin's vision
of a unified Russian Empire, resulted in Finland's and Sweden's applications for membership of NATO after many decades of cherished
neutrality.[120] Giving up their in-between positions created sharper and
more rigid boundaries between East and West, with Ukraine left as a
country more than ever torn between its Western and Eastern parts. The
unification from the one side is responded to by a similar unification from
the other side, so that both parties become involved in a process of far-
reaching polarization that, once started, is very difficult to stop.

As described earlier in this chapter, the combination of internal unification and external division stands in sharp contrast to the desirable
functioning of the self as proposed by DST. As the I is always positioned
in time and space, the self is constantly drawn in different directions so
that different and contradictory positions strive for expression. At the same
time, the unity of the self is preserved by attributing an "I," "me," or
"mine" imprint to the different positions, so that they are felt as belonging
to the self in the extended sense of the term (e.g. "my mother as a
pessimist," "my lovely children," "my competitive colleagues"). Similarly,

---

[119] For an extensive clarification of the boundaries of the self, see Hermans (2018).
[120] During a two-day visit to Stockholm in March 2023, Secretary General Jens Stoltenberg said that
it is time to welcome Finland and Sweden as NATO allies.

the notion of the "we-position" refers to a contrasting and contradictory variety of positions, while, at the same time, it keeps them together as members of a cohesive social group, society, or even humanity (we as world citizens, we all as neighbors, all our children; see Chapter 6). As differentially positioned in time and space, the self, like a social group, functions as a unity-in-multiplicity and multiplicity-in-unity. On the social level, this implies that ingroup unity exists in the midst of multiplicity. Instead of external division, there is – or should be – internal unity as coexisting with and enriched by internal multiplicity, which allows for discussion, contradiction, and opposition – in short, a dialogue – within the ingroup and in communication with any outgroup.

Enemy Image Construction

We need to determine what an enemy image is and how the self is involved. First, as the word "image" signifies, it should be distinguished from what we define as reality. An image does not automatically coincide with reality but is a construction. In this construction we put together particular elements derived from reality in such a way that it becomes an identifiable pattern. Second, the self is involved as an "I" or a "we" that appropriates this image as belonging to the extended self (my enemy, our enemy). An enemy image can be clarified by the distinction between internal positions in the self (e.g. I as hating them, I as fearful) and external positions in the self (e.g. they as dangerous, they as wanting to destroy us). Usually, an enemy image involves resistance to seeing or even an inability to see the distinction between the other as a construction (external positions in the self) and the other as "real." When we see the real other and our construction of them as identical and when we do not see that this construction is, at least partly, the result of our own internal positions ("We as a proud nation" or "We as in need of protection"), then we erroneously see our construction as coinciding with reality. When the distinction between internal and external positioning is not clear and their interconnections are disregarded, the enemy image is susceptible to a "reality claim" that, on emotional grounds, evokes a strong and persistent anti-positioning against the outgroup with no space for constructive counter-positioning. When both parties, involved in an internal unification and external dividing process, are blind to their subjective contribution to the image and its persistence, the anti-positioning process ends in toxic polarization, which, via a process of over-positioning of the original impulse, can result in war, destruction, or genocide.

Dictatorial leaders in particular make active use of such emotional positioning processes as part of their propaganda machinery. Putin warns his nation of an aggressively expanding West that purposefully wants to destroy Russia. In this way, he increases the anxiety level of his citizens, which allows him to place himself in a savior position and gives him the "noble" task of protecting his own people. Hitler used the same strategy by selecting the Jews as the main threat to his nation and race so that he could present himself as the strong Führer who, as the savior of his nation, would be able to lead the Germans to racial purity and victory over evil. One of the differences between Hitler and Putin is that the latter has nuclear weapons that he might use as a threat against NATO countries in his (psychological) war against Ukraine. Threatening with nuclear attack, he deliberately elevates the "bomb anxiety" in Western populations, hoping that NATO's willingness to become more decisive in actively halting the atrocities by the Russian army in Ukraine is reduced.

In the several stages, eloquently described by Reicher and colleagues (see earlier in this chapter), I see a process of transpositioning at work. In their five-step model we could see a succession of: (1) creating a cohesive ingroup; (2) excluding people from inclusion via boundary setting; (3) perception of the outgroup as threatening ingroup identity; (4) representing the ingroup as uniquely good; and (5) annihilation: praising inhumanity as a defense of virtue. So, the process starts with creating a cohesive ingroup (unification) and ends with annihilation, evaluated as morally "good." In other words, the energy invested in the first step (unification) is, via a stepwise process of transpositioning, finally expressed in deeds of annihilation. Or, phrased differently, the energy invested in annihilation receives an *initial* push by unification as a welcome way of bringing people together. Apparently, acts that are initially evaluated as morally good or neutral have, on a hidden level, the potential of ending in destruction, legitimized as the defense of virtue. In moral good lie the seeds of moral bad as a potential position.

Does a Moral Middle Ground Exist?

As long as individuals or groups consider each other as enemies, they look at the other and the world from their own perspectives in the internal domain of the self: I as good. The corresponding position in the external domain of the self is: the other as bad. However, the actual other is involved in the same "game": They see themselves as good in the internal domain of their self with the corresponding position in the external domain of their self as bad. As long as both parties stick to this simplistic pattern, they both have a reason to entirely reject the other and see them as dangerous. They both do this on the assumption that they are fighting for the sake of virtue, which is placed exclusively on the side of the self, with "vice" located exclusively on the other side. As long as they are imprisoned in this position pattern, they have moral reasons to fight against the enemy and to support political leaders who motivate them to do so, certainly when these leaders emphasize the necessity of defense. As long as people are confined in this pattern, they don't see that the opponent is actually locked in the same pattern. The absurdity of war is that people who are willing to kill each other are motivated by the same positions, but, blinded as they are, they don't see that the enemy is, basically, thinking along the same lines.

As long as people are subjected to the construction of enemy images, there cannot be any moral middle ground because good and bad are *mutually exclusive*; that is, purely located at opposite sides. Good and bad are not brought together and there is no interface that allows them to see their intimate relationship. Right and wrong are separated from each other so that people can convince themselves that they are fighting on the right side and for the "good cause." However, this way of positioning, widespread as it may be, is not the only one because human beings are always able to step out from established position patterns and take a critical look at their own behavior. To understand this, we need a special position that appeals to the classical formula of "know thyself" and that enables us to look at ourselves from the outside in. In DST, this is known as taking a "meta-position."[121] Let's first consider this crucial position before examining how it gives access to the moral middle ground.

Meta-Positions as Helicopter Views

The main characteristics of meta-positions are the following:

(1) They provide an optimal *distance* vis-à-vis a plurality of more specific positions, which prevents us from being entirely determined by only one of them or by a limited pattern. This distance allows us to take a critical view of ourselves and acknowledge that there are *alternative perspectives* from which one can look at a particular topic. In the case

---

[121] Hermans (2018).

of enemy image construction, this position allows us to identify the
position of the other and to see what occurs on their side.

(2) They allow taking an *overarching perspective* so that a diversity of
I- and we-positions, both internal and external ones (others-in-the-
self), can be observed at the same time. This perspective allows us to
see the *patterns* of positions and the *processes* that are involved (e.g.
from unification to annihilation). They also permit a longer time
perspective so that we can grasp the long-term consequences of being
imprisoned in particular position patterns and processes.

(3) They lead to an *evaluation*, including a moral evaluation, of positions
that are facilitating or inhibiting the development of the self and the
other-in-the-self. They also allow us to see whether a particular
position has an *access* to other ones and an *exit* that allows us to leave
that position. In that way, we can see which I- and we-positions are
liberating and which ones are imprisoning. Evaluating them from the
broadly scoped and long-term perspective of a meta-position creates
opportunities for innovation of significant parts of the self.

(4) They acknowledge not only one's *personal history*, in the form of
changing I-positions and their patterns, but also how our personal
I-positions are influenced by our *collective history* (e.g. the influence
of political propaganda or educational materials that give biased views
on history). At the same time, we can notice how our own personal
positions contribute to the maintenance or change of collective
positions. Recognition of the close interconnection of personal and
collective histories allows us to see that one's personal concerns are
not purely individual constructions but are permanently under the
influence of collective we-positions and vice versa.

(5) They help us to assess the *developmental direction* in which we want
to move as participants of a personal and societal process of change.
Meta-positions have a signaling function: They act as a stop sign for
automatic and accustomed behavior and offer trajectories for
becoming liberated from rigidly established or maladaptive patterns
of positions, such as "I'm good, the other is bad." They give us an
opportunity to see which *counter-positions* are needed for giving a
different or new direction to existing I- and we-positions.

(6) They offer a broad *dialogical space* with a wide horizon where specific
positions of self and other can be explored in their mutual
relationships and interchanges. When the dialogue evolves from one
position only (e.g. I speak as a citizen of this country or as a
representative of a particular religious or cultural group), then the

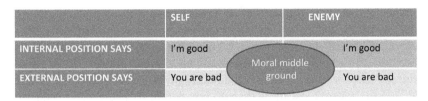

Figure 3.7   Positions "I'm good" and "you are bad" and the moral middle ground that interconnects them.

> dialogical reach is more limited than when we transcend these limits and take a look over the boundaries of our own specific positions and collective positions (e.g. I speak as a human being).[122]

Meta-positions have the potential of liberating ourselves from the fixed patterns and processes of positioning in which we imprison our enemies and ourselves. As these patterns are based on moral dualism, they block us from entering the meeting space of good and bad on the moral middle ground. Well-developed meta-positions may overcome the often-dramatic consequences of sharply demarcated, dualistic perspectives in which good and bad are always on one side and never on both sides.

Meta-positioning allows us to identify ourselves not only with our own internal positions, but also with those of other people, including our opponents or enemies as significant but negatively experienced others-in-the-self. The meta-position enables us to include not only the enemy as another in the self, *but also our perception of the other as positioning us as enemies of them.* The way we feel positioned by the other is then part of our extended self, which we can confirm, reject, correct, or include in the dialogues with others and ourselves. If we bring the positioning of ourselves as good together with our perception of the actual other as seeing us as bad and if we reflect, from a meta-position, on our *extended* selves as good *and* bad (the two rows in Figure 3.7), then this meta-position provides access to the moral middle ground. This extension can take place not only in our own self but also in the self of the actual other. If participants do so, a dialogical space opens up that goes beyond any imprisoning stereotype or prejudice and beyond any individualized self-ideal.

However, assuming a meta-position in which we pretend to take the position of our enemy requires our image of the enemy to be sufficiently

---

[122] For an overview of the democratic organization of the self, see Hermans (2018, 2020).

realistic – realistic in the sense of *their* perspective, not as a projection from our own part. Take the following example that I present *not* as a justification of the Russian invasion in Ukraine but as an exercise in taking the position of the other as *different* from our current position in Western Europe and the USA. It runs as follows: Many Russians know that during WWII the country lost more than 20,000,000 of its soldiers and civilians. Contemporary Russians are aware of the fact that they suffered the greatest losses of all countries during that war, and stories about lost ancestors are passed down through the generations. Films about the "Great Patriotic War," as it is called in Russia, are abundant. These films are not simply about the past; their stories are felt as "present," as they are kept alive by a powerful propaganda machine that convinces Russian citizens that Nazism is still active in Ukraine. Since the collapse of the Soviet Union, NATO has expanded to countries that previously were under the Russian sphere of influence, and many Russians believe that the populations of those countries are increasingly "indoctrinated" by "corrupt" Western values. By now, many Russians feel that since the Ukraine war the "whole world" has united against them, and they feel increasingly threatened by the advancing "enemy." In such a situation, they feel the need for a "strong leader" who is seen as capable and willing to defend them and restore their national pride. If you put yourself in *their* shoes, would you be critical enough to *not* support such a leader?[123]

The central question behind Figure 3.7 is: Are we willing to include the way we perceive others' perceptions of us in our self-construction? When we stick to dichotomous "we versus they" thinking, the answer will be: no. If we are willing to see the other and the other's perception of us as part of our extended self, then we may be inclined to enter a dialogue between others and ourselves that has the potential of transcending any enemy construction *image*, based as it is on an irreconcilable opposition and separation of us versus them. In fact, enemy image construction functions as the shadow of our attachment to certainty and dichotomous thinking. As a correction to this process, a well-developed meta-position gives access to a moral middle ground where the good perceived in our self and the bad attributed to us by our enemy come together and create space for tension-loaded and dissonant dialogues.

To avoid misunderstandings, it should be added that there is a difference between *understanding* the position of the enemy as part of one's

---

[123] In the context of a broadened identity definition, it makes sense to see any individual or group defined as "enemy" by our allies or ourselves also as a human being just like us (see Chapter 6).

extended self and *acting* on the basis of this position. The fact that one has insight into the motivations of the enemy or "wrong other in the self" (see also Chapter 4) as an external position in the extended self does not mean that this position takes exclusive priority over other extensions of the self (children, family, fellow citizens) at the level of action. In agreement with the principle of the relative dominance of positions in DST, the self has the right to prioritize these other extensions in case of the necessity of defending them against any enemy if necessary.

Practical Implications

This chapter allows for some practical implications. First and most significantly, I would like to emphasize the *moral multiplicity* of the self as a counterforce to any premature definition of the self as morally unified. In this chapter, I argued that both Hitler and Putin developed worldviews aimed at realizing a purification of their empires by setting up a powerful propaganda machinery. The consequence was that Hitler became engaged in a project of removing and even destroying a group of people – the Jews – that he defined as polluting the purity of the Aryan race. Likewise, Putin's goal seems to be to cleanse the population of Ukraine, which he sees as polluted by a process of "Nazification" and under the threat of moral degeneration by Western sexual liberties, gender liberties, and same-sex marriage. As both dictators place the moral bad purely outside, in enemies or dissidents, they reject any internal moral multiplicity, a process that results in moral dualism with sharp boundaries between good and bad. The principle of moral multiplicity recognizes that good and bad are both *within* the self and within the other.

The recognition of the multiplicity of self and identity can be fostered by *avoiding the identification of people on the basis of one category only*. Research in the field of morality[124] has compared multilevel categorization of a target (e.g. "Giuseppe is a black male young person. He was born in Italy, and his parents are immigrants") with simple categorization where the target is described on the basis of their skin color only (i.e. "Giuseppe is a black person"). It appeared that in the multiple categorization condition participants endorsed human rights values (e.g. equality, liberty, security) in favor of the target to a higher degree than in the simple categorization condition. This suggests that when people are seen as representing a

---

[124] Albarello and Rubini (2012).

multiplicity of identity categories, they are perceived as more human than in the case where this multiplicity is stripped from them.

It should be added that, in a more general sense, "categorical thinking" predisposes people to use stereotypes that don't give full weight to people's multiplicity of self and identity and, thereby, to their full human potential. Yet, we use categorizations as a necessary process in the construction and organization of social knowledge. As Allport acknowledged in his milestone work *The Nature of Prejudice*, "Categorical thinking is a natural and inevitable tendency of the human mind"[125] because categorization allows people to impose structure on the world so that they can cope with its complexity. However, at the same time, social categorization makes people believe that a social category captures a collective "essence." In Allport's view, this belief in the essence of social groups is a central characteristic of the prejudiced personality who tends to use race, sex, ethnicity, age, and other categories as a basis of social categorization.[126]

Given our ingrained use of social categories and the associated tendency to categorize people, I want to go one important step further than the employment of categorizations and even multiple categorizations and propose to *conceive of identity as a dynamic multiplicity of I-positions*. Very differently from objectifying, impersonal, and static categories, I-positions are based on the assumption that people live as *subjects* who, from a first-person perspective, give meaning to themselves and the world. And as *persons* rather than representatives of categories they deserve to be recognized in their unique place in time and space. Moreover, I-positions, including we-positions as their extension, are basically expressions of highly *dynamic processes*, as demonstrated in Reicher and colleagues' five-step model for explaining enemy image construction (discussed earlier in this chapter). Such processes demonstrate that the self can make transitions from one position to another one and that positions that are initially seen as morally neutral or good may carry the seeds of later dehumanization, purification, and enemy image construction, as illustrated by Hitler's and Putin's worldviews and by all those ideologies that express a longing for a purified group or nation in a utopian future (see also former US president Donald Trump's slogan "Make America Great Again").

In specific threatening situations, categorical thinking can be very effective and helpful. When you meet a group of hooligans leaving a café at night after their favorite team has been defeated and you pass them by dressed in a showy shirt covered in symbols of the winning team, it might

---

[125] Allport (1954), quoted by Roets et al. (2015, p. 257).   [126] Roets et al. (2015).

be wise to categorize them as "dangerous" and make a detour. But it is also very practical not to use social stereotypes as ways of systematically degrading other individuals or groups, as this may lead to fierce aggression, discrimination, and even murder. My purpose is to emphasize that recognizing the other as "another I" prevents considering them merely as representatives of a social category, and that categorization, like stereotyping, is a *first* step toward dehumanization. So, a practical way of acknowledging the other as another I is to pose questions such as: "How would they think about this?" "How would they feel about this?" "How would I feel if I stood in their shoes?"

Another practical implication of the presented view is that it is beneficial to self and society to *broaden one's moral circle* beyond one's favorite ingroup. As we saw earlier in this chapter, ingroup unity is protected by the construction of a moral circle that includes those who belong to one's own community and the simultaneous exclusion of those who are perceived as a threat to or moral contagion of the ingroup. The coexistence of inclusion and exclusion creates razor-sharp and rigid boundaries between the "good people" located within the moral circle and the "bad people" outside this circle. Only those who are included in one's own circle are within the scope of moral concern. For example, the citizens of many countries in Western Europe were spontaneously and rapidly inclined to provide support to refugees from Ukraine. In contrast, refugees from Syria during the violent conflict between prodemocratic insurgents and Syrian president Bashar al-Assad's long-standing dynastic regime faced more resistance and less social support, although their suffering was very similar. (For broadening the circle of moral concern, see Chapter 5.)

An essential element of expanding our moral circle to the other is the stimulation of *intergroup contact* as a powerful strategy to break through the closed boundaries of moral bifurcation. Social psychological research[127] has shown that high-quality intergroup contact leads to fewer dehumanizing perceptions of outgroups. The already-mentioned contact hypothesis of Gordon Allport has inspired a meta-analytic study[128] that assessed more than 500 publications on the reduction of prejudice toward physically and mentally disabled people, individuals with black or brown skin color, women, and LGBTQ+ people. The main conclusion of that research was that intergroup contact typically reduces intergroup prejudice.

Another road to the reduction of prejudice toward outgroups is to promote a *superordinate identity* as a way to emphasize the similarities

---

[127] Haslam and Loughnan (2014).   [128] Pettigrew and Tropp (2006).

and shared fate of different subgroups. Social psychologists have proposed a common ingroup identity model[129] that assumes that cooperative contact would reduce separation between social groups by favoring the adoption of a superordinate goal to which both ingroup and outgroup are devoted. A redefinition of groups from "us" versus "them" to a superordinate, more inclusive "we" creates a common ingroup identity. This redefinition of the boundaries in the direction of a larger group has the effect that the motivations and emotions initially limited to the ingroup are broadened to the former outgroup.[130]

A widely scoped perspective can be achieved by *taking a meta-position*, as this allows us to look beyond our limited I- and we-positions and to enlarge our moral circles. Meta-positions provide an overarching perspective, allow the possibility of alternative routes, and show how our present view emerges from our individual and collective history, and thus they have the potential to open the boundaries of our limited I- and we-positions. Our inclination is to see others as our "mirrors." The more similar others are to ourselves, the more morally concerned we are about them. Meta-positions allow us not only to take the specific positions of others, but also to look *through* the mirror so that we have access to the positions of others; not only those that are similar to our positions, but also those that are different. As I have argued elsewhere,[131] in a globalizing world in which we are highly interdependent but at the same time different, we need the precious capacity of imagination, which enables us to look beyond our inclinations and limitations and place ourselves in the positions of others who are different from us on an individual as well as a collective level.

Meta-positions give us *access to the moral middle ground.* They enable us to include not only *our* enemy as another in our selves, but also our perception of the other as positioning us as enemies of them. Being positioned by the other is then part of our extended self and, via our meta-positions, we can confirm, reject, deny, or include the positions that we have in the eyes of the other and include them in dialogues with ourselves. If we bring together our position as good in the eyes of ourselves with our perception or imagination of the actual other as seeing us as bad and if we have the courage to reflect on our extended selves as good *and* bad, then we find ourselves on the moral middle ground. For sure, this brings us into a situation of uncertainty (see Chapters 5 and 6) that contrasts strongly with the more easy and comfortable view of ourselves as exclusively located on the right side and as belonging to the "better

---

[129] Gaertner and Dovidio (2000).   [130] Capozza et al. (2013).   [131] Hermans (2022).

group." However, circling around in this comfort zone may not be the ideal starting point for finding solutions in situations where individuals and groups are separated from each other by the combination of internal unification and external division.

Summary

Whereas in Chapter 2 I examined the implications of reversing bad into good, in the present chapter I was interested in the rejection of bad by putting it entirely outside one's own self or group. I selected two shocking examples of the latter response: Hitler's worldview as embraced by Nazi Germany in the previous century and Putin's worldview as an ideological legitimation of his invasion of Ukraine in the present century. A comparison of these two figures gives access to some deeper commonalities in the social identities they propagated as part of their worldviews.

In analyzing the two ideologies, I found four common features that I qualified as the "dead ends" of identity construction, as I see them as being based on illusions that seem to offer a promising future but actually lead to aggression, violence, and even genocide. These common features are purification, dehumanization, internal unification in combination with external division, and enemy image construction.

Then I analyzed the moral implications of the four dead ends by placing them in the context of recent developments in the psychology of morality. I devoted special attention to Albert Bandura's model of self-sanction, as it delves deeply into what happens in the self when good people do bad things, and I discussed the highly dynamic five-step model proposed by Stephen Reicher and his colleagues.

I provided insights into the four dead ends from the perspective of DST. This led to the conclusion that the strategy of morally elevating the self by placing "evil" entirely outside does not leave any space for the existence of a moral middle ground. However, by considering that we are positioned as "bad" by our enemies and accepting the view that *our* enemies are extensions of our own selves, we notice that the moral middle ground becomes accessible.

I concluded this chapter with some practical implications: recognizing the existence of moral multiplicity instead of moral dualism; avoiding the identification of people on the basis of one category only; replacing social categories by personalized I-positions; broadening one's moral circle beyond one's favorite ingroup; intergroup contact; promoting a superordinate identity; developing an overarching meta-position; and creating access to the moral middle ground.

CHAPTER 4

The Vitality of the Moral Middle Ground

No morality "wants there to be many moralities, they want no comparison and no criticism; just absolute faith."

Friedrich Nietzsche[1]

In this chapter, I want to explain in greater detail what I consider to be the specific nature of the moral middle ground and to show its variation, breadth, and significance for the moral functioning of the self. With this purpose in mind, I want to analyze some phenomena in which good and bad aspects are combined and how I consider them as productive coalitions on the moral middle ground. This middle ground is without any form of moral dualism, a view that considers good and bad, or right and wrong, as two separate, antagonistic, or conflicting moral realms. The following phenomena are discussed: healthy selfishness, enlightened self-interest, Machiavellianism, the case of Oskar Schindler, black humor, grey hat hackers, transgressive art, the combination of the pure and impure, and the bad other-in-the-self. After offering a definition of the moral middle ground, I discuss some practical implications: (1) the positive evaluation of transgressive art; (2) controversies in the abortion debate in the USA; and (3) recent developments in the #MeToo movement.

Healthy Selfishness

Usually, selfishness is regarded as an undesirable or even immoral attribute, whereas altruism is considered desirable and virtuous. However, as psychologists Scott Barry Kaufman and Emanuel Jauk[2] have demonstrated, recent research data suggest a more complex picture: Not all selfishness is necessarily bad and not all altruism is necessarily good. Based on the

---

[1] From Nietzsche's *Beyond Good and Evil* and *Sämtliche Werke. Kritische Studienausgabe*, quoted by van Tongeren (2006, p. 392).
[2] Kaufman and Jauk (2020).

psychological literature and their own research, they discuss two concepts: healthy selfishness and pathological altruism. Overall, they found that healthy selfishness is associated with higher levels of psychological well-being, adaptive psychological functioning, and a genuine prosocial (helpful) orientation. In contrast, they demonstrated that pathological altruism is associated with maladaptive psychological outcomes, vulnerable narcissism, and selfish motivations for helping others. Together, these results underpin the paradoxical nature of both constructs.

The authors were inspired by an essay[3] of Abraham Maslow in which he argues that a distinction should be made between healthy selfishness and unhealthy selfishness. He writes: "It may be that at certain times, selfish behavior is good, and at other times, it is bad. It also may be that unselfish behavior is sometimes good and at other times bad." And he adds that "a good deal of what appears to be unselfish behavior may come out of forces that are psychopathological and that originates in selfish motivation."[4]

Likewise, in his 1939 essay "Selfishness and Self-Love," Erich Fromm remarked that "[m]odern culture is pervaded by a taboo on selfishness. It teaches that to be selfish is sinful and that to love others is virtuous."[5] He emphasized that this cultural taboo has had the unfortunate consequence of making people feel guilty when they experience healthy self-love, which he, instead, welcomed as the passionate affirmation and respect for one's own happiness, growth, and freedom.[6] And he added that the kind of selfishness that society disapproves of – an interest *only* in oneself and the inability to care for the dignity and integrity of others – is actually the *opposite* of self-love.[7]

Whereas selfishness is often looked upon with disapproval, altruism is typically viewed as desirable and morally good. Indeed, altruism is healthy as long as it is associated with openness to new experiences and a desire for personal growth. However, there are forms of altruism that can be considered as unhealthy and undesirable. What is known as "pathological altruism" can be defined as "the willingness of a person to irrationally place another's perceived needs above his or her own in a way that causes self-harm."[8] A major motivation for individuals driven by pathological altruism is to please others, gain approval, and avoid criticism and rejection.

To clarify my arguments in this book, it is relevant to note that there is a significant difference between healthy selfishness and pathological

---

[3] Maslow (1943/1996).   [4] Ibid., quoted by Kaufman and Jauk (2020, p. 2).
[5] Fromm (1939), quoted by Kaufman and Jauk (2020, p. 2).   [6] Ibid.   [7] Ibid.
[8] Bachner-Melman and Oakley (2016), quoted by Kaufman and Jauk (2020, p. 3).

altruism. Although they both can be regarded as paradoxical phenomena, healthy selfishness is associated with a sense of vitality, whereas pathological altruism leans toward a self-sacrificing or, even worse, self-destructive behavior. In their research, Kaufman and Jauk found a positive relationship between healthy selfishness and what they called "social vitality," described as a combination of social dominance and caring. In contrast, the relationship between pathological altruism and social vitality was slightly negative, suggesting that pathological altruism was associated with a somewhat lower degree of social vitality.[9] These data are in accordance with the main thesis of this book that the moral middle ground is an in-between area where good and bad have the possibility of forming coalitions that serve as sources of energy and vitality. These qualities would be lost when bad is separated from good as a form of moral dualism that considers good and bad as mutually exclusive or opposite forces.

It strikes me that, probably as a result of our upbringing and social training, we have the spontaneous tendency to organize our position repertoire in such a way that some positions are easily or self-evidently intertwined, whereas other ones are regarded as opposites and as not belonging together. Nobody would be surprised to see that "I as a hard worker" coexists with "I as a sports lover." Likewise, it is obvious that "I as a jealous person" may go together with "I as angry." And it is easy to position another person as striving for social power and, at the same time, as abusive. However, it is *not* self-evident that "I as a moral person" can coexist or even be integrated with "I as selfish." Apparently, the coalition of "I as dominant" *and* "I as loving," like positioning another person as dominant *and* as loving, brings us into a field of uncertainty, as we intuitively feel these positions are contradictory and that they cannot, or cannot easily, go well together. To see ourselves as loving increases our self-esteem, whereas seeing ourselves as selfish decreases it. It requires some internal dialogical effort to see and accept that, *as part of a coalition with a morally righteous position*, selfishness can be beneficial to self and society. (For the topic of contradiction in relation to self-esteem, see Chapter 5.)

Enlightened Self-Interest of Moral Exemplars: Unusual but Possible

People who embody the phenomenon of healthy selfishness are similar to those who became known as "moral exemplars." These are individuals who

---

[9] Kaufman and Jauk (2020, p. 10).

achieve power *with* conscience and brilliance *with* wisdom and in their extraordinary commitments promote benevolence, justice, or basic human welfare.[10] Jeremy Frimer and colleagues, who proposed this term, objected against the usual dualism of self-interest versus morality:

> Our primary contention is that this dualistic rendition (self vs. morality) may capture some aspects of moral reasoning but fails to adequately explain optimal moral identity and motivation … This dualism between self-interest and the dictates of one's moral code may be typical for most persons; however, our claim is that exemplars are an exception to this rule. We posit that they defy this dualism by integrating their personal ambitions with their moral convictions, yielding a state of "enlightened self-interest" in which their own interests become aligned with the interests of others; therein lays the motivation to lead the virtuous life.[11]

Based on these considerations, the researchers investigated twenty-five recipients of the Caring Canadian Award, a national honor given to individuals who have spent years, in some cases decades, in extraordinary voluntary service, supporting people in their community, or advancing a humanitarian cause. After their initial nomination by members of the general public, the recipients of the award were nominated by an independent committee and finally decorated by the governor-general, the representative of the British Queen (and now King) in Canada. This group was compared with twenty-five demographically matched participants.

Frimer and colleagues studied both groups regarding two basic motives: "agency" and "communion," which are often conceptualized as being in conflict. Agency was defined as the motive to advance oneself within a social hierarchy expressed as striving for achievement, social power, or material wealth. Communion was described as striving for the benefit of significant others or through a concern for the well-being of disadvantaged, distant others or the ecological well-being of the planet. The results of this research revealed that "exemplars" displayed not only more agency and communion than participants in comparative groups, but they were also more likely to integrate these motives into their own personality.

This research on agency and communion has a strong appeal to me as I was, over several decades, involved in research into two basic motives: Self-motive (referring to self-assertion and self-enhancement) and Other-motive (longing for contact and union with somebody or something else). As a personality psychologist, I collaborated with psychotherapist Els Hermans-Jansen, and together we constructed the Self-Confrontation

---

[10] Frimer et al. (2011).   [11] Ibid. (p. 150).

Method.[12] Within a broad population of clients, we found that when the Other-motive was supported by a strongly developed Self-motive, they formed a combination that was associated with high levels of personal well-being and coexisted with concern for the well-being of others. In contrast, those clients whose position repertoire was structurally dominated by aggression and anger showed a combination of high self-enhancement and low well-being. They were frustrated and disappointed by not reaching their goals and responded to this frustration with a persistent anti-positioning stance: systematically going against other individuals, being opposed and rebelling against them, sometimes culminating in hate. These clients were clearly not able to combine their striving for a self-enhancement motive with a sense of communion with others. The application of the Self-Confrontation Method in a larger group of subjects confirmed this finding: Clients who were motivated by a combination of high self-enhancement and *low* communion were characterized by distrust in others and a high need for control.[13]

Go Ahead and Go Along: Machiavellian Youngsters

Only in recent decades have developmental psychologists been asking the question as to whether human aggression can be fruitfully viewed through an evolutionary developmental lens. The function of aggression has been of central interest in fields traditionally guided by evolutionary theory. Animal researchers, ethologists, and anthropologists have long regarded phenomena like status attainment, the acquisition of material resources (e.g. food) and social resources (e.g. mates), and defense against intruders to be important functions of aggression and aggressive displays. Under certain conditions, aggression is considered to be adaptive both ontogenetically (for the individual) and phylogenetically (for a species or group).[14]

On the basis of these considerations, developmental psychologist Patricia Hawley[15] studied children of grades 5 through 10 and distinguished three groups: (1) *Prosocial controllers*, who put "getting along" over "getting ahead," assessed as agreeable/sociable, socially skilled, conscientious, and, as a result, enjoying a most favorable peer regard; (2) *coercive controllers*, with a profile opposite to that of the prosocial controllers – they are more concerned with getting ahead than getting along and experience

---

[12] Hermans and Hermans-Jansen (1995).   [13] van Geel et al. (2019).   [14] Hawley (2014).
[15] Hawley (2003).

negative feedback from the social group for this; and (3) *bistrategic controllers*, who combine prosocial and coercive control.

In this context, Machiavellians,[16] describing those youngsters who used both strategies of resource control, emerged as possessing a combination of positively and negatively valued characteristics and, despite their aggression or even due to it, were rated as socially recognized, liked by peers, socially skilled, and well-adjusted. They seemed to command a great deal of attention from the peer group and were admired by them. Interestingly, teachers rated bistrategic controllers as socially accepted to the same degree as prosocial controllers. Hawley suspects that teachers may not be able to differentiate prosocial and bistrategic controllers in this age group because bistrategists are skilled at hiding their aggression from authority figures.

Hawley concludes that Machiavellianism refers to an apparently effective approach that entails a careful balancing of "getting along" and "getting ahead." These youngsters admit that they are aggressive, claim to be hostile, and confess that they are involved in cheating behavior. They are cast in a similar light by their peers, who report them to be the most aggressive children in the schoolyard. At the same time, they are also regarded as effective and socially central, and they are reasonably well liked. Not surprisingly, Machiavellians enjoy a higher-than-average social self-concept and positive affect.

In a relativizing way, Hawley notes that Machiavellian children are not to be evaluated as model citizens nor as shining examples of social competence. By their own admissions, they sometimes behave badly. Without doubt, the prosocial controllers stand out as the ones who are most agreeable, socially skilled, and conscientious. Moreover, prosocial controllers report that they generally conform to societal expectations and they rate themselves as well below average on aggression and hostility, a combination of characteristics that makes them popular in the eyes of their peers. Not surprisingly, they are respected as friendly, competent children with leadership skills and positively evaluated by their teachers.

Reading about Machiavellians, my memories went back to my high school years when I demonstrated some features of this type of behavior. At that time, I was frequently involved in cheating, like copying during an

---

[16] Niccolò Machiavelli (1469–1527) was an Italian Renaissance political philosopher whose most famous work, *The Prince* (*Il Principe*), earned him a reputation as an atheist and an immoral cynic; *Encyclopedia Britannica*, www.britannica.com/biography/Niccolo-Machiavelli, retrieved June 30, 2022.

exam, and sometimes I joined in with bullying behavior. Moreover, I felt a strong opposition to any authority figure and, if possible, violated the strict social regulations of the school. However, I was clearly aware that I could not express my revolting attitude directly. So, my friends and I developed strategies of sabotage that would make it difficult for teachers to unmask the perpetrator. But this was not always successful. Once, we were practicing singing religious songs in a church under the supervision of our religion teacher. I joined in with the singing, but, with my low-pitched voice, I started to sing one octave lower than the rest, knowing that this would be very irritating to the teacher. I assumed that he would not be able to localize the source of the deviant voice. However, to my surprise, he suddenly appeared next to me and angrily sent me out of the church with the command to report myself to the rector (a priest) of the school, which I did not do. The next day, I had to appear in the rector's room, and he was extremely angry at me. The only thing I could do was look straight into his eyes as a nonverbal form of opposition. My eyes were "telling" him: "I don't care about you, I'm not afraid of you!" This made him even more angry, and he started circling around me, shouting that if I hadn't been so tall, he would have hit me. While he was shouting so loudly, I could smell the gingerbread he'd had for his lunch on his breath. As a punishment, he expelled me for one day from school and called my parents to inform them about my misbehavior.

It was in that period that one of our teachers decided to choose a class representative, which took place by anonymous vote. To my great surprise, my name was the most frequently mentioned of the twenty-five students in the class. Then, the teacher invited me come to the front of the class and say a word of thanks. I stood there, entirely unprepared. Not one word passed my lips. Teacher and students were waiting, but I was mute and deeply embarrassed (not a real Machiavellian at that moment!). After a tormenting minute passed, the teacher spoke some words that I just had to repeat. To my great relief, I could return to my place. When I look back at these incidents after reading the research on Machiavellian youngsters, I realize that, in that period of my live, I was a boy who preferred to combine prosocial and coercive strategies in my contacts with both classmates and teachers, and I suspect that my peers appreciated this behavior.

The Case of Oskar Schindler

Oskar Schindler (1908–1974) was a German industrialist who, with the aid of his wife and staff, sheltered approximately 1,100 Jews from the Nazis by giving them employment in his factories, which supplied the German army during World War II (WWII).[17]

In 1935, Schindler joined the pro-Nazi Sudeten German Party in Czechoslovakia, which had the official aim of breaking the country up and joining it to the Third Reich. The next year, he began collecting counterintelligence for the Abwehr, the German military intelligence agency. In 1938, he was arrested by Czechoslovak authorities, accused of espionage, and sentenced to death. After the annexation of the Sudetenland by Germany in the same year, Schindler was pardoned by the Reich and rose through the ranks of the Abwehr. His application for membership in the Nazi Party, probably submitted out of pragmatism rather than ideological affinity, was accepted in 1939.[18]

In the same year, Schindler journeyed to Kraków, where he became active in the emerging black market. Making use of his network of German contacts through bribes, he leased a formerly Jewish-owned enamelware factory and renamed it "Deutsche Emailwaren-Fabrik Oskar Schindler." Some months later, he had several hundred employees, seven of whom were Jewish. By 1942, nearly half of the workers at the expanded plant were Jewish. As "cheap labor," Schindler paid their salaries to the SS.[19]

In the fall of 1942, a concentration camp, the "Płaszów work camp," was opened in the neighborhood of Kraków that, in 1943, came under the command of the notoriously sadistic SS officer Amon Göth. Knowing of the officer's appetite for drink and other luxurious items, available mainly on the black market, Schindler cultivated a friendship with him by providing a constant stream of these luxuries. He then proposed to Göth to create a separate camp for his Jewish workers, where they were actually shielded from the abuses of Płaszów. Although it is not exactly clear what Schindler's motivations were prior to this point, many scholars interpret his efforts to save his workers from Płaszów as a sign that his concern for them was not purely financial.[20]

When his factory was decommissioned in August 1944, Schindler successfully petitioned to have it moved to Brněnec (Brünnlitz) in the Sudetenland, which was part of Czechoslovakia. Together with associates, he composed a list of Jewish workers that he "deemed essential" for the new factory and submitted it for approval to the Jewish labor office. Finally, he

---

[17] Encyclopedia Britannica, www.britannica.com/biography/Oskar-Schindler, retrieved July 1, 2022. The novel *Schindler's List*, written by Thomas Keneally in 1982, was later adapted by Steven Spielberg in his 1993 film with the same title.
[18] Ibid.   [19] Ibid.   [20] Ibid.

ensured that 700 men and 300 women arrived at Brněnec, who were later joined by 100 more Jews from another concentration camp. Those who reached the camp worked there during the remaining months of the war on the manufacturing of munitions that were rigged to fail. A final head count listed 1,098 Jews as inhabiting the camp at the end of the war.[21]

In his book *Varieties of Moral Personality*,[22] Owen Flanagan argues that the very qualities that most of us would consider to be morally problematic in Schindler – his hedonism, his avarice, and his ability to maintain convivial but actually instrumental relations with others – were precisely the qualities that put him in a position to save so many Jews from Hitler's *Sonderbehandlung* (special treatment), which was actually an euphemism for mass murder by Nazi functionaries and the SS. Precisely these qualities made him an attractive person to various SS officers, who remained ignorant of Schindler's actual purposes.

What Flanagan finds fascinating about Schindler is "that he remained every bit the hedonist, a hard-drinking womanizer remarkably uninterested in his familial responsibilities, as he began to display his moral nobility."[23] He was so convivial in his contacts with SS officers – keeping a good stock of brandy and enjoying the company of beautiful women – that he succeeded in keeping his "social friends" from carrying out their horrible project. Had the SS men realized what Schindler was doing, they certainly would have killed the Jews. Because of his ability to calmly enjoy the company of despicable men and deceive them, he was able to keep the SS from knowing what his real plans were.

In Flanagan's view, Schindler's case is deeply paradoxical. The best way to understand him is to acknowledge that he possessed a set of vices that he developed to a fairly high degree and that were, at the same time, *causally implicated* in the good acts he performed. This makes Schindler different from other moral icons, who are generally celebrated as heroes or saints. For example, Martin Luther King Jr. was a frequent adulterer, but overall this is not considered as nullifying his main ethical merit. Gandhi is known for sharing his bed with naked young women and for his apparent lack of deep and healthy relations with members of his own family. Both Luther King Jr. and Gandhi were driven by moral principles, such as justice and equality, but this hardly indicates that they lived their whole lives, in all domains, guided by these principles. Their difference from Schindler is that their vices were not causally implicated in the benefits they provided for their societies.

[21] Ibid.   [22] Flanagan (1991).   [23] Ibid. (p. 8).

"Comfort girls" during World War II as an example of the moral middle ground

The terms "comfort women" or "comfort girls" refer to females who were forced into sexual slavery by the imperial Japanese army in occupied countries and territories before and during WWII. Below is the story told by an eighty-five-year-old person who remembers the time when she as a nine-year-old girl, together with her mother, was incarcerated in such a camp in the Dutch East Indies (now Indonesia) during the period 1944–1945.

> We lived in the camp in appalling conditions and suffered under the harsh and cruel regime of the Japanese officers. The food that we received was extremely sober: a lump of bread with some tea in the morning, a small piece of tasteless meat at noon and, again, a lump of bread with some tea at the end of the day. We were forced to stay for many hours in a bowed position outside, as a reverence to the Japanese authorities. When one of the strict rules was violated, we were punished to stand a whole day in the heat of the sun without any water and food. Sometimes a whole group was punished with deprivation of food and water during three successive days. I remember very well that some adolescents of our barrack were selected as comfort girls and forced to have sex with Japanese soldiers. When they came back to the barracks, most of them were crying and extremely upset about what had happened. However, there were girls who came back with food! This was reason for some of the girls to offer themselves for prostitution so that they could get some extra food for their families and themselves. I also wanted to join but this was not allowed because of my young age . . .

Making oneself available for prostitution in the service of survival in these extreme circumstances: Was it good or bad?

Source: Lecture by Paula Cremers-Cardynaals for the Society Jansberg, February 17, 2022, Milsbeek, the Netherlands. Published with her permission.

Apparently, moral heroes such as Mahatma Gandhi and Martin Luther King Jr. had a position repertoire in which their moral positions stood *side by side* with their positions judged as vices by the communities of their time. These vices were not actively contributing to their virtues and were not necessary for the realization of the moral good. Rather, these vices may be seen as a stain on their moral blazon. This is very different from Schindler's case. He organized his life in such a way that his moral position – saving the Jews – was actively stimulated and even made possible by the immoral positions in his repertoire. In other words, moral and immoral positions formed a coalition in which not just one of them, the good one, was contributing to the welfare of society (as was the case for

Martin Luther King Jr. and Gandhi), but *both* the moral *and* immoral positions contributed in their unique combination and mutual dynamics. If one of them had been absent, it would not have been possible for Schindler to save the lives of the Jews. Because good and bad were productively working together, this coalition of positions is located on the moral middle ground.

Black Humor

Black humor treats sinister subjects like death, deformity, disease, physical disability, or warfare with bitter amusement and presents such tragic, distressing, or morbid topics in comic terms. Often indicated as morbid, grotesque, gallows, or sick humor, it is used to express the absurdity, cruelty, insensitivity, and paradoxical nature of the modern world. Usually, characters or situations are exaggerated far beyond the limits of normal satire or irony and often require increased cognitive efforts to get the joke. Furthermore, black humor is sometimes associated with tragedy and equated with tragic farce. It is perceived as nasty, morbid, psychopathic, twisted, and often very funny.[24]

Here are some examples of black humor[25]:

- Death, represented by a skeleton in a hooded coat holding an hourglass and a sickle, stands in front of a man on the doorstep of his apartment. The man says: "I am sorry, we do not die at the front door."
- A man scratching his chin apparently out of confusion is clutching the receiver of a public phone. The voice coming from the receiver says: "Here is the answering machine of the self-help association for Alzheimer patients. If you still remember your topic, please speak after the tone."
- In an operating theatre, a surgeon has one arm deep in an opened-up body. Another surgeon explains the situation to a man in a suit: "The autopsy is finished; he is only looking for his wrist watch."

In their study on black humor, developmental psychologist Ulrike Willinger and colleagues invited 156 adults to rate black humor cartoons on a number of variables (e.g. surprise, difficulty, vulgarity). Moreover, they measured the verbal and nonverbal intelligence, aggression, and mood disturbance of the participants. The results of this study, characterized by the researchers as "surprising," showed that participants with the highest levels of *preference* for and *comprehension* of black humor had high levels of

---

[24] Willinger et al. (2017).   [25] Ibid. (p. 161).

intelligence, high education levels, and low levels of aggression and mood disturbance. On the other hand, participants with low verbal and nonverbal intelligence, high mood disturbance, and high aggressiveness scores showed low levels of comprehension of and preference for black humor. The researchers concluded that understanding black humor, due to its combination of emotional and cognitive aspects, is a complex information processing task.[26]

However, what is the function of black humor, and what accounts for its popularity in films, magazines, newspapers, and other media? Russian psychologist Nikolay N. Gubanov and colleagues[27] believe that "psychological distance" plays a critical role in forming a humorous reaction to a tragic event and that this is significant for its moral evaluation. They analyze this concept as including the following four components: temporal distance, spatial distance, social distance, and hypothetical distance. Let's consider each of them in more detail.

- *Temporal distance:* The well-known expression "time heals" is reflected by Mark Twain's idea that "humor is tragedy plus time." The more time has passed since a tragic event, the more tolerant one is vis-à-vis black humor as a response to the event. For example, making jokes about a recently murdered politician who has the status of a national hero is unacceptable, whereas humorous remarks about the same event thirty years later meets less resistance.
- *Spatial distance:* The farther we are from the scene of the tragedy, the easier we can joke about it, as reflected in the formula of "involvement depends on the number of deaths divided by geographical distance." For example, the farther away a hurricane is, the more people tolerate humor about it.
- *Social distance:* It is more pleasant to joke about what happened not to us but to another person. The essence of this statement was well phrased by the comedian Mel Brooks: "Tragedy is when I cut my finger. Comedy is when you fell into an open manhole and broke your neck." Jokes about the accident of a colleague with whom one has frequent contact meet more resistance than jokes about a similar accident of a colleague who works in the same organization but with whom you have never had a talk.
- *Hypothetical distance:* Black humor in a story that is fictional is perceived better than black humor in a real one. "Tearing off the head" of a figure in a cartoon film is much easier, both from a technical and

[26] Ibid. (p. 165).   [27] Gubanov et al. (2018), elaborating on McGraw et al. (2014).

from a psychological point of view. Cartoons allow us to achieve a certain level of unreality, which provides an ideal base for the use of black humor. This is easier when it concerns abstract, faceless, almost inanimate objects. The constantly recurring death of a faceless "little boy" can be found in the popular animated series *South Park*. In this series, a boy, Kenny, dies in the most ludicrous ways: One of the characters bites off his head; the police shoot him when he approaches them with a white flag; he is pecked to death by turkeys; and in one episode he even dies of laughter.[28]

In summary, black humor about tragic events is most acceptable and successful when it is about events that have not happened to us (social distance), that occurred at the other end of the world (spatial distance), that happened long ago (temporal distance) and that are fictional (hypothetical distance).

What is the specific nature of black humor, and in what respects it is different from "normal" humor? We may laugh at a classic comedy scene in which we see a man fall over. However, we understand that this is not really serious and that the man will get up, shake himself off, and go on. In contrast, black humor contains an element of *irreversibility*: The dead person will not come back, the terminally ill patient will not be cured, and the severed limb will not grow again. As Gubanov and colleagues argue, black humor has the potential of transforming the tragic events of our lives into abstract ideas by taking a certain degree of psychological distance from them. Due to this distance, the psycho-traumatic perception of real phenomena is reduced.[29] The traumatic event is neither denied nor emotionally overwhelming but rather relativized. Black humor has the power of creating a coalition of good and bad that offers a unique perspective on irreversible damage, loss, or bad luck. Making jokes about a tragic experience is a way of positioning that may be regarded as morally rejectable, but if it is combined with giving support and even solace to oneself or another, it is a way of positioning oneself that may be helpful in a situation in which one is faced with an irreversible setback.

On July 5, 2022, the day when I was writing this text, I saw on the Dutch TV news channel NOS a fragment of a performance of an art group from Kyiv called Underground Standup Club. The performers were making "black jokes" about the Ukrainian war. One of them said that she worried that, if a missile were to hit the walls of her house, people would see what a mess it was inside, and she joked that she would probably

[28] Ibid.   [29] Ibid.

die on the toilet. Another artist, referring to the atrocities of the war, added: "We have to cope with that." Indeed, as one commentator wrote: "The war isn't remotely funny, but Ukrainians are learning to laugh about the awfulness of it all. Not necessarily because they want to, but because they have to – to stay sane in the brutality that has killed tens of thousands of people …"[30]

The Grey Hacker

Under the title "Hackers: The Good, the Bad, and the In Between," Sedona Du[31] wrote a research paper in which she posed the questions: Who are hackers? What do they do? And are they evil people? She notes that the majority of pieces published by the media about hackers have a negative overtone. In contrast to this overall view, she argues that, in spite of the fact that hackers break laws and cause harm, they are necessary to society and do not deserve to be labeled, in an overgeneralizing way, as "villains" or "criminals." In order to substantiate her thesis, she distinguishes three types of hackers, denoted as black, white, and grey hats.

Black Hats

Black hat hackers are those who are traditionally considered to be "cyber criminals" and are regarded as "bad guys" in the eyes of the government and majority of the general public. The reasons and aims behind these hackers reveal great variation. They can be motivated by financial gain, revenge, creating chaos, and shutting down servers. An example of a hacker with financial gain as his goal is the American Kevin Poulsen, also known as Dark Dante. In 1994, he pleaded guilty to seven counts of conspiracy, fraud, and intercepting wire transmissions in connection with a radio station contest. Poulsen took over all of the telephone lines for Los Angeles radio station KIIS-FM, which enabled him to be the 102nd caller and win the prize of a Porsche 944 S2.[32]

White Hats

In the world of hacking, white hat hackers are considered to be "the good guys." Often hired to do "penetration testing," they have the task of hacking into their own company's system in order to find flaws in their software. Once they get through the system's security, they report this

---

[30] Leicester (2022).   [31] Du (2017).   [32] Ibid.

back to the company and are involved in closing these gaps and in creating a more secure network. They are different from black hats because they never hack into a system without permission and don't use the information obtained in an illegal or unethical way.[33]

Facebook and other companies sometimes give financial rewards to people who find and report a security breach in their own companies' software. Although such people are not hired specifically to do "penetration testing," they are still given an incentive when they report a breach in security. In many cases, the government relies on white hat hackers. The Australian government, for example, started a competition called the "Cyber Security Challenge Australia." The intention behind this competition was to find the new wave of technological geniuses who are able to help the government to achieve strict security and to prevent future security breaches.[34]

A person who became famous as a white hat hacker is Kevin Mitnick, initially known as "the condor" or "the darkside hacker." His case is exceptional because he actually started out as a black hat hacker. During that period, the US Federal Communications Commissions called him "the most wanted computer criminal in U.S. history." He was known as an infamous hacker of private information and to have been involved in a string of other Internet crimes. After he was arrested in 1995 and served five years in jail, he made a complete 180-degree turn. He transformed himself from one of the most notorious black hat hackers to one of the most highly regarded white hat hackers in history. Generally speaking, white hat hackers behave "correctly" and abide by the law. They are viewed as "knights in shining armor" because they protect companies from being hacked and help the government to protect confidential information.[35]

Grey Hats

Not all hackers are purely benevolent or purely malevolent. There is a middle group, the grey hat hackers, who break laws just like black hats do. However, in most cases they don't have any malicious end goal as is typical of the black hats. Although grey hat hackers often hack their way into systems without permission and behave in illegal ways, they do not intend to cause harm or to steal money. They are motivated to improve Internet security by revealing security breaches or exposing vulnerabilities. Many webpage owners are thankful to the hackers who notify them of breaches

[33] Ibid.   [34] Ibid.   [35] Ibid.

because this helps them to prevent further damage in the future. These hackers may sometimes distribute stolen information when they think the general public has the right to know about it.

The most famous grey hat hacker is Julian Assange, the creator and figurehead of WikiLeaks, a website that distributes information that hackers submit to be published. The dark side of this activity is that the information that is posted on WikiLeaks is stolen and confidential. Yet, Julian Assange is not to be considered a black hat because WikiLeaks is not made with malicious intentions. He and other hackers who publish information via WikiLeaks (e.g. serious violations of human rights) are fighting for transparency, as they believe that confidential information that has societal relevance should be available for public viewing. However, in the eyes of governments, WikiLeaks is a threat to national security, and some people think that WikiLeaks does more harm than good. This is a huge "grey area" laden with controversies because a choice of greater transparency may have the consequence that confidentiality is violated, while a choice of greater confidentiality implies that the public will remain ignorant of moral transgressions. After an evaluation of the pros and cons, Sedona Du concludes: "Although grey hats commit illegal acts and can cause adverse reactions, they have good intentions. Sometimes they over-step boundaries and can do some harm. However, overall grey hats have a positive effect on society because they monitor the government and look out for the general population."[36] In agreement with this view, I see grey hat hackers as "workers on the moral middle ground" who, despite their controversial methods and illegal procedures, add value to society and invite people to compare arguments for and against in dialogical ways.

Transgressive Art

Art has great power to allow people to explore a diversity of perspectives and their moral implications. Great works of art can be influential, informative, and sometimes can even change social attitudes about certain topics. However, moral and aesthetic judgments of artworks are not always in accordance with each other. Sometimes they clash. A well-suited example of a form of art that has evoked hot controversies about its moral meaning became known under the label "transgressive art." Such art aims to outrage or violate basic morals and sensibilities. The term "transgressive

[36] Ibid. (n.p.).

art" was first used by the American filmmaker Nick Zedd and his Cinema of Transgression in 1985.

Transgressive art refers to a form of art that forcefully pushes us out of our comfort zone. Its traces can be found in any art that is considered offensive because of its shock value. Examples are the French *Salon des Refusés*, referring to exhibitions of works rejected from juried art shows; Surrealism, in which artists depicted unnerving, illogical scenes that allow the unconscious mind to express itself; and Dada, an art movement of the European avant-garde in the early twentieth century consisting of artists who rejected the logic, reasoning, and aesthetics of modern capitalist society and instead expressed irrationality and antibourgeois protest in their artistic productions. Transgressional books share some themes with art that deals with psychological dislocation and mental illness. Examples are Albert Camus's *L'Étranger* (*The Stranger*) or J. D. Salinger's *The Catcher in the Rye*. Also, some musical genres are regarded as expressions of transgressive art, such as black metal, death metal, and various bands within the avant-garde rock genre.[37]

In order to explore the relationship between transgressive art and morality, I refer to Kieran Cashell's[38] book *Aftershock: The Ethics of Contemporary Transgressive Art*, which provides an excellent basis for understanding this art as falling squarely on the moral middle ground. The author starts by observing that transgressive art, by its shocking, disturbing nature and its tendency to subvert conventional beliefs, is regarded by many as "going too far" and violating the transfer of higher culture. Yet, he notes that this art has genuinely expanded the horizon of artistic expression and constitutes a vital aesthetic force in post-twentieth-century vanguard culture.

To clear the way for a proper understanding of transgressive art, Cashell is opposed to the notion of "disinterestedness" as a basic principle in the aesthetic conception of the German philosopher Immanuel Kant (1724–1804). In Kant's view, disinterestedness is a prescribed aesthetic concept that starts from the assumption that the rational appreciation of artistic beauty should be disengaged from all practical contexts and from all emotional, sexual, or moral feelings. For Kant, a judgment of aesthetic value can only have universal validity if any motivation toward the object that involves desire is absent. For example, in order to appreciate the

[37] Art and Popular Culture, www.artandpopularculture.com/Transgressive_art. See also Wikipedia, https://en.wikipedia.org/wiki/Transgressive_art, retrieved July 7, 2022.
[38] Cashell (2009).

aesthetic value of the nude, one must learn to suspend any erotic desire evoked by it. If the body were to become the object of sexual desire, this would prevent pure artistic contemplation, and it would not be possible to dwell exclusively on the aesthetic significance of the nude and appreciate its artistic value.[39]

According to Cashell, Kantian disinterestedness has had an overwhelming influence on later conceptions about the philosophy of art. It continues to exert a palpable magnetism on philosophers of art, and it has been followed by many contemporary art critics. Yet it is precisely this concept that representatives of transgressive art try to sabotage by engaging with the "extra-aesthetic" contexts of very emotional, sexual, and especially moral life-worlds.

Drawing on a variety of authors, Cashell notes that there is "something fundamentally wrong" with Kant's conception of aesthetic value. He refers to passages in Kant's work where the philosopher argues that it is impossible to render beautiful "that which excites disgust," because disgust, as an intense emotion, cannot be assimilated to disinterested contemplation. In this aesthetic tradition, a visceral reaction to an artistic product is necessarily in conflict with forms of aesthetic appreciation that require an attitude of critical and emotional distance.

Consider Paul McCarthy's (1945–) *Bossy Burger* (1991), a combination of performance and video installations that constitutes a clear assault on post-Kantian aesthetics. In the claustrophobic confines of a plywood studio set, the artist is dressed as a *chef de cuisine* with yellow rubber gloves and wearing a mask. Grumbling and moaning, he smears every surface around with ketchup and mayonnaise. Narcissistically absorbed in his purposeless business, and finally completely covered in mess, he kneels on a table and begins to apply coats of the ketchup to a shabby armchair. The work expresses zero tolerance for any orthodox aesthetic value.[40]

As a stark violation of the conventional aesthetic principle, transgressive art aims to produce a direct, uncomfortable effect upon us. If it didn't shock, it would cease to have its desired function. This art form is explicitly intended to make us involuntarily exclaim: "*Stop!* This is wrong!" Yet it is precisely this kind of moral reaction to art that the practitioners of this kind of art have in mind when they violate the aesthetic feelings and expectations of the viewer. Performances like those of McCarthy reflect transgressive art's "predatory relation with what is forbidden."[41] Yet, art critics have defended his disturbing, perverse, and obscene performances as not only artistically significant but also enriching. They enable audiences

[39] Ibid.   [40] Ibid.   [41] Ibid. (p. 3).

Figure 4.1   "Civilización Occidental y Cristiana" or "Western and Christian Civilization",
1965, by León Ferrari.
Source: ALBERTO PIZZOLI/AFP/Getty Images.

to experience, vicariously, a violent regression without becoming directly
involved, similar to the cathartic relationship that emerged between the
protagonists and antagonists of ancient Greek tragedy and
their audience.[42]

However, where is the moral middle ground in transgressive art, and in
what ways do these artists bring good and bad close together? In the
following subsections, I present two famous and controversial works that,
in my view, are clearly located on this middle ground: "Western and
Christian Civilization" (Figure 4.1) by the Argentine artist León Ferrari
(1920–2013) and "The Holy Virgin Mary" (Figure 4.2) by the British
Turner Prize-winning painter Chris Ofili (1968–).

---

[42] Ibid.

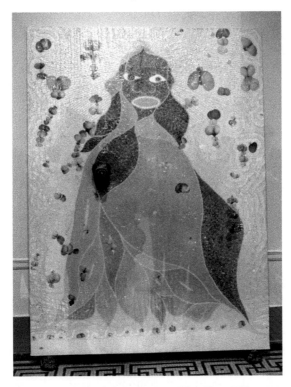

Figure 4.2 "The Holy Virgin Mary" by Chris Ofili, 1996.
Source: DOUG KANTER/AFP/Getty Images.

León Ferrari's Controversial Artistic View

Mara Polgovsky Ezcurra, a lecturer in contemporary art at the University of London, wrote an article in which she examined the moral implications of León Ferrari's transgressive art. In the beginning of her exposé, she goes back to December 1, 2004, when the former archbishop of Buenos Aires, Jorge Mario Bergoglio, the later Pope Francis I, published an open letter in response to León Ferrari's retrospective exhibition, opened at Centro Cultural Recoleta in Buenos Aires. The letter expressed concerns about certain "offences directed at our Lord Jesus Christ and the Holy Virgin Mary" that he criticized as "blasphemy."[43] By treating Ferrari's art as a religious offence, Bergoglio triggered what Ezcurra considered to be "the

---

[43] Ezcurra (2018, p. 21).

most important debate on the relationship between art and religion in recent Argentine history."[44] This debate was accompanied by legal disputes aiming to close the show, recurrent bomb threats to the art center, the destruction of some of the artist's works by religious fanatics, and the organization of mass prayers outside the art center in an attempt to exorcise "evil" from the venue. Aware that the artist and his work were under threat, a variety of local and international artists, curators, academics, and art organizations responded with a solidarity campaign to support Ferrari and the organizers of the exhibition, followed by a number of public demonstrations in defense of freedom of expression. After a temporary closure and later reopening of the exhibition, Ferrari decided to put an end to the ongoing scandal and the many risks to his life and works.[45]

Ezcurra's purpose was to argue that despite the polemic nature of several of Ferrari's works, reading them as an attack on Christianity, as asserted by then-Bishop Bergoglio, allows only a superficial understanding of the artist's work. As a correction to a religiously Manichaean approach of good (Christian values) versus bad (blasphemy), she aims to place Ferrari's art in a broader historical context in order to deepen the meaning of his work. Part of this history includes the period of Jorge Rafael Videla (1925–2013), an Argentine military officer and dictator and member of the military junta who became president of Argentina from 1976 to 1981. His government was held responsible for human rights abuses during Argentina's "Dirty War," which started as an attempt to suppress terrorism but resulted in the deaths of thousands of mainly left-wing civilians. The official estimate of those killed was 9,000, but other sources estimate that between 15,000 and 30,000 people were murdered by military and right-wing death squads during Videla's presidency, and many others had to suffer torture and imprisonment.[46]

The Argentine dictatorship – together with the Holocaust – belongs, in Ezcurra's view, to the grand political projects that have led to the mass annihilation of human lives in the name of the protection of Western Christian civilization. Therefore, neither the dictatorship nor the Holocaust is a singular event or expression of absolute evil. Rather, each belongs to the long history of the West, marked as it is by conquest, imperial expansion, religious conversion, and racist dehumanization (see Chapter 3).[47]

---

[44] Ibid.   [45] Ezcurra (2018).
[46] Jorge Rafael Videla, president of Argentina, *Encyclopedia Britannica*, www.britannica.com/biography/Jorge-Rafael-Videla, retrieved July 8, 2022.
[47] Ezcurra (2018).

It is in this context that we have to evaluate the moral significance of Ferrari's earlier and probably most famous work "La civilización occidental y cristiana" ("Western and Christian Civilization"; Figure 4.1). Originally, it was conceived for the Instituto Di Tella Prize and expressed a vehement protest against the Vietnam War, but it was excluded from the contest on the basis of the argument that it could offend the religious sensibilities of the institute's personnel. The work is a two-meter-long scale replica of a North American bomber jet hurtling downward with a wooden figure of the crucified Christ on its fuselage. With this combination of elements Ferrari suggested that the colonial massacre of the Vietnamese population by the American military ensued from the conviction that the US had the moral duty to bring Western values to the Asian country that they saw as ostensibly corrupted by communism. For the artist, the value-laden argument was used as a rationale for the use of physical violence and to conceal the sheer brutality of waging a colonial war.[48]

This brings us back to Cashell's reflections on the title of his book *Aftershock*, which he sees as an epitome of transgressive art:

> Typically, reaction to transgressive art assumes the artist was wrong to have done this. Such work may, however, motivate the subsequent, (re)considered and highly complex, indeed, tortuous response: this is difficult, may appear indeed to be wrong, or immoral, but the artist was ultimately right to engage this difficult and contentious subject-matter – because its overall ethos demands approval and establishes that *the transgression the work entails is ethically justifiable*. This phenomenon of reflective moral response I shall later identify as the ethical aftershock of the work.[49]

When the author later comes back to the title of his work, he adds a remark that clearly explains why it makes sense to shock the viewer:

> ... shock is often required for the development of an ethical perspective that is sensitive to the moral distinction between good and bad, right and wrong. ... When confronted with art that shocks as a result of the moral transgression it performs, there is real danger here. Such work shakes us, *makes us think twice*. The danger is that something fundamental will occur as a result, that we will be changed in some way, that the work will have more than an aesthetic effect.[50]

The phrase "makes us think twice" suggests that there are two successive ways of positioning oneself toward the work. The first response is: This is wrong! The second response is: Let's see – why is the artist doing that? The

---

[48] Ibid.   [49] Cashell (2009, p. 12, emphasis added).   [50] Ibid. (p. 15, emphasis added).

second position is more reflective, more distanced, more open, and less emotional. This is precisely what meta-positioning is doing: taking some distance, reconsidering the initial emotional response, asking questions of oneself or others, looking beyond one's first impulse so that this impulse can be viewed and evaluated from another, *broader* perspective. At this meta-positional level, a dialogue is stimulated, either with oneself or with others who are able and willing to enter a moral middle ground where nothing is definitely fixed or clear but where a field of uncertainty opens itself up for posing deeper moral questions that don't permit an immediate answer.

Note that a basic assumption in Dialogical Self Theory (DST) is that *one position can be viewed and evaluated from the perspective of another position* and, as a result, receives an additional or new meaning. For example, from a gourmet position, an excessive meal can be purely enjoyable, but from a meta-position, the same meal can be critically evaluated from a perspective that takes one's health into account. Not only can a particular action be viewed from different positions, but also the position as a whole can be critically evaluated (e.g. I as looking for pleasure is too significant in my life).

Chris Ofili's Controversial Virgin

Chris Ofili is a British Turner Prize-winning painter with roots in Nigeria, and he is best known for his paintings that incorporate elephant dung. His most representative work is "The Holy Virgin Mary" (Figure 4.2), in which he uses various materials, such as acrylic material, oil, polyester resin, glitter, paper collage, etc. The most controversial material, named "sick," is a lumpy form of elephant dung. Dried and polyester resin-coated elephant dung is placed on the right breast of the Virgin. Around her figure he collages paper-printed pictures of black female genitals that he had cut from pornographic magazines. The visual forms and textures of these materials are very varied. Together, these materials create a strong impression of conflict.[51]

This painting, "The Holy Virgin Mary," was a controversial issue in a lawsuit between the then-mayor of New York City, Rudy Giuliani, and the Brooklyn Museum of Art when the work was exhibited there in 1999 as a part of the "Sensation" exhibition. The mayor had threatened that the museum would lose its annual $7 million City Hall grant unless it

---

[51] Yang (2021).

canceled the opening of the exhibition. Giuliani, who was at that time preparing to defend his office in the polls against Hillary Clinton, argued that his ultimatum to the museum should not be seen as censorship but as a correct use of public funds: "You don't have a right to government subsidy for desecrating somebody else's religion," he said. Although he had not seen the exhibition himself but only examined the show's catalog, he declared: "The idea of having so-called works of art in which people are throwing elephant dung at a picture of the Virgin Mary is sick." Religious campaigners also spoke out against the show: "I think the whole city should picket the show . . . [it] is designed to shock, but instead it induces revulsion," said William Donohue, President of the Catholic League for Religious and Civil Rights. A spokesperson for Chris Ofili responded to the threats by calling them "totalitarian and fascistic."[52]

According to the Turkish art critics Mehmet Güney and Emin Kayserili, Ofili's work takes an artistic stand against racist approaches around the world, especially in Europe and America. In this view, the use of elephant dung should be associated with Ofili's roots in African culture, as it imposes a sacred meaning on the black body that is treated as "other" in white Western traditional cultures. In this view, Ofili's art is regarded as a reaction to the white perception of superiority over black bodies, and his art represents a search for answers to the otherized identity problem.[53]

In this alternative view, the blessed body of Holy Mary has been removed from the authoritarian powers of the Middle Ages and Renaissance. As a sign of cultural protest, it can be approached critically, ironically, secularly, politically, or personally by contemporary artists who liberate the art from any duty to "serve" dominant artistic traditions. Ofili went beyond cultural limitations by linking Western and African artistic traditions through the colors and materials he included. His respect for the Renaissance is expressed through the classic blue robe of the Black Mary and her African origin through the elephant excrement. Elephant dung expresses the roots of African and Asian societies and, at the same time, serves as a protest against racist attitudes.[54]

Ofili's work is particularly significant from a cultural point of view. Art can serve as a moral middle ground where symbols of holiness or fertility for one society are confronted with judgments of ugliness, abomination,

[52] BBC News, "Sensation Sparks New York Storm," September 23, 1999, http://news.bbc.co.uk/1/hi/entertainment/455902.stm, retrieved July 25, 2023.
[53] Güney and Kayserili (2020).   [54] Ibid.

and moral rejection from another culture. This brings us back to Kieran Cashell's phrase that transgressive art "makes us think twice," inviting us to take a meta-position from which we can see and evaluate one and the same piece of art as morally good and bad *at the same time.* This is precisely what meta-positioning is doing: taking some distance by viewing something from a broader historical and cultural viewpoint and including our initial impulsive position as part of a more comprehensive reflexive and culture-transcending dialogical process. Especially in a globalizing era in which different cultural traditions meet and clash, an artistic moral middle ground is needed where we stand with one leg in one culture and with the other leg in another culture. We can achieve this when standing still in front of an intriguing piece of transgressive art in a museum that invites us to step beyond our culturally determined moral limitations.[55]

Perhaps it is striking and insightful to quote Friedrich Nietzsche's critical observation that there is only one type of morality left that claims to be the only one: "[I]t says stubbornly and inexorably, 'I am morality itself, and nothing besides is morality.'"[56] This is, according to Nietzsche, charac-teristic of all moralities. No morality "wants there to be many moralities, they want no comparison and no criticism; just absolute faith."[57] As long as one sticks to one kind of morality and denies its actual historical and cultural contingency, there can be no appreciation of culturally determined trans-gressive art as an entrance to a moral middle ground.

The "Wrong" Other in the Extended Self

In this chapter, I want to illustrate some phenomena that are located on the moral middle ground, their specific nature, their variation, and how they are related to DST. In this section, I want to outline a phenomenon that refers to moral bad *not* located in the self as an individualized entity and *not* in the other as having an existence outside of the self, but as located in the *extended* domain of the self. To clarify this, we have to acknowledge that the dialogical self is not limited to processes that happen "within the skin." Other people, animals, nature, and even physical objects can become part of the extended self. Typically, they are felt as "mine," such as my child, my parent, my friend, my dog, and even my opponent or

---

[55] For more examples of transgressive art, see www.artspace.com/magazine/art_101/body-of-art/body-of-art-transgressive-performance-53294.
[56] From Nietzsche's *Beyond Good and Evil* and *Sämtliche Werke. Kritische Studienausgabe,* quoted by van Tongeren (2006, p. 392).
[57] Ibid.

enemy. The external I-position, as located in this extended domain of the self, does not imply that the other is an exact copy of the other in their actual existence. Rather, DST assumes that external positions are, to some extent, constructions produced by the needs and aspirations associated with internal positions. However, if external I-positions were to become *entirely* subjective constructions, they would ultimately result in a confusing mixture of fantasy and reality or even delusions. Therefore, the self, including its external I-positions, needs contact with the actual other, or with a reconstructed image of the actual other, in order to maintain or develop a minimally realistic image of the other as part of the extended self; that is, the other as not entirely constructed by the wishes and anxieties of the internal domain of the self. In the following, I will give an example of the morally bad behavior of a person located in the external domain of the self as evoking a response in the internal domain.

In her book titled *Geheim: Het oorlogsverhaal van mijn vader*[58] (*Secret: The War Story of My Father*), Leoni Jansen, a Dutch singer, actress, and TV presenter, describes how vividly her deceased father enters her self when walking alone in a quiet environment:

> I look around me, 360 degrees. I'm still alone in the landscape. Yet, I hear those footsteps. I "feel" someone walking next to me at the left side. This person says in my head: "I told you the names of these flowers, when we were walking in the meadow?" It is my father. I'm not afraid, yet very surprised. I feel my father . . . it is really like that, I feel my father walking next to me.[59]

When Leoni is sixteen, her father tells her that he had worked for the Nazis during WWII, something that was judged as "being wrong" by most Dutch citizens during and after WWII. From that moment on, her relationship with her father becomes problematic and deteriorates. She loves him but morally rejects his behavior. The "secret" remains hidden in the family because if it were to become known, her father would be at risk of losing his job. Ten years after his death, when Leoni makes a pilgrimage to Santiago de Compostela in Spain, she feels that her father walks with her. This is for her the starting signal to unravel her father's past. She visits places in Tunisia where he fought in the German army, in America where he was treated as a war prisoner, and several locations in the Netherlands. During her quest, she remembers other secrets emerging from the fog of her past. Her father had revealed to her that he had a six-year-long

---

[58] Jansen (2013).   [59] Ibid. (p. 6), translated by HH.

extramarital relationship with another woman but that she should also keep this as a secret, and he forbade her from telling it to her mother. She also discovered that her mother, before she gave birth to Leoni, had an illegal abortion, which was also kept as a secret in the family.

At the end of her quest, she concludes: "It did not become a rehabilitation of my father. I don't need to rehabilitate him. I only wanted to know how it was. And I'm glad that I figured it out. It increased my consciousness and, at the same time, it made me humble regarding humans and their choices."[60] And she became aware of the relevance of the historical context of her father's decisions: "You know if you did well in the light of history. In retrospect it is always much easier to give an interpretation than at the moment itself."[61]

At the end of her writing, her father appears once more in her imagination:

> Then he lifts his head and looks at me: "Why did you not interview me?" I'm startled, indeed I did not do that. But then I realize: "You are still dead?" "Oh yes," my father says, with a slight smile, "that's right, I'm dead." Then, satisfied, he lies back, his eyes shut again, to enjoy an unknown sun.[62]

This story lends itself to an interpretation that touches some central DST concepts. It can be read as an internal dialogue of Leoni with her father, who, although having passed away long ago, feels to her as almost physically present during her pilgrimage. Her relationship with him is loaded with ambivalence. Although she loves him, she morally rejects his behavior as being "wrong" in the war, which makes it impossible for her to find peace in herself. Her quest through the different places in the world where he spent his time during the war represents a form of vicarious travel and, at the same time, a quest through the unknown spaces in herself. She felt and still feels "locked up" in several family secrets that brought her into an I-prison from which she wants to liberate herself. Finally, her physical quest and simultaneous self-exploration bring peace to her own mind and also allow her father to find rest and pleasure under an "unknown sun."

In the context of this chapter, the most significant aspect of Leoni's story is that not she but her father as part of herself is felt as morally wrong. He is so intimately involved in her life and so nearby that he became part of her (extended) self. She experiences the immoral behavior of her father as part of her own life that she wants to reconcile with. She cannot reject him entirely, as she would then reject a significant part of her own life.

---

[60] Ibid. (p. 218).   [61] Ibid.   [62] Ibid. (p. 219).

By visiting the places where he traveled during the war, she starts a journey in her inner self and becomes involved in inner dialogues that finally bring the peace she feels in her (reconstructed) relationship with him. This helps her to understand her father's behavior in the historical context of the war without approving of it. During her travel, she creates a moral middle ground in which her good and (extended) bad sides become engaged in a dialogical encounter that led to some peace of mind regarding her own past.

There lived a villager. He made his living by selling seeds in the market. He had ten bags with him, which he would carry to another village to buy the seeds.

Of the ten bags, one was different from the rest. It had many holes and was torn in a few places. But, despite its poor condition, the villager would carry it regularly together with all of his other bags to gather the seeds from another village.

One fine day, the torn bag started thinking, "I am but a torn bag. I have so many holes. I don't understand why my master takes me along for bringing seeds. Why doesn't he throw me out?" He decided to ask the villager.

"O my master, why don't you just throw me away? You know I am no use. I don't serve you honestly. I spill all the seeds you fill me with all along the way. By the time you reach home I have no seeds left to offer you. Please, may I know why you don't do away with me?" asked the bag.

The villager patiently listened to the torn bag. Then, he smiled and said, "My dear bag, who told you that you are bad? You don't know how good you are! Come, I will tell you what good you have done for me, and for others as well."

So saying, the villager took the torn bag into his arms and took it outside to show it something. The villager then said, "Do you see all these trees? These trees are there all along the way from this village to the next, from where I buy seeds. These trees have grown from the seeds you have been spilling along the way for so many years."

The villager then paused for a second and continued, "These trees give cool shade to the tired passers-by on hot sunny days. They also give oxygen to living beings and fruits to birds, animals, and humans. Can't you see of what great service you have been to the world?!"

The torn bag was happy to learn all this. It had realized that everyone everywhere had something good to offer the world!

The moral: Accept all people the way they are. You never know what good they may be doing for you.

Source: Short Stories for All Ages, https://shortstoriesshort.com/story/people-good-and-bad/.

Durkheim on the Pure and Impure

In the preceding sections, I presented and discussed several examples of the moral middle ground in the social sciences and the arts. The question arises as to whether there exists literature outside these domains in which instances of this concept can be found. The work of Émile Durkheim and related literatures are particularly relevant.

Émile Durkheim (1858–1917) was a French sociologist who, along with both Karl Marx and Max Weber, is generally regarded as one of the principal architects of modern social science. As Alexander Riley[63] indicates, Durkheim became, perhaps unwittingly, the founder of an intellectually iconoclastic school of surprising originality and scope. In particular, his ideas about the "impure sacred" presented in his work *The Elementary Forms of Religious Life*[64] are particularly relevant to the concept of the moral middle ground.

Whereas the polarity of the *sacred* versus the *profane* is one of the key conceptual tools in Durkheim's sociology of religion, it is not the only set of oppositions he proposed in his wish to understand religious experiences and rites. He also introduced the distinction between the *pure* and the *impure*. In Durkheim's view, the pure maintains societal order and moral awareness, but at the same time it is closely associated with the impure and evil that produce disorder, sacrilege, disease, and death. In the early Durkheimian school, this ambiguous purity led to the distinction between the "right sacred" that was regarded as pure and benevolent and the "left sacred" that was seen as impure and transgressive.[65]

As Riley notes, the relationship between pure and impure sacred is a rather complex one, as they are not always clearly distinguishable. In Durkheim's view, a pure sacred object can become impure while it *remains* sacred at the same time, and also vice versa. He refers to certain societies who have specific rituals for treating a dead body as impure and as frightening because of the risk of evil contagion. However, later it may receive the status of a venerated sacred object that can even be ingested by surviving members of the family or clan as a form of protection against evil forces.[66]

In order to broaden his analysis to other cultural groups, Riley refers to Brahmanic religion, where the "impure sacred" has played a more important role than in analogous groups in Judaism and Christianity. For example, religious adepts of Gnosticism in Christianity, of Tantricism in

---

[63] Riley (2005).   [64] Durkheim (1912).   [65] Riley (2005).   [66] Ibid.

Hinduism, and of Buddhism are in certain cases no longer bound to particular moral limitations and are permitted to heighten their spiritual level by deliberately transgressing moral rules. This contrasts with the emphasis on the pure sacred in the history of Christianity, which led to the crushing of Gnosticism in the first centuries of the Church.[67] For present purposes, it suffices to observe that in the sociology of religion there are also instances of the combination of the pure and the impure that are close to our notion of the moral middle ground. (For an elaborate discussion of Durkheim's work and related developments in sociology and philosophy, see *The Cambridge Compendium to Durkheim.*[68] That volume also contains chapters that deal with works from other French philosophers, such as Michel Foucault and Jacques Derrida, who have presented similar ideas on the combination of the pure and impure. See also Chapter 3 of the present book for the problem of the obsession with purity by political figures such as Hitler and Putin.)

The Moral Middle Ground: How to Define and Understand It?

In this chapter, I brought together some concepts that, despite their apparent psychological differences, have some basic characteristics in common: What initially seems morally good and what initially seems morally bad are closely brought together to form coalitions that transcend any form of moral dualism. I will summarize the different concepts and then propose a definition of the moral middle ground.

Healthy selfishness, not to be confused with the concept of narcissism, is associated with higher levels of psychological well-being, adaptive psychological functioning, and a genuine prosocial orientation. This goes against the dominant view that being selfish is always sinful and loving others is always virtuous. This cultural taboo has had the unfortunate consequence of making people feel guilty when they experience healthy self-love as an affirmation and respect for their own happiness, growth, freedom, and vitality.

Similar to healthy selfishness is the existence of *moral exemplars*, described in terms of "enlightened self-interest." People qualified in this way bring together social power and conscience, combine brilliance with wisdom, and in their extraordinary commitments promote benevolence, justice, or basic human welfare.

---

[67] Ibid. (p. 277).   [68] Alexander and Smith (2005).

Machiavellians are portrayed as bistrategic controllers who combine prosocial and coercive control strategies. In their social behavior they use an approach that entails a careful balancing of "getting along" and "getting ahead." Despite their aggression or even because of it, they are rated as socially central, liked by peers, socially skilled, and well-adjusted.

The case of *Oskar Schindler* showed that the very qualities that most of us would consider to be morally problematic – hedonism, avarice, and maintaining instrumental relations with others – were precisely the qualities that put him, in his contacts with Nazi officers, in a position to save more than 1,000 Jews from Hitler's genocide.

Black humor treats sinister subjects like disease, death, deformity, physical disability, or warfare with amusement and presents tragic, distressing, or morbid topics in comic terms. The "surprising" finding of the study reviewed in this chapter was that participants with the highest levels of black humor preference and comprehension scored high on intelligence and had high education levels but showed low levels of aggression and mood disturbance.

In addition to so-called white and black hat hackers, there exists a middle group, the *grey hat hackers*, who break laws just like black hat hackers do. Although they often hack their way into systems without permission and behave illegally, they do not intend to cause harm or to steal money but rather are motivated to improve Internet security by revealing security breaches or publishing sensitive information in the service of transparency.

Transgressive art refers to art forms that aim to transgress and outrage or violate basic mores and sensibilities, and such art is considered offensive because of its shock value. However, the phrase "makes us think twice" suggests that there are two successive ways of positioning oneself toward such artwork. The first response is: This is wrong! The second response is: Let's see – why is the artist doing that? This response has the potential of revealing the often-hidden moral meaning of the work.

The morally wrong other in the extended self was exemplified by Leoni Jansen's story about her deceased father who was "wrong" during WWII. Although she loved him, she morally rejected his behavior. By visiting the places where he had traveled during the war, she started a quest in her inner self and became involved in inner dialogues that finally brought the peace she felt in her (reconstructed) relationship with him.

The *impure sacred* has received attention in the sociological work of Émile Durkheim. A pure sacred object can become impure while remaining sacred at the same time, and also vice versa. In some societies, a dead body is regarded as impure and as frightening because of the risk of evil contagion. However, it may later receive the status of a venerated sacred object and be treated as a protection against evil forces.

The first and most basic commonality of these phenomena is that in them judgments of good and bad in a person or object are not separated from each other and not considered as mutually exclusive opposites but brought together in coalitions that contribute to the vitality of self and society. On this basis, two different forms of coalition can be distinguished. One is a coalition of positions where good and bad go together as sponta-neous allies without much cognitive dissonance or internal dialogue. Healthy selfishness, which combines selfishness with a prosocial orientation, and Machiavellianism are typical examples. They function as stable person-ality characteristics. Another category requires a significant degree of internal dialogue as a way to combine good and bad with the purpose of reconciling them in one way or another. Typical examples are transgressive art forms, which require a second thought that may contradict the first impulse, and the wrong other in one's extended self, which also requires a significant degree of cognitive effort and dialogical processing in an attempt to reconcile inner conflicts or dilemmas. (For another example of a moral dilemma, see the description of white lies in Chapter 3.)

Also, in Schindler's case there seem to be some signs of inner moral dialogue. On multiple occasions after the war, Schindler faced the question of why he helped Jews survive the Holocaust. To some extent, his answers changed over time, making it difficult to find a clear, concise explanation for his behavior. In a 1964 interview, he said, "I had to help … I had no choice." To survivor Murray Pantirer, a "Schindler Jew," he gave a more elaborate answer: "I was a Nazi, and I believed that the Germans were doing wrong … when they started killing innocent people, it didn't mean anything to me that they were Jewish, to me they were just human beings, Menschen. I decided I am going to work against them and I am going to save as many as I can."[69]

The example of black humor lies somewhere between a self-evident coalition and active dialogical processing. The people who like such humor may need to undergo some inner deliberation before expressing their opinion.

In sum, the moral middle ground can be defined as a space in the self where moral positions, judged as good or bad in their isolation, come together in coalitions in which they form vital combinations. When these positions are evaluated as contradictory, they stimulate internal and/or

---

[69] Merrill (2018).

external dialogical relationships. This may result in agreement, disagreement, conflict, or reconciliation of good and bad positions as a basis of decision-making. Moral positioning is a highly dynamic process that is personally, socially, and culturally contingent and may change across history. Positioning on the middle ground is not fixed and static. Positions that are usually considered to be exclusively good or bad can enter the middle ground and be explored regarding their differences and dynamic relationships. An important implication of this definition is that there are situations in which positions that in a particular social or cultural context are evaluated as "bad" (e.g. transgressive art), as opposite to good, can be introduced into the moral middle ground, where they can be reevaluated in terms of their moral meaning.

A central thesis in this book is that the energy of one position can be transferred to another position with the implication that the specific energies of positions can profit from each other's energy. This process is called "transpositioning" (see Chapter 1). The assumption is that two positions as coalitions on the middle ground create forms of energy in the self that cannot emerge when the positions are working in isolated or opposite directions. As a productive combination, they have the potential to enhance the vitality (zest, enthusiasm) of the self.

Practical Implications

Arriving at the final part of this chapter, I would like to briefly discuss two practical implications. The first is an educational guideline to evaluating artistic expressions beyond one's first impulse. The second is applying the concept of the moral middle ground, tentatively, to two of the most controversial issues of our time: abortion and the #MeToo movement.

Looking at Art Beyond the First Impulse

Art is one of the most important ways to broaden our emotional, cognitive, and moral outlooks. It stimulates us to explore scenarios in unexpected ways, challenges our imagination, involves us emotionally, and provides us with alternative viewpoints. It can exaggerate certain aspects of reality to such a degree that they are brought to the center of our attention and fuel dialogue and debate.[70] This is certainly applicable in the realm of transgressive art forms that exaggerate particular aspects of a work to such a

---

[70] Roeser et al. (2018).

degree that they can become highly controversial. The question is: What can we learn from this art form and what are its practical implications? Therefore, let's return, by way of example, to León Ferrari's work "Western and Christian Civilization" (Figure 4.1), judged as "blasphemy" by then-archbishop of Buenos Aires, Jorge Mario Bergoglio. As has already been said, reducing Ferrari's art to an attack on the Catholic Church would overlook its broader critique of modernity and colonialism. As Mara Ezcurra notes, numerous spectators, including some Christians, have been perceptive of the wider moral claims of this work. For example, after attending the 2004 retrospective of Ferrari's work at Recoleta (a neighborhood of Buenos Aires), one viewer wrote the following comment in the visitors' book:

> My name is Isabel, I am 16 years old. This is the second time that I have seen the exhibition, but this time I examined it more carefully. I must say that the church's reaction to your work was very unnecessary. The church creates a paradox by promoting good will and equality, but then opening the doors of hell to those who are different.[71]

This remark is particularly relevant to Cashell's remark that transgressive art "makes us think twice." After the first shock, a process of self-reflection and dialogue starts that results in "second thoughts" that ask us to view the work in an alternative way and reveal its complexities and moral aspects that may have been hidden at first sight.

Another commentor, Marcela, a self-proclaimed Christian, even regarded Ferrari as a true believer:

> When I saw Christ nailed to the aircraft, I remembered what he said: "Whatever you did for one of the least of these brothers and sisters of mine, you did for me." In the end, I feel that you [Ferrari] are the most Christian of us all. A very nice guy, full of smart, beautiful, and unique things to show that one can always be a better person, and that the only hell is blindness, madness, and ignorance.[72]

Indeed, to stop looking at transgressive art after the first shock, reject it, and turn one's attention away can be regarded as a form of moral blindness or ignorance. A next step is needed that enables us to delve deeper into the artistic and moral meaning of the work and reveal its complexities and contradictions. Yes, this applies to many other forms of art, but it applies to transgressive art in particular.

---

[71] Ezcurra (2018, p. 37).   [72] Ibid. (p. 38).

The Moral Middle Ground in the Abortion Debate

Initially, I was very hesitant to apply the concept of the moral middle ground to abortion because the debate on this topic recently became very emotional and politically controversial in the United States. On June 24, 2022, the Supreme Court in the US overruled *Roe v. Wade*, terminating the constitutional right of a woman to have an abortion, a right that had been in place for fifty years. I hesitated to address this topic as, at the time of writing this text, the debate seems to be more polarized than ever. During the heat of the debates and controversies, it seemed almost impossible not to be placed in one of two camps: pro-life *or* pro-choice. However, my reservation lessened when I found an article written by journalist Caitlin Geurts, who addresses the topic in a way that convinced me that discussions on abortion may profit from taking the *possibility* of a moral middle ground into account.

Before I provide some brief reflections on the issue, I want to make clear that my aim in this section is not to deny the claims of either of the two moral views on abortion, pro-choice or pro-life, but to explore the existence of a moral middle ground, where judgments of good and bad have a chance to meet each other. My main argument will be that the *deep exploration of the individual case* and its context offers an interface where arguments and emotions for and against can come closer to each other than in an overly polarized debate on the level of *principles only*.

During a walk on January 21, 2020, Caitlin Geurts[73] went into the Wisconsin State Capitol. Thankful for its open-door policy to the public, she waltzed right in and stumbled upon the State Assembly in session. Out of curiosity, she sat down in the public gallery. After some time, the Speaker opened debate on a new resolution, Assembly Joint Resolution 118, concerning January 22 as "Protect Life Day" in Wisconsin. Geurts writes that her eyes were wide with fascination as different representatives said their piece, and she noted that almost every person who stood up showed clear emotion behind their words. For her, it was most striking that when a representative on either side of the debate, be it pro-choice or pro-life, was giving what seemed like the speech of their lifetime, they weren't even paying attention to their opponents.

This visit to the Assembly made her reflect on the nature of the debate in relation to herself. She was born and raised Catholic and is still practicing her faith proudly. However, she is also a proud Democrat

---

[73] Geurts (2020).

who knows the problematic ramifications of restricting personal liberties. For her, as for many others, this clearly represents cognitive dissonance and calls into question the way in which abortion is being discussed: as a polarized topic where there can only be a right or wrong view.

On the historic day of January 22, 2020, Geurts felt the urge to share a statement from columnist Sydney Harris. Writing about those who find themselves with an unplanned pregnancy and unmarried in college, he declared that "anyone who takes a black-or-white position on the subject of abortion is either a fool or fanatic. *It is the grayest moral area I can imagine*, and I myself am torn in two each time it happens."[74] Geurts ends her column by writing: "On the anniversary of Roe v. Wade, I just want to say that it is imperative that *some* things are left in a gray area."[75] Acknowledging the existence of "grey areas" in the abortion debate may serve as a counterweight, or even as a buffer, in overly polarized debates.

As I have already argued in Chapter 2, moral mandates, including those on abortion, euthanasia, suicide, same-sex marriage, and other prevalent moral issues, are typically formulated at an abstract level, often in terms of for or against, with the risk that debates and convictions become strongly polarized. However, when we think about actions and events in a *concrete and specific situation*, we tend to concentrate on the specific details of the situation and focus on the immediate experience. Conversely, if we think in a more abstract and general manner and on the level of strict moral principles *only*, we focus on more global, overarching features that are more distant from the specific situation. Focusing on a specific person, located in this specific situation, with a particular age, with this background, and with this probable future may give more access to the moral middle ground than keeping a fixed stance in an either/or way of positioning. And precisely on this middle ground there is more chance of becoming involved in critical self-reflection and dialogue than continuing to stick to abstract moral positions only.

From a DST perspective, moral principles are abstract and valuable ways of positioning oneself to the world and to oneself. However, these positions are not dogmatic "truths" that are fixed forever, culturally invariant, and irrevocably applicable to every specific case. Instead, they have to be checked regarding their validity and moral significance through a deep exploration of individual cases. In addition to individual cases, one must look at the social world when considering the morality of these choices as well. So, the case of the individual must be seen in light of society and its

[74] Ibid. (n.p., emphasis added).   [75] Ibid. (n.p., emphasis added).

provision of care. This is indeed a complex issue with many dimensions. My main argument is against being caught in rigid positions – rigid moral I-prisons, one might call them – and instead is in favor of looking at each situation, including its social and societal context, in its complexity and contradiction. In other words, morality can be understood as a multiplicity of moral positions, where abstract principles and analyses of individual cases have to *complement* each other. The final decision is the result of a productive dialogue between the voices of abstract and specific ways of positioning. However, it should be added that in the absence of legal access to abortion, the choices resulting from (inner) dialogue regarding abortion are seriously restricted. Abstract and specific ways of positioning would be neither welcome nor useful in any public sphere where choices are made impossible.

In regard to these limitations, I also want to emphasize the importance of meta-positioning (see also Chapter 3), as this allows us to identify ourselves not only with our own internal positions (for or against), but also with opponents who disagree with us as significant but negatively experienced others-in-the-self. These others are part of our extended self, as they are constructed not only based on interactions with actual others, but also on the basis of the needs, anxieties, anger, and hate that are part of the internal positions in the self. The image of the opponent, as a construction in the external domain of the self, is strongly influenced by the convictions and emotions associated with the internal positions. The meta-position enables us to include not only the opponent as another in the self, but also our perception of *the other as positioning us* as opponents of them. The way we find ourselves positioned by the other is part of our extended self that we can confirm, reject, deny, or include in the dialogues with others and ourselves. If we bring the positioning of ourselves as "right" together with our perception of the actual other as seeing us as "wrong" and if we reflect, from a meta-position, on our extended selves as good *and* bad (see Figure 3.7 in Chapter 3), then we gain access to the moral middle ground. If participants achieve this, a dialogical space opens itself up that goes beyond any dogmatic conviction and also beyond a conception of the self as a purely individualized entity.

The Moral Middle Ground in the #MeToo Debate

Stories like that of "Grace" and Aziz Ismail Ansari became well-known in the fight against sexual assault and for gender equality. Grace is a Brooklyn-based photographer, then aged twenty-two, whose real name is not mentioned to protect her identity. Aziz Ismail Ansari (1983–) is a well-known American actor, comedian, writer, and filmmaker.

Their story is one that is all too common. When their contact begins with some flirting and a date, Ansari anticipates sex with Grace, while Grace does not. It ends with Grace feeling disrespected and violated because all of her signals and statements of discomfort toward sex have been disregarded.[76]

American writer and journalist Fiona Chen observes that the case of Grace and Ansari has created a relatively large rift in the #MeToo movement. Many people have expressed support for Grace, but many others have argued that the story is detrimental to the movement's momentum or represents an "excess" of the movement in punishing innocent men. Some even expressed some sympathy for Ansari's failure to fully comprehend Grace's "mixed signals" and claimed that the account was far from describing a sexual assault.[77]

In Chen's view, the negative responses to the case show that our society faces a significant problem so long as people look at sexual assaults solely in the most extreme terms (e.g. Harvey Weinstein) and neglect the more everyday forms of gendered violence. Grace's story demonstrates that there exists a "grey area" in sexual assault and that various kinds of violence in this grey area have become highly normalized. A demonstration of this normality is the fact that many people found that they could express sympathy for Ansari and consequently called his actions ordinary, while many others made clear that they could relate to Grace and could tell similar stories as having happened to them.

As Chen argues, this normalization stems to a great extent from limited understandings of coercion. Many overlook the fact that coercion can operate in many subtle ways and doesn't necessarily require direct force, physical actions, or spoken threats. Most typically, sexual transgressions stem from power imbalances produced by social norms and structures. Such imbalances are associated with gender stereotypes that teach men to be tough and aggressively masculine rather than empathetic, whereas women have learned to be docile rather than outspoken.

Also, Jill Filipovic, an American journalist and feminist, touched on a related theme when writing: "Girls are raised with a contradictory set of expectations: Be kind and acquiescent, but also be the brakes on male sexual desire. We are taught to reflexively say yes except for when we're supposed to definitively say no, but we don't learn how to know when we

---

[76] Chen (2018).   [77] Ibid.

want to say either . . ."[78] Elaborating on Filipovic's statement, Conor Friedersdorf, an American journalist and a staff writer at *The Atlantic*, states: "I agree that men are too often socialized to be sexual aggressors who meet all resistance as an obstacle to overcome – or if you're of another perspective, that inborn aggression in men is too seldom mitigated by socializing them to 'do unto others' rather than to 'catch as can.'"[79]

Friedersdorf expects that the #MeToo movement is going to produce sustained culture change. Rather than simply weeding out the worst actors in a broken system, it is necessary to renegotiate sexual narratives that have been accepted for too long. This involves becoming engaged in conversations about sex that is violating but not criminal. Friedersdorf is very explicit about the relevance of grey areas in these discussions: "The sexual encounter Grace described falls into what I see as a gray area of violating, noncriminal sex – the kind of sex that Rebecca Traister described in 2015 as 'bad in ways that are worth talking about'; and what Jessica Valenti described as an interaction that the 'culture considers "normal," but is "oftentimes harmful."'"[80] Friedersdorf adds, "This is a kind of sex that is not only worth talking about, but necessary to talk about. Behavior need not fall under the legal definition of sexual assault or rape to be wrong or violating or upsetting."[81]

In my reflections on the #MeToo debate, I arrive, within the confines of this book, at conclusions that are basically similar to those I came to when writing on abortion earlier in this chapter. When moral mandates are mainly formulated at an abstract level, often in terms of right or wrong, there is a risk that debates and convictions might become strongly polarized. However, when we think about actions and events in a concrete and specific situation, we tend to concentrate on the specific details of the situation and focus on the immediate experiences of the men and women who find themselves on the moral middle ground. Focusing on living people finding themselves in situations of ambivalence, in a *particular* social, cultural, and historical background, may give more access to this moral middle ground than keeping a fixed stance in an either/or way of positioning. By meeting on that middle ground, men and women are invited to become involved in critical self-reflection, mutual questioning, and shared decision-making.

Writing on abortion and the #MeToo movement, I'm rather ambivalent about the question as to how far grey areas, as reported by the writers

---

[78] Filipovic (2018), quoted by Friedersdorf (2018).   [79] Friedersdorf (2018, n.p.).   [80] Ibid.
[81] Ibid.

in this section, fit with the conception of a moral middle ground as proposed in this book. I assume that these grey areas and the moral middle ground have in common that they serve as a meeting space where good and bad come close together and are sometimes indistinguishable. However, in several parts of the book, I have argued that on the moral middle ground good and bad form coalitions that add to the vitality of self and society. At this point in my thinking, I just don't know whether right and wrong in the case of abortion and the #MeToo movement can be understood as coalitions of I-positions, which would imply that the two positions *energize* each other and can work as a vitalizing combination. Perhaps this might become possible, but for the time being I don't clearly see how. In any case, I found the abortion and #MeToo debates relevant enough to relate them, in a tentative way, to the notion of the middle ground, but this topic needs further exploration.

Taking into account the differences between the moral middle ground and the grey areas in the abortion and #MeToo controversies, a distinction is needed between energy and vitality. Doubtless, these controversies create strong energies, in the form of tensions, oppositions, and disagreements, both between social groups and within the self. Although vitality is related to energy, it can be a bit misleading to use the word "energy" as a synonym for vitality because vitality entails mainly energy experienced as positive and adaptive. Somebody who is tense, nervous, or angry is energized, but not necessarily in a vital way in the sense of being driven by zest, enthusiasm, and strength. In the case of insoluble intrapersonal or inter-personal conflicts, energy may be high but vitality low.[82] When it is very difficult to solve conflicts, there may be much energy in the self but a low degree of vitality. Strong conflicts can occur in the grey areas of the abortion and #MeToo debates, but it is not certain that these areas are identical to the moral middle ground, because they are different from the other phenomena described in the present chapter (e.g. healthy selfishness, Machiavellianism, etc.) that have in common that they arouse *both* energy and vitality.

Summary

In this chapter, I discussed some phenomena relevant to the workings of the self that have in common that good and bad are brought together as productive coalitions on a moral middle ground, a concept that reaches

---

[82] Peterson and Seligman (2004).

beyond any form of moral dualism. The following examples of phenomena on the moral middle ground were presented and discussed: healthy selfishness, enlightened self-interest, Machiavellianism, the case of Oskar Schindler, black humor, grey hat hackers, transgressive art, the "wrong" other-in-the-self, and the combination of the pure and impure in the tradition of Émile Durkheim.

I suggested paying attention to the notion of transpositioning as regards the process of transferring the energy of one position to another one so that the combined energy is more productive to the self than the two positions can be in isolation. Applied to the moral middle ground, this means that good positions may profit from the energy of bad positions if they work as a coalition.

I presented three practical implications of this chapter: a guideline to evaluate transgressive art beyond one's first emotional response; relating the concept of the moral middle ground to the existence of grey areas in abortion as one of the most controversial issues of our time; and considering grey areas in the #MeToo debate. In the cases of both the abortion and #MeToo debates, I proposed focusing moral discussions on specific cases, with attention given to their specific situations and social contexts, and not only on abstract moral principles. I emphasized the practice of meta-positioning in order to take into account the position of the other and the way the other positions us.

CHAPTER 5

Contradiction as Intrinsic to the Multiplicity of the Self

What we agree with leaves us inactive, but contradiction makes us productive.

Johann Wolfgang von Goethe[1]

The term "contradiction" is used in the sense of "lack of agreement between facts, opinions, actions, etc."[2] A chapter on contradictions is indispensable in this book, because the moral middle ground, as a hybrid combination of good and bad, is a contradiction in itself. Moreover, the main theory of this book defines the dialogical self as a dynamic multiplicity of I-positions in the society of mind that can only flourish if one is tolerant of contradiction and makes active use of it.[3]

In this chapter, I will explore why, in general, coping with contradictions is difficult for people living in the Western Hemisphere and why contradictions are generally experienced as threats to our self-esteem. Tellingly, people from some Asian cultures are, more than those living in Western traditions, inclined to tolerate contradictions in their selves and to experience those as less threatening to their self-esteem.[4] After a comparison of conceptions of the self in Eastern and Western traditions, I will explore, inspired by the work of Carl Jung, the meaning of "shadow positions" as undesired or rejected parts of the self. When positions are defined as morally bad, they are experienced in particular as contrary to feelings of positive self-esteem and, as a result, banned to the domain of shadow positions. Finally, I will detail some practical implications of this chapter, with a focus on the question of how tolerance of contradictions can contribute to the enlargement of the dialogical space in the self.

---

[1] Goodreads, November 29, 2022.   [2] Oxford Learner's Dictionaries.   [3] Hermans (2022).
[4] Boucher et al. (2009); Spencer-Rodgers et al. (2010).

Why Is Tolerance of Contradiction Difficult?

In Dialogical Self Theory (DST), a contradiction refers to a position that is felt as being in disagreement or inconsistent with another position. Apparently, a contradiction is harder to tolerate than elements that seamlessly fit together like pieces of a jigsaw puzzle. Dissonant statements are less easy to understand, and they require more cognitive processing than consonant statements. Let's illustrate this by referring to literary critic Andrew Wilson's[5] characterization of Patricia Highsmith, an American writer of psychological thrillers:

> Patricia Highsmith was a person of contradiction: she was lesbian but not very crazy about women, a writer who wrote very insightful psychological novels and who was often annoyed by other people; a misanthrope with a kind, loving attitude.

Suppose we change this sentence and remove the contradictions in the characterization. Then it would read as follows:

> Patricia Highsmith was lesbian and fond of women, a writer of very insightful psychological novels who was intrigued by other people; a philanthropist with a kind, loving attitude.

Certainly, this characterization is easier to understand in comparison with the previous description. We experience the parts as "fitting," "matching," and "corresponding." The same is true for the reverse:

> Patricia Highsmith hated women, was a writer of mediocre psychological novels who got irritated by her fellow human beings; a misanthrope with an unkind, harsh attitude.

We experience these latter two statements as consistent. Each part falls neatly into place and there is no dissonance. In contrast, the first statement is strongly dissonant, and we cannot easily make sense of it. We have to struggle hard to understand and accept its contradictory elements. More generally, evaluating another person in terms of "like" *or* "dislike" is easier than using the combination of "like" *and* "dislike." Nevertheless, just as in a musical composition, a combination of dissonant and consonant elements is needed when we want to characterize individuals in their complexity and inner diversity.

Or consider the following example: When someone aggressively robs an innocent passerby, we characterize him, as the perpetrator of the act, as

---

[5] Wilson (2008). See also Hermans (2020).

morally bad. We use and need the categorization of actors as "perpetrators" and "victims," including their moral connotations, in the service of a well-organized society that endorses the rights of individuals to live their lives in freedom and to be masters of their own bodies. Things may become more nuanced when we hear that the perpetrator was raised in a poor neighborhood with alcoholic parents and was a member of street gangs, and that, at the time of the robbery, he lived in a situation of serious poverty. When we get to know the complete story, we are inclined to see him not only as the perpetrator of the act, but also as a victim of his upbringing and past experiences. Only when we become interested in the man's present and past situation can we move beyond the simple categorization of the "criminal perpetrator" and become aware of his predicament as *both* perpetrator and victim. The more comprehensive story helps us to move beyond the mutually exclusive opposites of "perpetrator" and "victim," and we become more sensitive to the contradictory situation of being in both positions at the same time. And thus, the acceptance of this contradiction provides us with a more *complex* and also a more *realistic* picture of the man and his situation. However, due to its dissonant nature, such a realistic picture is more difficult to process than a consonant description.

Contradictions: Distrusted, yet Productive and All-Pervasive

As the science writer Ashutosh Jogalekar[6] noticed, researchers usually don't like contradictions, and, if they are found, they set off alarm bells and compel experimenters to double-check their research setup. Contradictions in theoretical work are considered undesirable or worse. Contradictions force scientists to go back to the drawing board and start anew.

Yet, Jogalekar continues, contradictions have a revered place in intellectual history. First of all, they are highly instructive simply because they force us to think further, broader, and deeper. Finding discrepancies in their understanding of the world motivates scientists to perform additional experiments and to make decisive calculations to settle the matter. The discovery of contradictions often points to a tantalizing reality that is begging for further explanation.

However, the potential of contradiction goes far beyond the opening of a window to abstract thinking. Fascinating developments in twentieth-century physics demonstrate that contradiction is part and parcel of reality itself. According to Niels Bohr, a main representative of quantum theory,

---

[6] Jogalekar (2022).

contradiction is not only an important aspect of reality, but even an indispensable one. In the wave–particle duality in physics we are faced with one of the most enduring and bizarre contradictions. This duality shows us that photons of light and electrons behave not as waves *or* particles, but as both waves *and* particles. Although the two qualities seem to be maddeningly at odds with each other, they are absolutely essential to grasping the essence of physical reality.[7] As Albert Einstein wrote: "It seems as though we must use sometimes the one theory and sometimes the other, while at times we may use either. We are faced with a new kind of difficulty. We have two contradictory pictures of reality; separately neither of them fully explains the phenomena of light, but together they do."[8]

Nobel Prize-winning Austrian-Irish physicist Erwin Schrödinger (1887–1961) highlighted an even more bizarre quantum phenomenon of particles that are completely separated from each other but are nonetheless closely interconnected. He coined the term "entanglement," which he described as follows: "When two systems, of which we know the states by their respective representatives, enter into temporary physical interaction due to known forces between them, and when after a time of mutual influence the systems separate again, then they can no longer be described in the same way as before …"[9] In a contradictive way, entanglement requires that two separated particles remain connected without being in direct contact. Therefore, Einstein famously called entanglement "spooky action at a distance," since the particles seemed to be communicating faster than the speed of light.[10]

Schrödinger metaphorically illustrated contradiction as an essential feature of entanglement with his famous thought experiment that became known as "Schrödinger's cat" (Figure 5.1). In its most simple terms, it postulates that if you place a cat and something that could, at any moment, kill the cat in a box and seal it, you can't know if the cat is dead or alive until you open the box. The outcome will be unknown until the box is opened. As long as it is not opened, the cat is both alive and dead.

In the purest realm of human thought, mathematics, the concept of proof by contradiction, or, in other terms, by "reductio ad absurdum," has been treasured for millennia. (A simple example of this way of reasoning outside mathematics: The Earth cannot be flat; otherwise, since the Earth is assumed to be finite in extent, people would be able to fall off its edge.) In mathematics, "reductio ad absurdum" is exalted as a method of proof

---

[7] Ibid.   [8] Quoted by Andrei (2015, n.p.).   [9] Schrödinger (1935, p. 555).
[10] California Institute of Technology (2022).

Figure 5.1   Schrödinger's cat is alive and dead at the same time.
Source: Andrzej Wojcicki/Science Photo Library/Getty Images.

that proceeds by stating a proposition and then showing that the outcome implies a contradiction. This then leads to the conclusion that the proposition is false. In his book *A Mathematician's Apology*, mathematician G. H. Hardy expressed his high evaluation of this potent weapon: "Reductio ad absurdum, which Euclid loved so much, is one of a mathematician's finest weapons. It is a far finer gambit than any chess gambit: a chess player may offer the sacrifice of a pawn or even a piece, but a mathematician offers the game."[11]

The creative tension between seemingly contradictory phenomena has also been observed in biology. Darwin felt confused when he observed examples of altruism in the wild, as these seemed to contradict his main thesis of the "struggle for existence." Later, during the twentieth century, theories of kin selection (stating that animals engage in self-sacrificial behavior that benefits the genetic fitness of their relatives) and reciprocal altruism (an individual acts altruistically in the hope of equal-value repayment in the future) attempted to resolve these seemingly paradoxical phenomena within the framework of modern evolutionary theory.[12]

Whereas contradiction in science can be disturbing but ultimately rewarding and fruitful, some religions and philosophies have taken it as

[11] Hardy (1967, p. 94).   [12] Jogalekar (2022).

Figure 5.2   Yin and yang as a union of opposites.
Source: Sergii Iaremenko/Science Photo Library/Getty Images.

fundamental to their worldviews over many centuries. For example, in Chinese philosophy, the union of yin and yang represents a state of equilibrium of non-exclusive opposites. The black (yin) and white (yang) are encompassed by a surrounding circle (Figure 5.2). A dot of yin exists in yang, and a dot of yang also exists in yin, indicating the coexistence of opposition and complementarity. In this model, yin represents feminine forces, such as the moon, darkness, water, passivity, intuition, softness, contraction, and yielding. Yang embodies masculine forces, such as the sun, light, fire, activity, rationality, hardness, expansion, and assertiveness. Thus, although the S line *divides* the circle into two sides, the small dots in the white and dark areas demonstrate the *interwoven* and dynamic nature of the yin and yang forces.[13]

---

[13] Liu and An (2021).

Montaigne's View on Contradictory Members of the Self

One of the most eloquent expressions of contradiction in the self is presented by Michel de Montaigne (1533–1592), a French philosopher, politician, and author of the classical work *Essais* (*Essays*). At the age of thirty-seven, he retired and withdrew from political life, seeking reclusion in his father's castle. From then on, he devoted his time exclusively to philosophy and self-reflection. In stark contrast to Descartes' unitary mind that was considered as functioning in splendid isolation from the external environment, Montaigne depicted the self as a confusing multiplicity of contrasting images and inner contradictions, in close connection with a constantly changing environment:

> Not only does the wind of accident move me at will, but, besides, I am moved and disturbed as a result merely of my own unstable posture; and anyone who observes carefully can hardly find himself twice in the same state. I give my soul now one face, now another, according to which direction I turn it. If I speak of myself in different ways, that is because I look at myself in different ways. All contradictions may be found in me by some twist and in some fashion. Bashful, insolent; chaste, lascivious; talkative, taciturn; tough, delicate; clever, stupid; surly, affable; lying, truthful; learned, ignorant; liberal, miserly, and prodigal: all this I see in myself to some extent according to how I turn; and whoever studies himself really attentively finds in himself, yes, even in his judgment, this gyration and discord. I have nothing to say about myself absolutely, simply, and solidly, without confusion and without mixture, or in one word. Distinguo [I distinguish] is the most universal member of my logic.[14]

Montaigne's celebration of the multiplicity of the soul mirrors DST's emphasis on the multiplicity of the self. He distinctly emphasizes the many opposites and contradictions of the soul and the many directions it can take. Writing about "the wind of accident" that moves him to different sides and emphasizing that he can hardly find himself twice in the same state, he has a sharp eye for the finest nuances of the human self. However, his hypersensitivity to the situation-contingent self may have led him, at least in this quote, to underestimate the fact that there are forms of positioning that, if repetitive enough, leave their traces in the self and become stabilized in the course of time. With a twist on Montaigne's quote above, some people position themselves, across a variety of situations, as more talkative, whereas others are quite taciturn. Or, some people

---

[14] Montaigne (2003, pp. 293–294).

can be safely considered as truthful, whereas some others (e.g. sociopathic or narcissistic individuals) are used to lying in strategic ways in order to reach their hidden purposes. In other words, the apparent multiplicity and changeability of I-positions don't exclude the existence of relatively stable ones, as a sign that stability and change coexist well together in one and the same self.[15]

Why Is Contradiction a Problem in the Western Conception of Self?

As I have summarized elsewhere,[16] Western identity ideals are highly individualized and, in their exaggerated form, have led to embracing an overly autonomous "container self."[17] Cultural anthropologist Clifford Geertz has characterized the Western conception of the self as "a bounded, unique, more or less integrated motivational and cognitive universe, a dynamic center of awareness, emotion, judgment, and action organized into a distinctive whole and set contrastively both against other such wholes and against a social and natural background ..."[18] Likewise, psychologist Edward Sampson[19] has depicted the Western ideal image of the self as an entity with razor-sharp boundaries between self and nonself, with the exclusion of the other as an intrinsic participant in the self and as persistently involved in a pursuit of having the environment under control. From the perspective of sociology, Peter Callero[20] has criticized mainstream conceptions of the self because they have put a strong emphasis on the stability of the self with a simultaneous underemphasis on its change, and on the unity of the self with a neglect of its multiplicity. Furthermore, philosopher Karsten Struhl critically qualified the Western self as incompatible with a Buddhist point of view: "Thus, what is being denied by Buddhism is the existence of a substantial, unchanging, independent and unitary entity with an essential core which is both the subject and possessor of my experiences and body ... which separates what is me from what is not me, and which is also the agent that controls my actions, desires, and thoughts. The belief that we have such a self is for Buddhism, a cognitive illusion."[21]

Western conceptions of the self have been, over the centuries, influenced by (or represented by) Descartes as the much-criticized father of modern philosophy. His dualism between an internal immaterial thinking

---

[15] Hermans (2022).   [16] Ibid.   [17] Callero (2003).   [18] Geertz (1979, p. 59).
[19] Sampson (1988).   [20] Callero (2003).   [21] Struhl (2020, p. 115).

self (res cogitans) and an external material world (res extensa) governed by mechanistic laws has led to the idea that material and spatial reality are not part of thinking itself but are located in the external world. The body as a material thing cannot be a part of the self and is deemed to become externalized as not belonging to the self.[22] There is an additional problematic implication of Descartes' dualism that touches the heart of DST. A significant consequence of his method of "systematic doubt" (being skeptical about the truth of one's beliefs) is that the existence of the other person is not self-evident. Even when we perceive a person with our senses and define them as reality, it is possible that this is not reality but a product of our imagination, like in a dream. Therefore, the other as an external reality has to be proven after the self has already been defined as an autonomous entity having an existence in itself. This means that Cartesian dualism implies a separation not only between body and mind, but also between self and other.

However, if we were to accept Descartes' dualism or any conception in which the other is placed as purely positioned outside, the dialogical self as an integrative construction would be entirely dismantled and divided into separate pieces. That is, the central concept of DST, the "I-position," would fall apart into two different essences. In Cartesian terms, the "I" (res cogitans) and "position" as a spatial phenomenon (res extensa) would be divided so that the I-position as a composite concept would become entirely inconceivable. However, the "I-position" can only be understood if one accepts that the self, as an I, *is itself spatially positioned*. DST is based on the idea that space, both one's body and the other as spatial reality, are *in* the self as extended toward the social environment. This construction enables the self to function as a society of mind with an intrinsic connectedness with society at large and with its history. The denial of this extension would result in a "self-sovereign mind" that, in the words of philosopher Joseph Dunne, would function as a rational knower whose I or ego is "immediately, transparently, and irrefutably present to itself as a pure extensionless consciousness, already established in being, without a body, and with no acknowledged complicity in language, culture, or community."[23] In contrast, the dialogical self functions as a society of mind populated by a multiplicity of others endowed with voices that are able to speak to others and oneself. Indeed, the disappearance of embodied voices would essentially silence the self and prevent it from using its

---

[22] See also Damasio's (1994) criticism of Descartes' body–mind dualism.   [23] Dunne (1996).

mouth, intonation, facial expressions, and posture as ways of speaking to others and itself in dialogical interchanges.

It should be acknowledged that within Western philosophical and social scientific traditions there have been developments that fully acknowledge the role of the multiplicity in the extended self. I limit myself to three of them. In his groundbreaking chapter "The Consciousness of Self," the American pragmatist and psychologist William James presented this frequently quoted sentence: "[A] man has as many social selves as there are individuals who recognize him and carry an image of him in their mind," and he added: "[H]e has as many social selves as there are distinct groups of persons about whose opinion he cares. He generally shows a different side of himself to each of these different groups."[24] In the same stream of thought, the philosopher and sociologist George H. Mead posed the thesis that a sense of self can only come to development if it learns to experience itself from the "particular standpoints of other individual members of the same social group, or from the generalized standpoint of the social group as a whole."[25] And the Russian literary scholar Mikhail Bakhtin[26] introduced, on the basis of his reading of Dostoyevsky's novels, the metaphor of the "polyphonic novel." The principle feature of such a novel is that it is composed of a multiplicity of independent and mutually opposing viewpoints, embodied by characters engaged in dialogical relationships. Each of these characters is "ideologically authoritative and independent"; that is, each character is perceived as the author of their own ideological perspective, not as an object of Dostoyevsky's all-encompassing artistic vision. Instead of being "obedient slaves," acting under the guidance of Dostoyevsky's centralized authorship, the actors are capable of standing beside their creator, disagreeing with him, and sometimes even rebelling against him. The polyphonic novel, populated by a multiplicity of contradictive voices, serves as a fertile metaphor for a dialogical self that gives up any ideal of an omniscient self that has itself under control.

The preceding exposé clarifies two things. First, the Western self is often criticized as a self-contained and unitary system defined as isolated from the body and the social (and natural) environment. This stream of thought certainly has had an enormous influence on common conceptions of the self, defined as having an existence within the skin or as a "ghost in the machine." Accordingly, it is difficult to accept and deal with the contradictions that are inherently present in the self as a dynamic multiplicity of relatively independent voiced positions that populate the self. This short

[24] James (1890, p. 294).   [25] Mead (1934, p. 138).   [26] Bakhtin (1984).

overview shows that there are theorists in the social sciences and philosophy who have recognized the multiplicity of embodied voices as a centerpiece of their conception and have given welcome impetus to the formulation of DST. However, if we assume that multiplicity is inherent to the self, the question can be posed as to whether a self that is typical of a culture that embraces the ideal of unity and continuity is able to deal with its own complexity, as associated with multiplicity and inner contradictions.

Don't Put All of Your Eggs in One Basket: The Problem of Low Self-Complexity

The complexity of the self was investigated by social psychologist Patricia Linville,[27] who noticed that people differ substantially in how they respond to positive and negative events in their lives. In response to the ups and downs of daily life, some individuals experience dramatic mood swings, while others are relatively unaffected by such mood fluctuations. Her "buffer hypothesis" states that individuals who experience greater swings in affect and self-appraisal following a success or failure experience have a low degree of self-complexity (in DST terms, the I-positions have a low degree of relative autonomy). As an illustration, she provides the following example: Suppose a scientist has a simple self-representation in which professional aspects are closely linked to other aspects of the self, such as family and other social relationships. Then the negative affect and self-appraisal associated with a distressing event, experienced as a profes-sional failure, will be widespread in the self, resulting in negative feelings not only in their professional position, but also in other areas of the self. However, when this scientist harbors a complex self, other areas are not highly dependent on one's professional self, and thus these areas will not be very much affected. In that case, the other areas (e.g. friends, family, nature) act as a buffer against negative events or negative thoughts about the professional area.

In a series of experiments, Linville tested her buffer hypothesis by investigating the differences between participants with high and low self-complexity. She found that those with lower self-complexity experienced greater swings in affect and self-appraisal following a failure or success experience. When she followed her participants over a two-week period, it appeared that those with lower self-complexity experienced greater affec-tive variability, implying more ups and downs. These findings led Linville

[27] Linville (1985).

to choose as the subtitle of her article: "Don't Put All of Your Eggs in One Cognitive Basket,"[28] indicating that the less complex self is more vulnerable to the distressing effect of failure experiences.

The buffer hypothesis, holding that self-complexity shields an individual from the negative impacts of stressful events, touches on a significant part of the nuclear definition of the dialogical self as a dynamic multiplicity of *relatively autonomous* I-positions in the society of mind. When the positions are relatively autonomous, as representing the complexity of the self, the disappointment or frustration of one position has a less generalizing influence on the other positions of the self-system. In other words, the relative autonomy of the positions works as a *buffer* against feelings of disappointment or frustration, because the positions are sufficiently independent of each other. The other positions function as a refuge in difficult situations.

Tolerance for Contradiction: Differences between Eastern and Western Selves

In a seminal paper, a group of cultural psychologists[29] reviewed a substantial amount of empirical research demonstrating that people differ in the degree to which they view the world as being in a state of constant flux and as inherently contradictory. The general finding was that members of some East Asian cultures provide, in comparison with those from Western cultures, more *contextualized explanations* for their own and others' behaviors and see these behaviors as dependent on changing contexts. Moreover, they demonstrate greater *tolerance for contradiction* in situations that involve contradictory information and are more in tune with the *changeable* character of reality.

The researchers found that the two features, changeability and tolerance for contradiction, are interrelated. For example, a person who views themselves as changeable ("In some situations I am extraverted, in other situations I am introverted") might be expected also to characterize themselves as comprising contradictory elements (e.g. "I am both extraverted and introverted"). In agreement with this expectation, they found that Korean participants who adhere to changeability (e.g. "Current situations can change at any time") are also inclined to agree with contradictory items (e.g. "It is more desirable to take the middle ground than go to extremes").[30] Similarly, they referred to research demonstrating that the

[28] Ibid. (p. 94).   [29] Spencer-Rodgers et al. (2010).   [30] Ibid. (p. 299).

tendency for one's emotions to change is correlated with emotional complexity; that is, the tendency to simultaneously experience opposing emotions. In their own research, they found that beliefs about change (e.g. "I often find that my beliefs and attitudes will change under different contexts") and contradiction (e.g. "When I hear two sides of an argument, I often agree with both") showed positive correlations across various national and ethnic groups.

From Western theories of cognitive dissonance,[31] we have learned that, when faced with inconsistent attitudes, beliefs, or behaviors, we feel uncomfortable, and this leads to an alteration in one of these attitudes, beliefs, or behaviors to reduce discomfort and restore balance in the self. In contrast, the self in some East Asian cultures is generally less clearly defined, less internally consistent, and less cross-situationally and temporally stable. Japanese, Chinese, and Korean individuals tend to exhibit less of a reduction of cognitive dissonance, less congruence between the actual, ideal, and ought selves, and less cross-situational self-consistency than do North American individuals.[32]

The researchers reasoned that the concept of contradiction implies that events, objects, and states of mind are thought to comprise opposing elements. In a universe that is considered to be in a constant state of flux, one realizes that what is true of someone or something at one moment in time is not necessarily true of that person or object at another moment: "In a world that is perceived as changing abruptly and rapidly (e.g., good becomes bad, but then bad becomes good), contradiction must be assumed and accepted (e.g., what is good is also bad)."[33] Eastern philosophies are characterized by *the doctrine of the mean*, or the belief that truth is always located somewhere in the middle, in contrast to Western folk theories that are guided by the *law of the excluded middle*, or the belief that propositions cannot be true and false at the same time. In their search for cognitive consonance, Westerners seek to reconcile contradictions and, with the powerful instrument of Aristotelian logic in their hands, reject the least plausible in favor of the most plausible proposition. Specifically, the feeling that cognitive dissonance is unpleasant results in a spontaneous and rapid rejection of one of the dissonant alternatives as an expression of a reduced tolerance of uncertainty.[34]

This leads to the following question: If some Eastern cultures, more than Western ones, are more sensitive and more tolerant to the existence of

---

[31] Aronson (1969).   [32] Spencer-Rodgers et al. (2010).   [33] Ibid. (p. 297).
[34] Ibid. For similar conclusions, see also Boucher et al. (2009).

Figure 5.3   One of the many variations of yokai: nonhuman beings with human forms.
Source: Pictures from History/Universal Images Group/Getty Images.

contradictions, then what are the consequences for understanding the relationship between moral good and bad? Before moving on to the role of shadow positions in our lives, let's have a look at a particular phenomenon that is popular in Japanese folklore where good and bad go together in one and the same figure.

Yokai: A Contradictory Figure in Japanese Folklore

Japanese folklore is full of monsters, ghosts, phantasmatic beings, and supernatural phenomena that are also abundantly present in popular culture. They appear in numerous shapes and sizes and are believed to exist as mountain goblins, water spirits, shape-shifting foxes, and long-tongued ceiling lickers. They often have animal features but may also appear humanoid in appearance (see Figure 5.3), and they are currently popular in film, computer-generated animation, graphic novels, and computer games.

In his monograph *The Book of Yokai: Mysterious Creatures of Japanese Folklore*, Michael D. Foster,[35] a specialist in the study of East Asian

---

[35] Foster (2015).

folklore, sees "in-betweenness" as a common characteristic of yokai. They are typically creatures living in the borderlands, on the edge of a town, in the eddies of a river, or in the mountains between villages. They often appear at twilight, when the familiar seems to be a bit strange and faces become less distinguishable. They haunt tunnels and bridges and lurk at crossroads. Today, "yokai" has become an umbrella signifier for a variety of phenomena such as monsters, spirits, demons, goblins, phantoms, lower-order deities, fantastic beings, or unexplainable occurrences.[36]

It is difficult, maybe even impossible, to provide a definition of yokai. Ultimately, they have no single definition. They appear as spooky, unexplainable things lurking at the edge of knowledge, sometimes scary, sometimes cute or goofy. An often-asked question is whether people actually believe in them. Implicit in this question is that there are only two possibilities: belief or doubt. However, yokai teach us that between belief and doubt, or between the literal and the metaphorical, lies a zone of contradiction as a fertile ground for imagination. As Foster phrases it:

> Humans seem to have a tremendous capacity to embrace different ideas, even ones that may seem contradictory. Any time we hear a story, read a novel, or watch a movie with fictional characters, we allow ourselves to "believe" in people and activities we know are not "real." But of course in one sense they *are* real: they make us laugh and cry, and they stay with us as memories, affecting the way we think and feel. We often express strong emotions about fictional characters – love and hate and everything in between.[37]

Instead of cognitive dissonance, Foster introduces the term "cognitive resonance," the balance of seemingly contradictory ideas that, in their combination, are realistic and meaningful. For this combination, the Japanese use the term *hanshin-hangi*, which means "half-believe/half-doubt." In DST terms, this would refer to a coalition of I believe and I doubt, without any exclusion of one of the possibilities. This combination does not require a decision one way or the other. The two halves are brought together in a whole within which they can harmoniously cooperate. Therefore, the main question is not whether or not people believe in yokai, but why we find it so important to find a yes-or-no answer to this question in the first place.[38]

In grasping the special quality of yokai, Foster proposes the term "interstitial," referring to gaps as the zones of uncertainty existing between

---

[36] Ibid.   [37] Ibid. (p. 30).   [38] Ibid. (p. 31).

two possibilities. The interstitial can also refer to a space where different, seemingly incompatible elements are brought together in a new whole. This space is not empty or meaningless, but rather the opposite: a space for communication, contact, and dialogue, and where meanings may emerge.[39] In logical terms, yokai thrive in the excluded middle, where there lies the possibility of a third, often unimagined choice (the third position in DST[40]). Here, the negative connotations of the experience of uncertainty are replaced by an open space of uncertainty, not laden with negative value but an invitation to seeing things in new and fresh ways, an opportunity for finding things that we otherwise would not look for.[41]

In Foster's view, yokai operate in a tricky middle zone that challenges our powers of empathy. As they are partly human, they allow us to place ourselves in their shoes, but at the same time they remain alien and strange because it is very difficult to fully recognize ourselves in them. The familiar and unfamiliar merge together in a mysterious assembly. There are all sorts of humanlike yokai with exaggerated characteristics, such as a long neck or a long tongue. Many of them are extraordinary: They hop on one leg or are depicted as having just one eye (Figure 5.3).[42]

A key concept that is associated with yokai is *kami*, a kind of god or deity that may be worshipped or prayed to, although they don't possess the all-powerful status of the almighty god from the main monotheistic religions. They are part of the yokai cluster that functions as a continuum. At one end of this cluster, there are those entities that are regarded as troublesome, dangerous, undesirable, and not to be worshipped. At the other end, we find the helpful, friendly, desirable, and worshipped entities, who are generally called kami. Foster adds that these identities are not set in stone, as they are contingent upon the perspectives of the people who are interacting with them. Through rituals and peaceful acts, a troublesome spirit can be transformed into a gentle, cooperating power. A yokai that threatens human actions can be transformed into a gentle spirit and changed from a bad yokai into good kami. So, if a "bad" yokai does something good for society it is considered a kami, but when a kami becomes annoyed it can transform into a bad yokai.[43]

I'm aware of the fact that in other folk traditions and religions illustrations can also be found of gods and goddesses who are seen as good and bad at the same time or who are changeable from good to bad and vice versa, particularly but not exclusively in Hinduism and Buddhism.

[39] Ibid. (p. 89).   [40] Hermans (2018).   [41] Foster (2015, p. 90).   [42] Ibid. (p. 88).
[43] Ibid. (p. 21).

I selected the yokai as an old tradition that persists even in our modern computerized society, in the form of videos, movies, and games, in order to give an example of an entity that demonstrates the possibility of transcending any moral dualism. In this tradition, as in other East Asian ones, good and bad, although regarded as distinguishable, are accepted in their contradiction. Actually, the yokai illustrate a continuous process of moral positioning, counter-positioning, and repositioning where judgments of good and bad are not stable and opposed but flexible and open to reconciling good and bad as hybrid positions in the self (e.g. enemy and friend).

The Risk of Removing Moral Bad from the Self

The example of yokai as a folkloristic figure in Japanese culture can easily be dismissed from our Western lifestyle and, certainly, from the reality of our own selves. Apparently, as we have seen earlier in this chapter, it is difficult for Western cultural traditions to accept certain aspects, judged as morally problematic, as part of one's own self. This acceptance is made difficult when, in the Cartesian tradition, the self is regarded as an undifferentiated unity and defined as an entity apart from its social and natural environment. This unitary quality of the self is highly vulnerable to reductions of self-esteem, particularly when the self has a low degree of complexity. Because shadow positions, considered as rejected positions in the self (e.g. I as hating, I as greedy, I as possessive, I as envious, I as cruel), have a morally inferior quality, such positions are threatening to one's self-esteem *par excellence*.

One of the main assumptions of DST is that our individual I-positions are strongly influenced by we-positions, given the fact that, from a historical perspective, the latter positions are often present before we are born. Utopian worldviews, in particular, are reflected as we-positions in the self, and their powerful influences on our lifestyles start from birth onward before we are explicitly aware of them. As detailed in Chapter 2, utopian ideals have demonstrated the far-reaching consequences of a lack of moral multiplicity. They typically start with good or noble intentions, but after their institutionalization, they can transform, via a process of over-positioning, into "giant monsters." Over the course of history, many social, political, and religious utopias have nurtured the illusion of complete purity, goodness, and perfection as the end position of an idealized future. This final salvation is to be realized by transforming an imperfect society into a heaven of ultimate happiness and moral goodness. Christianity aims to achieve this ideal state by promising an eternal afterlife of ultimate goodness, a mission that has caused rampant wars and led to the extermination of heretics (e.g. the Spanish Inquisition), legitimized by the moral conviction that they were inherently evil. Communism, rejecting religion as the opium of the masses, painted the vistas of a class-free society of freedom but ultimately resulted in the mass killings of the Stalin and Mao Zedong regimes. The ideology of Nazism envisioned an ideal society in which only one supreme group, the Aryan race, was depicted as the superclass, but it led to the killing of millions of people in the disaster of the Holocaust. More recently, President Putin of Russia has caused mass killings and destruction by invading Ukraine in February 2022, guided by his ideal of bringing back the tsarist Russian Empire of the past (Chapter 3). Some Islamic groups embrace the original teachings of Mohammed as "holy," but in their political manifestation they have produced the horrors of killing "nonbelievers." Neoliberal capitalism has preached the message of salvation of the free market, but this finally led to the worldwide exploitation of natural resources, poverty among large parts of the global population, and sharp economic divides. As these examples show, many generations are educated by institutions based on beliefs in "pure religion," "pure race," "pure empire," "pure liberty," and even the "pure ideology of the free market," all of them advertised as representing moral goodness but actually associated with a simultaneous blindness to their shadows. These shadows should not simply be considered as undesirable side effects of a valuable aim but as *potential positions* inherent to the original, mono-positional ideal itself (e.g. a "true" believer who becomes a religious fanatic). The problem with these ideals is that they lack moral multiplicity and the correcting influence of counter-positions that have the potential of preventing any conviction or moral mandate from undergoing a process of over-positioning of the original impulse. I repeat the words of the personality psychologists Walter Mischel and Harriet Mischel: "History is replete with atrocities that were justified by invoking the highest principles and that were perpetrated upon victims who were equally convinced of their own moral principles. In the name of justice, of the common welfare, of universal ethics, and of God, millions of people have been killed and whole cultures destroyed."[44]

In order to gain some deeper insights into the meaning of shadow positions, let's have a look at the work of Carl Jung, who has published extensively on this subject (Figure 5.4). I will then explore how DST

---

[44] Mischel and Mischel (1976), quoted by Skitka and Mullen (2002, p. 39).

Figure 5.4   Jung's archetype of the shadow.
Source: Klaus Vedfelt/DigitalVision/Getty Images.

differs from the Jungian view vis-à-vis shadow positions and in what respects they share some similarities.

Jung on Shadows

In one of his last articles, titled "Good and Evil in Analytical Psychology,"[45] Carl Jung (1875–1961) exposed his view that good and bad are not intrinsic in themselves and are not to be discovered in reality but are always *judgments* of reality: "When we speak of good or evil we are speaking about what men call good or evil, about what they perceive as good or evil."[46] People can talk with great certainty about good and evil: "But perhaps the view which the speaker has of the world does not agree with the real facts at all, so that an inner, subjective picture is substituted for objectivity."[47] Therefore, Jung thinks that good and evil are judgments based on the application of certain standards: "At most we can say cautiously: judged by such and such a standard, such and such a thing is good or evil."[48]

After this relativizing remark, Jung continues to write about clients who are confronted with bad in themselves but are scared to face it: "He sees his

[45] Jung (1960).   [46] Ibid. (p. 91).   [47] Ibid. (p. 91).   [48] Ibid. (p. 92).

own shadow, his crookedness, but he turns his eyes away, does not confront himself, does not come to terms with himself, risks nothing – and then boasts before god and his fellows of the spotless white garment which in reality he owes only to his cowardice, his regression, his super-angelic perfectionism."[49]

Jung notes that it may be very good indeed for the person to be confronted with moral bad in themselves: "Perhaps he has to experience the power of evil and suffer accordingly, because only in that way can he give up his Pharisaic attitude to other people. Perhaps fate or the uncon-scious or god – call it what you will – had to give him a hard knock and roll him in the dirt, because only such a massive experience could strike home with him, pull him out of his infantilism, and make him more mature."[50]

Along these lines, Jung arrives at a point where he sees not only the possibility but even the necessity of bringing judgments of good and bad together as opposite members of the self:

> When we observe how people behave who are confronted with a situation that has to be evaluated ethically, we become aware of a strange double effect: *suddenly they see both sides.* These people become aware not only of their moral inferiorities but also, automatically, of their good qualities. They rightly say: "I can't be as bad as all that." Confronting a man with his shadow means showing him his own light. Once one has experienced a few times what it is like to stand judgingly between the opposites, one begins to understand what is meant by the self. *Anyone who perceives his shadow and his light simultaneously sees himself from two sides and thus gets in the middle.*[51]

In this quotation, Jung comes very close to what I propose as the moral middle ground in this book. First of all, it should be clear that there are three things that he is *not* telling us: (1) He does not advise mixing up good and bad so that they are no longer indistinguishable – he writes about a "middle," where the opposites meet each other; (2) he does not recom-mend suppressing the bad side or the good side in favor of the other; and likewise (3) he does not address the one side at one moment and the other side at the next moment but configures them simultaneously. These three features allow the possibility of a dialogical relationship between the two sides when we consider them as two I-positions. When the two sides are moving in tandem and go together on the moral middle ground, where they are recognized in their differences, they are valued as "equals" insofar as having the right to express themselves with their own voices *before* arriving at a decision or conclusion.

[49] Ibid. (p. 94).   [50] Ibid.   [51] Ibid. (p. 96, emphases added).

In an insightful article on Jung's concept of the shadow, a student of his work, Murray Stein, agrees fully with Jung's view that a judgment of good and bad depends on the perspective one takes:

> The source of what we perceive as evil, then, is a mixture of psychological content (the shadow) and psychological dynamics that allow for, encourage, or require shadow enactments. This is different from saying that the shadow is evil per se. What is in the shadow may well, under certain conditions, be seen as good and useful for promoting human life and well-being. Sexuality and aggression are cases in point. Any archetypal image and any instinctual drive may yield evil action *under psychological conditions of inflation* and identification with primitive archetypal contents accompanied by social conditions of permission or secrecy. Used under other conditions and governed by more favorable attitudes, these same psychological contents and drives can yield benefit and goodness.[52]

This quotation adds an element that is useful for understanding the specific nature of the moral middle ground: Any archetypical image may yield evil action under the psychological condition of inflation. This is in accordance with the notion of over-positioning in DST and with the thesis, emphasized several times in this book, that one of the positions on the moral middle ground can be dominant over the other positions located on this middle ground. When the bad position of the coalition becomes involved in a process of over-positioning, it can finally disappear from the middle ground, so that it can be seen as entirely belonging to the realm of bad.

Shadows in Jungian Psychology and in Dialogical Self Theory: Differences

Besides evident similarities between Jungian shadows and shadow positions in DST, there are also some conceptual differences. It is difficult, even risky, to briefly summarize the main differences because a detailed exposure would need a new book.[53]

Universal or Situational

Most typically, Jung considers shadows as archetypes of a universal quality that can be found in all cultures. Generally, archetypes exist in different forms – for example, as the child, the wise old man, the trickster, the jester,

---

[52] Stein (1995, n.p., emphasis added).
[53] For a profound exposition of Jungian archetypes, see Jacobi (1999).

the shadow, the mother. In order to characterize the universal quality of the archetype, Jungian psychologist Jolande Jacobi sketches the mother archetype in the following way: "... the individual is no longer confronted with his own mother, but with the archetype of the 'maternal'; no longer with the unique personal problem created by his own mother as a concrete reality, but with the universally human, impersonal problem of every man's dealings with the primordial maternal ground in himself."[54] DST does not assume the existence of universal I- or we-positions, because positions are conceived of as contingent on personal, social, and cultural characteristics and circumstances. I-positions can be unique for this person, they may emerge from membership of a particular social group, or they may be embedded in the values or traditions of a particular culture (recall the example of yokai as a folkloristic figure specific to Japanese culture).

Instinctual or Social and Personal

In Jung's vision, archetypes are instinctual, partly due to their biological origin. In his view, the archetype has one aspect oriented "upward" (i.e. toward the world of images and ideas), but it also has another aspect oriented "downward" (i.e. toward the instincts as natural, biological processes).[55] I- and we-positions, on the other hand, are primarily learned over the course of one's individual and collective history. Certainly, some I-positions have a genetic basis. For example, a position like "I as always stressed" may well be an expression of the personality trait "emotional instability" that has, as is generally accepted, a genetic component.[56] However, the majority of positions have a social or cultural origin. A child that does not meet the expectations of its parents may position itself as "I as a failure." A child that goes to school for the first time has a new position added to their repertoire of I-positions: "I as a pupil."

Different Emphasis on Coalitions

As they are contingent on a great variety of individual, social, and cultural circumstances, I- and we-positions are virtually unlimited in their configurations. Not only is there an endless multiplicity of actual and possible I-positions, they can also create a multitude of combinations, described in this book via the concept of "coalition." Moreover, these coalitions are

[54] Ibid. (p. 26).   [55] Ibid. (p. 39).   [56] For a review, see Hermans (2022).

involved in processes of transformation and change. In one of my case studies,[57] I worked with a client who had three main positions in his present life: "I as doubter," "I as perfectionist," and, somewhat in the background but very important to him, "I as enjoyer of life." The latter position seemed to be an enduring feature of his personal history, but this position was suppressed by the strong coalition between the doubter and the perfectionist, the second one compensating for the anxiety aroused by the first one. After a year of counseling, we decided to investigate his position repertoire again. Most significant was the finding that the perfectionist and the enjoyer had formed a new coalition that was strong enough to push the doubter into the background of the self-system. Whereas at the beginning of the counseling process the perfectionist was in a maladaptive coalition with the doubter, over the course of a year this position changed camps and joined the enjoyer of life in a new coalition that produced a third position (having fun with work) that was strong enough to push the doubter into the background. As this example illustrates, not only positions but also coalitions can change over the course of time.

Jungian archetypes, including the shadow, are *typically* not easily changed and not involved in cooperation with other archetypes. However, this is not always the case. There was a period in his life in which Jung was driven by the desire to replace the one-sided Christian God image with one that encompasses evil within it.[58] In Jung's fantasies during World War I, a new God had been born in his soul, the God whom he described as the son of the frogs or the son of the earth, and he called him Abraxas, a God who was difficult to grasp: "His power is greatest, because man does not see it. From the sun he draws the *summum bonum*; from the devil the *infinum malum*; but from Abraxas LIFE, altogether indefinite, the mother of good and evil."[59]

Jung considered Abraxas as representing the unification of the Christian God with Satan, symbolizing his vision of a transformation of the Western God image. In his audacious thinking and rich experience he brought the opposites of a good God and a bad God closely together: "If the God is absolute beauty and goodness, how should he encompass the fullness of life, which is beautiful and hateful, good and evil, laughable and serious, human and inhuman? How can man live in the womb of the God if the Godhead himself attends only to one-half of him?"[60] In this integrative image of God, the energy of LIFE did not escape his attention.

---

[57] Hermans (2018, pp. 283–285).   [58] Jung (2010).   [59] Jung (2009, p. 350).
[60] Ibid. (p. 243).

This corresponds with one of the main themes proposed in this book: The coalition of good and bad has the potential to add, in particular situations (see Chapter 4), to the *vitality* of the self.[61]

Collective Unconscious or Internal and External Shadow Positions

Finally, Jung's archetypes, including shadows, are central elements in the collective unconscious. Their existence may be inferred from art, stories, myths, religions, fairy tales, or dreams, and they are actualized when they enter consciousness as images or become manifest in one's behavior in interactions with the outside world. In DST, shadow positions are contextual phenomena that may result from personal experiences that are rejected as undesirable members of the self on the basis of social or cultural preferences or judgments. To understand their functions, it makes sense to make a distinction between internal and external shadow positions and acknowledge their interwovenness. Let's take a look at the following example: At primary school, a young, introverted student has a socially isolated position and never plays with his peers. As a result, he is systematically and persistently bullied by his classmates. He feels rejected, despised, and devaluated by them, at the cost of his self-esteem. In order to compensate for his feelings of inferiority, the boy tries to excel in sports and to achieve high grades in school. However, his despising classmates as well as others who devalue him (as shadows positions in the external domain of this self) and his hidden feelings of inferiority (shadow positions in the internal domain of his self) remain vulnerable parts of his self for the rest of his life. His successes in sports and his excellent school performance make him feel better through recognition by adults and his peers, and his self-esteem is restored. However, in the hidden areas of his self, the external and internal shadows remain present and may suddenly resurface when he comes into contact with others who show signs of depreciation of him. At the surface he is successful, and also he feels that way, but at a lower level of consciousness he feels as if he is a failure and experiences nonintimate others as *potential* threats. His outward achievements were motivated by the shadows of his past, but in some situations he is vulnerable enough to regress to the "monsters" of his past. As this example suggests, his shadow positions are unacceptable internal and external members of his self that are rooted in his personal history and

---

[61] For my earlier thoughts on the relationship between shadow and shining positions, see Hermans (2018, pp. 285–287).

in collective norms that prescribe that a boy of that age should be tough and strong.

Accepting shadow positions is one of the greatest challenges to the dialogical self as a society of mind. Let's make a comparison with society at large. When the differences, contrasts, and contradictions between individuals and between groups greatly increase, there comes a point at which these differences become unbridgeable, as the common ground between them shrinks. Likewise, when the tensions among acceptable I-positions and unacceptable (shadow) I-positions culminate, this may put a heavy burden on the self to hold them together and to interconnect them. Yet, the acknowledgment and integration of opposite and conflicting I-positions are preconditions not only for the psychological health of the individual person, but also for human society as a whole. In my view, Jung had a keen eye for this challenge when he wrote: "If people can be educated to see the shadow-side of their nature clearly, it may be hoped that they will also learn to understand and love their fellow men better. A little less hypocrisy and a little more self-knowledge can only have good results in respect for our neighbor; for we are all too prone to transfer to our fellows the injustice and violence we inflict upon our own natures."[62] I hold that the best way to deal with the increasing tension between strongly contradicting I-positions in the self is a well-developed dialogical capacity.

Dialogue and Contradiction

Given the general tendency to see good and bad as just mutually excluding opposites and to reject our shadow positions as purely bad members of ourselves, it is difficult to keep good and bad together on a moral middle ground and to create a space for dialogical relationships between them. In this section, I want to present the thesis that dialogue is the process *par excellence* not only to *face contradictions*, but also to *respond to them* in ways that are productive to the self as a society of mind. After elaborating on this thesis, I will in the next section of the chapter formulate a series of practical implications that may be helpful for dealing with contradictions in everyday life.

First, I want to stipulate that dialogue allows us to face contradicting positions and bring them together in a highly dynamic way. I will present here an example of a dialogical process that I have described several times

---

[62] Jung (1966, p. 26).

in previous publications.[63] I repeat it here because I consider it as one of the deeper layers of dialogue. The essence of the argument is that we can understand dialogue and its relationship with contradiction only if we acknowledge its *spatial* basis.

The spatial nature of dialogue can be clarified with the following Bakhtinian example about the difference between logical and dialogical relationships.[64] Take two identical phrases: "life is good" and, again, "life is good." In terms of Aristotelian logic, these two phrases represent *identity* as, in fact, they are one and the same statement. However, from a dialogical point of view, they are different as they are expressed by the voices of two spatially separated people who entertain a relationship of *agreement*. The two phrases are identical from a logical point of view but different as utterances: The first is a statement, the second a confirmation. Similarly, we can compare the phrases "life is good" and "life is not good." From a logical perspective, one is a *negation* of the other, and, as such, they are contra-dictive. However, as the utterances come from the mouths of two different speakers, a dialogical relation of *disagreement* (literally, contra-diction) exists.

To understand the nature of contradictions, an additional difference between logical and dialogical relationships has to be added. While the latter are open, the former are closed. Dialogical relationships are open in the sense that they move toward an unknown future. As the process develops, every speech act *opens* a dialogical space that allows a range of *possible* statements in the future, but the next step is largely unpredictable. In contrast, logical relationships are *closed* as they do not permit any alternative conclusion due to the limits of the logical rules that govern the relationships among the statements. For example, a syllogism starts from a set of premises, leading, through a number of logical steps, to a conclusion that is necessarily true. Contradiction is excluded, and any alternative conclusion is not possible. Nothing is left to be said, and there is no opening to the domain of the unexpected. It is this openness to the unexpected and its association with uncertainty that Descartes wanted to avoid in his journey that brought him, along logical pathways, to the perfect certainty of his *Cogito*. Dialogue, in contrast, embraces the unexpected of an open future and profits from the potential of creative uncertainty, as greatly welcomed by Montaigne's central philosophical adage "*Que sais-je?*"[65]

To describe the generative potential of dialogue, a more detailed analysis is needed. Generative dialogue as a meaning-making process involves three steps: (1) an individual or a social group takes a particular position and,

---

[63] For example, Hermans (2022).   [64] Vasil'eva (1988).   [65] Montaigne (2003).

from this voiced position, they address another individual or group and send a message to them; (2) the addressee, who occupies a different spatial position, receives this message and answers it by addressing the first speaker by sending a message to them from their own specific perspective; and (3) the first speaker receives this message and *revises, nuances,* or *expands* their original position under the influence of the message of the other speaker, with recognition of its original intention. Let's illustrate this process by elaborating on the "life is good" example. Note that this example is simplified to clarify the conceptual argument.

(1)   First speaker: "Life is good."
(2)   Second speaker: "Life is not good."
(3)   First speaker: "Well, life is good, but it also has its shadow sides."
(4)   Second speaker: "Which shadow side do you have in mind?"
(5)   First speaker: "Good question! I think . . ."

In this example, the first speaker takes a *position* toward the second one (step 1). The second speaker takes a *counter-position* and sends from their own specific perspective a response to the first speaker (step 2). Then, crucial to a generative dialogue, the first speaker *repositions* themselves and revises their original message under the influence of the comment of the second speaker and resends it to them (step 3). The second speaker follows up on this comment and its intention by posing a question or bringing in a new point of view, which deepens the dialogical process (step 4). As a response to this challenging question, the first speaker is invited to start a process of *internal positioning and repositioning*, in the form of self-questioning and self-answering (step 5). As a product of this internal questioning, a more detailed and more developed message is shared with the second speaker, in whom the same internal self-exploration may take place, resulting in new thinking, or new feeling, on both sides. Along these lines, the external dialogue is expanded and enriched by the internal dialogue and vice versa. In this way, the process evolves further in an unpredictable direction, providing the participants with the opportunity to gain *new* and *shared* insights and unexpected discoveries. To acquire such insights, the participants have to modify their initial points of view, and, in this sense, they "lose" something. However, one of the features of generative dialogue is that it requires something to be given up, with the possibility of receiving something better or different some moments later. Generative dialogue profits from its own contradiction: It decentralizes the self, but it also has the power to recentralize it.

Let's now apply this stepwise procedure to a moral dispute in which two individuals talk about Andrew Carnegie as representing a figure on the moral middle ground (see Chapter 6):

(1)   First speaker: "Carnegie was a selfish predatory capitalist."
(2)   Second speaker: "But he also did good things, like establishing many libraries."
(3)   First speaker: "Well, he did that to become famous."
(4)   Second speaker: "Even if that were true, many uneducated people could profit from his gifts."
(5)   First speaker: "Yeah, I never looked at it this way. Maybe he also did good things . . ."

In this dissonant dialogue, the two speakers addressed an issue of common interest and were willing, despite their disagreement, to listen to each other. They were, moreover, able and willing to take the perspective of their opponent into account when exploring Carnegie's status on the moral middle ground. If their interchange were to have continued, they *might* have discovered that Carnegie, or any figure like him, had the opportunity to contribute to the welfare of society not *despite* but rather *due to* his selfishness.

If this process of positioning and counter-positioning continues, both between and within the participants, a dialogical space is created that emerges as an experiential field that is felt by both of them. This field was not there before the interchange started but develops when the participants listen carefully to each other, have the chance to speak from their own original points of view, and allow each other to broaden the bandwidth of I- or we-positions relevant to the topic discussed, with an absence or minimum of nondiscussible areas. This space is experienced by both parties as emerging between them and is felt as something that they have in common. This virtual space functions as fertile ground for new insights and discoveries shared by the participants.[66]

Some Crucial Features of Generative Dialogue

For the dialogical process to take place productively, it is necessary that participants not only respond to the other's words, but also attend to their *intentions* at different intentional levels (I know that you know what

---

[66] For a more comprehensive treatment of contradiction and dialogue in the context of inner democracy, see Hermans (2020); Hermans and Bartels (2021).

I mean). To understand what the other intends to express, we need to listen to what is said "between the lines" (I think what you want to say is that ... Is that right?). The advantage of dialogue at different intentional levels is that misunderstandings can be detected and corrected.[67]

It is far from self-evident that participants are willing and able to change their initial position. Once established, I-positions have the tendency to stick to themselves and even defend themselves against any other positions that challenge them. Changing or giving up an initial position is often felt as decreasing one's self-esteem, and this is associated with negative emotions. In such a case, the initial position becomes *rigid*, with the consequence that the openness of the self, which is of vital importance for generative dialogue, is reduced. The opposite occurs when an initial position is given up prematurely. This happens when individuals change or give up their position in every new encounter, resulting in a rapid change of positioning in different directions with a high degree of instability (flip-flopping). In such a case, the initial positioning is *overly flexible* and not stable enough for comparison with another position that enters the dialogue. The result is a decision process that gets stuck in indecision. In other words, generative dialogue needs an optimal degree of positional flexibility.

When a position is loaded with emotions, a generative dialogue with other people needs an *internal dialogue between reason and emotion*. Reason has the power of comprehending, inferring, or thinking in orderly, rational ways. Reappraisal of an initial emotion by one's reason occurs when participants are contemplating why they are responding in this particular way and whether there is good reason to experience this emotion. Reason–emotion dialogue has the potential of opening up the otherwise closed boundaries of emotional positions in search of an exit in the direction of different emotions or alternative explanations. Our reasoning processes have some potential to act as a counter-position that weakens the initial emotion and takes it in another direction.[68] However, we have to take into account that emotions need more processing time than reasoning. Particularly when the interchange is very fast, there is insufficient time for the expression and dialogical processing of emotions, with the result that these emotions go underground and require space for expression at some later moment in time.

Moments of *silence* have an organizing function during dialogical interchange, and they are crucial for the fluency of the process of interchange.

---

[67] For dialogue at different intentional or meta-positional levels, see Hermans (2022, p. 274).
[68] Feinberg et al. (2012).

Dialogical turn-taking is based on a *rhythm* – a regular, repeating pattern of question and answer or stimulus and response. Brief pauses between the words or sentences give structure and organization to the content of the interchange. However, when during this back-and-forth process the phase of silence takes too long, the rhythm is interrupted and the focus of attention decreases. In contrast, when brief pauses do not occur and the speakers chase each other or they interrupt each other frequently, there is no time for listening and no space for internal dialogue as an original source of new content, with the result that the external dialogue is impoverished.

Generative dialogue and the creation of a dialogical space are *not limited to verbal interchange*. Two people who embrace each other after a conflict or misunderstanding can experience a form of commonality that renovates their relationship. And moments of silence can produce a similar effect. As Martin Buber said: "Dialogue is not merely the interchange of words – genuine dialogue can take place in silence, whereas much conversation is really monologue."[69] Dialogue without words, although less precise, is more direct, immediate, and oriented in the here and now than any verbal dialogue can be. More generally, giving attention to body signals, such as changes in breathing, heartbeat, muscle tension, and relaxation, may significantly influence the dialogical process of question and answer or agreement and disagreement (e.g. taking a deep breath before answering in case of disagreement). Also, discrepancies between the verbal level of interchange (the words) and the nonverbal level (body language) are signals with far-reaching impacts on the ways words and sentences are interpreted.[70] Differently from purely textual forms of dialogue, like that offered by ChatGPT, dialogue in this book is understood as embodied dialogue.[71]

Typically, *implicit* forms of positioning, if they are conflicting with explicit ones, such as nonrecognized shadow positions, have the tendency to narrow the dialogical space and can even disturb the dialogue. They limit or "pollute" the space beyond the awareness of one or both participants. In such a case, participants may pretend to be involved in a "good" dialogue, but this interchange is not associated with awareness of obstacles

---

[69] Buber (1965, p. xvii).

[70] For a more extensive exposé on nonverbal factors in relation to dialogue, with special attention given to the emotion-regulating function of the right brain hemisphere, see Hermans (2018, pp. 158–161). For the connection between the orbitofrontal cortex and the amygdala in the context of a discussion of dialogical relationships between I-positions, see Lewis (2002). For the importance of the expression of emotions during dialogues in family therapy, see Seikkula and Trimble (2005).

[71] For the effects of priming different I-positions on motor behavior in the dialogical self, see Suszek et al. (2023).

that may, often nonconsciously, narrow the dialogical space. There are various shadow positions that participants may reject as undesirable and "not belonging to me" and which they exclusively attribute to other people. For many people, it is difficult to acknowledge the role of shadow positions in themselves, such as "I as hateful," "I as vengeful," "I as taking pleasure in the bad luck of my competitor," "I as having a big ego," "I as jealous," "I as wishing the death of the person who damaged me," or "I as scared of my own death." As warded-off positions, located in no-go areas of the self, they have a low degree of I-ness (the feeling that this position belongs to me),[72] and therefore they are isolated from other I-positions, with the consequence that they are not accessible and cannot be actively and consciously connected with more acceptable positions. This is particularly true for positions that are candidates for inclusion in the moral middle ground. Because of the pervasive tendency to separate good and bad positions and to see them as mutually exclusive, they are prevented from entering *together* on the middle ground. The consequence is that they cannot be recognized as part of a coalition with acceptable positions and their dialogical processing becomes blocked. Because many positions – explicit or implicit ones, morally good or bad ones – have a productive or inhibiting influence on the dialogical process, DST, like any dialogical theory, needs a positioning theory as its conceptual basis.[73] This basis is needed because dialogue is a moral process in any society that celebrates "freedom of speech" as a necessary condition for the expression of opposite, conflicting, or minority positions, and this also applies to the self as a society of mind.

Finally, I want to emphasize that generative dialogue is not a shortcut to a solution or decision. Particularly on the shaky moral middle ground, dialogue, often of a dissonant nature, needs a series of dialogical steps in the direction of a solution to a moral problem or dilemma. When good and bad positions are conflicting, dissonant dialogues are unavoidable, both between participants and within the self. Such dialogues will proceed into an unknown future and lead to unpredictable decisions. However, generative dialogue, particularly in its dissonant version, is a slow process and always needs a "second thought" that goes beyond any direct impulse or automatic response.

Why would I want to advocate for the recognition of the value of contradiction? It's because our usual, spontaneous, automatic response to contradictions is to "solve" them via dissonance reduction. However, this

---

[72] Hermans (2022).   [73] Hermans and Hermans-Konopka (2010). See also Raggatt (2012).

reduces the space for dialogue, because one of the positions is dominated and pushed back by the other one, with the result that the positions cannot profit from one another in their problem-solving process. Dialogue, and certainly dissonant dialogue, profits from difference, disagreement, and conflict *before* achieving consonance. It stimulates the analysis of problems from divergent or opposing perspectives and widens the dialogical space. Contradiction is the basic stuff of generative dialogue among positions and counter-positions both between participants and within the self, and it is an essential precondition to the development of a dialogical capacity.

Practical Implications

Given the all-pervasive presence of contradictions in the self, and especially the functioning of shadow positions, the first practical implication of this chapter would be the fostering of *self-empathy*. The idea behind this concept, which has been expressed in various ways in the psychological literature, was first described by developmental psychologist Heinz Kohut, who introduced it as the "ability of empathizing with ourselves, i.e. with our own past mental organizations."[74] Central to DST is that a position, as a spatial concept, has boundaries that can be open, closed, soft, rigid, or flexible.[75] Self-empathy requires that the boundaries of positions, referring to present or past experiences, are open or flexible enough to make it possible to enter them and experience, both cognitively and affectively, their specific nature with a minimum of projection. This is particularly relevant for shadow positions that usually have closed or rigid boundaries, as they are in contradiction to one's positive self-esteem and, therefore, separated and isolated from more positive positions in the self at the risk of projecting them onto others. The psychotherapist Judith Jordan expressed a keen insight regarding the relevance of self-empathy when she argued that the observing, often judging self can't make empathic contact with some rejected aspect of the self: "To be able to observe and tolerate the affect of that state in a context of understanding becomes a kind of intrapsychic empathy which actually can lead to lasting structural change in self-representations." In addition, she suggests: "Unlike empathy with another, where the self-boundaries undergo more temporary alteration and the final accommodation may be slight, with intrapsychic empathy there is more opportunity for enduring change . . ."[76] Precisely

---

[74] Kohut (1959), quoted by Jordan (1984, n.p.).   [75] Hermans (2018).
[76] Jordan (1984, n.p.). See also her concept of self-boundary flexibility.

for that reason, I would like to suggest that practices that open the boundaries of shadow positions are crucial to integrating them as original positions in the self. This requires a well-developed meta-position with a broad reach that enables us to see the connection between the protection of high self-esteem and the tendency to ward off shadow aspects of ourselves. The motivational and attitudinal characteristics of nonjudgment and openness may contribute to important shifts in the inner experience of troublesome self-images.

When shadow positions are open and addressable and receive a voice in the self, it becomes possible to become involved in a dialogue with them. A crucial question arises here: *When I unveil a shadow position in myself, is it possible to give it a place on my moral middle ground?* This can be realized by searching for possible coalitions between this position and other, more desirable and morally acceptable positions. In Chapter 4, we saw a variety of examples of phenomena in which such coalitions are realizable: healthy selfishness, enlightened self-interest, Machiavellianism, the case of Oskar Schindler, black humor, grey hat hackers, transgressive art, and integrating the "wrong" other-in-the-self. In Chapter 6, I will elaborate on the example of Andrew Carnegie in order to illustrate that a certain degree of selfishness can, under particular conditions, even be profitable in terms of doing philanthropic work. In invite you as a reader to search in your own self for a shadow position (e.g. I as greedy, I as egoistic, I as aggressive, or any other) and to pose the question to yourself as to how this position can be combined with a morally acceptable position and transferred onto the moral middle ground. Simply said, your ego is a wolf – don't try to slay him, but make use of him in the service of benefiting yourself and others.

As many coaches, counselors, and psychotherapists emphasize, *the art of listening*, both to others and to oneself, is worth practicing when one wants to open up the boundaries of positions in the self. There is perhaps no one who has expressed greater insight into this process than the celebrated psychotherapist Carl Rogers, sometimes called "the best listener in the world," who knew what listening can evoke in the mind of the speaker:

> In this atmosphere of safety, protection, and acceptance, the firm boundaries of self-organization *relax*. There is no longer the firm, tight gestalt which is characteristic of every organization under threat, but a looser, more uncertain configuration. He begins to explore his perceptual field more and more fully. He discovers faulty generalizations, but his self-structure is now sufficiently relaxed so that he can consider the complex and *contradictory* experiences upon which they are based. He discovers experiences of which

he has never been aware, which are deeply contradictory to the perception he has had of himself.[77]

Inspired by this insight, a group of Israelian psychologists[78] decided to investigate the nature of inner contradictions more profoundly by proposing a distinction between two kinds of contradictions that I would like to emphasize here because they often get confused. The first is what they called *objective ambivalence*. This can be observed when a person has simultaneously positive and negative feelings or thoughts about a certain person, object, or issue, but these attitudes do not necessarily interfere with each other (e.g. "On the one hand I appreciate that they . . ., on the other hand I experience some difficulty with their . . ."). In this form of ambivalence, one realizes that two realistic aspects of someone or something contradict each other, but one is able and willing to distinguish and compare them. The second kind is *subjective ambivalence*, which refers to a sense of being confused, being torn, and having unclear and mixed feelings about something. This happens if we cannot create order in our thoughts or feelings and end up profoundly confused. I think this distinction is relevant to responding to contradictions because objective ambivalence is needed for a well- balanced evaluation, whereas subjective ambivalence is something that one typically wants to avoid because it interferes, at least for some time, with reaching reasonable conclusions and clear decisions. Admittedly, this does not exclude the possibility that a period of confusion or chaos can function as a welcome start to a subsequent process of creativity!

The researchers then wanted to know what the effect was of *high-quality listening* on subjective and objective ambivalence. When collaborators in these experiments listened to speakers in an empathetic, nonjudgmental, and respectful way, labeled as "high-quality listening," they found that the speakers suffered less from social anxiety, were less defensive, and experienced more objective ambivalence compared to a situation in which listeners reacted in a rather absent-minded way and let themselves be distracted, labeled as "low-quality listening." These findings suggest that high-quality listening opens up the boundaries of positions, creates space in the self to tolerate inner contradictions, and leads to more objective ambivalence than in the case of low-quality listening. High-quality listening seems to be particularly difficult to achieve in situations requiring quick responses, when there is an overload of stimulation and information,

---

[77] Rogers (1951, p. 193, emphases added).   [78] Itzchakov et al. (2017).

or when one feels under pressure to perform in a highly effective manner. Taken together, this provides reason to consider the precious quality of good listening as an art form in itself.[79]

To recognize, understand, and, if possible, solve some of the many complex problems of our time (e.g. climate change, pandemics, international conflicts, economic divides, the power of digital and technological giants), we need to acknowledge the inherent complexity of the self (see also Linville's buffer hypothesis as described earlier in this chapter). As argued in this book, this is a self that has a broad, multiple, and highly dynamic position repertoire at its disposal, capable of positioning itself in the minds of other people, listening to itself and others, and being involved in an ongoing process of trying out, learning, and trying out again. Because there is often "not just one correct solution," a considerable *tolerance for uncertainty* is required, because nobody can give, as an individual, social group, or government, definitive answers. That is why dialogical relations are crucial between individuals, between social groups, as well as within oneself in order to explore alternative positions and their possible temporal consequences. Perhaps the term "tolerance for uncertainty" doesn't express the full potential of this capacity. The Czech-born French writer Milan Kundera[80] used the phrase "worlds of ambiguity," in which no absolute truth exists. In his view, these worlds manifest a "confusing manifold of contradictory truths" in which the only certainty is the relevance of the "wisdom of uncertainty."

There are cultural differences concerning the tolerance of contradictions. As management consultant Karl Albrecht[81] argues, we have a tendency to engage in *dichotomized thinking*: to think in terms of two possibilities, typically two opposite and mutually excluding potentials. We are for or against a particular proposal, winner or loser in a game, left or right in political matters, high or low in mood. We are used to evaluating a performance as good or bad and evaluating a person as intelligent or stupid. As Albrecht continues, given this tendency to think in mutually exclusive dichotomies, we are less sensitive to realistic in-between possibilities. There is day and night and there is also twilight (compare the example of yokai from earlier in this chapter). There are two sexes, male and female, but what about the LGBTQ+ community? There are winners and losers in games of sport, but some of them result in a tie or, in the case of chess, stalemate. When we categorize people as left or right in politics, we neglect the silent majority. We embrace or reject a

[79] Hermans (2020).   [80] Kundera (1988, pp. 6–7).   [81] Albrecht (2010).

particular view or theory, but we know that creativity thrives on sensitivity to contradictions.[82] Dichotomous thinking carries the risk of casting aside the diverse alternatives and variations that are the outcomes of sensitivity to contradictions.[83]

Elaborating on Albrecht's observations, I propose some specific guidelines that might be useful for broadening our view beyond dichotomous thinking and for dealing with contradictions within the self:

- Keep opinions and conclusions on probation. See them as beginning positions but not as end positions and keep them open to dialogue. See opinions as preliminary points of view, open to revision, expansion, or improvement, because better information, knowledge, or insights may become available at some later moment.[84]
- Abandon the wish to be rigidly and firmly certain about everything. Train yourself to be comfortable with a certain amount of contradiction and ambiguity. Concentrate on this contradiction, at least for a while, because it entails the possibility of productive thinking and generative dialogue.
- Modify your language by sometimes substituting words such as "or" with "and" to suggest that there might be multiple options, not just two. Where applicable, use verbs instead of nouns.
- Train yourself in taking meta-positions from which you consider and evaluate the dynamic relationship between I-positions, including their contradictions, conflicts, and limitations.
- Try to construct "third positions,"[85] in which two different or conflicting I-positions are combined so that their energies can strengthen each other (e.g. combining work and relaxation; being alone, yet feeling together with someone; bringing your shadows together with morally good positions on the moral middle ground).
- Look for the existence of grey areas and try to bring shadow positions together with more morally acceptable positions in coalitions on the moral middle ground.
- Train yourself in conducting dialogues – not only consonant dialogues, with an emphasis on agreement, but also dissonant dialogues, with tolerance for differences and disagreement. The latter ones, although more difficult to practice, thrive on the fertile soil of disagreement and often lead to creativity and innovation. Remember

[82] Miron-Spektor et al. (2022).   [83] Ibid.   [84] See also van Loon (2017).
[85] Hermans and Hermans-Konopka (2010, ch. 3).

that an unambiguous and premature focus on achieving consensus has the disadvantage that central elements of the dialogical process, such as contradictions and differences, are disregarded.[86]

In this chapter, I elaborated on the notion of dialogical space as emerging during a generative process of back-and-forth utterances between two or more participants involved in a dialogue or between two or more I-positions in the self of an individual. This dialogical space functions as a field of tension in which a multiplicity of positions mutually influence each other in such a way that the starting positions change over the course of an interchange and develop further under the influence of contradicting remarks or evidence. The emergence of a unique dialogical space allows the interchange to rise to a higher plateau because new and commonly shared elements are added and become integrated. In these ways, the content gets enriched and the contact gets strengthened.[87]

In the present era, many people have the feeling that we live in a world that is frightening and challenging at the same time. It is Orwellian insofar as we are threatened by increasing forms of authoritarianism, the widespread preference for strongmen, and the growth of autocratic regimes. It is also Kafkaesque, subjected as we are to high levels of uncertainty resulting from technological advances that not only provide us with new communication and information channels, but also produce a great variety of (self-learning) algorithms that are only partly under human control. In such situations, we are in need of well-informed and inspiring teachers and mentors who actively and creatively share with their students and coworkers the exciting challenges and complex problems of our time – teachers and mentors who are inspiring enough to be incorporated as promoter positions in the external domains of their students' selves.[88]

Summary

I started this chapter by showing that contradictions, although hard to understand and tolerate, have a hallowed place in intellectual history, as exemplified by scientific discoveries in physics and biology. Contradictions are also pervasive in the human self, as vividly demonstrated by Montaigne's prolific self-investigation. I elaborated on the value of complexity of the self as symbolically expressed by Linville's recommendation: Don't put all of your eggs in one basket. A central part of this chapter was

---

[86] Andersen and Hovring (2020).   [87] Hermans (2020).   [88] Ibid.

devoted to the finding that some East Asians view the world as being in a state of constant flux and are tolerant of contradictions. This tolerance is more problematic for Western individuals, who tend to experience contradiction as a threat to their self-esteem. The Japanese folkloristic figure of yokai was presented as an example representing a coalition of good and bad in one and the same character. Furthermore, utopian ideals were critically discussed as embracing one ultimate end position, with the denial of the fundamental contradictive nature of human beings and their moral multiplicity. Then I turned to the work of Carl Jung, who introduced the "shadow" as one of his main archetypes and argued that it is possible to take a position in the middle of good and bad, comparable to the moral middle ground in DST. The main differences between Jung's concept of shadows and the notion of shadow positions in the dialogical self were outlined. The process of generative dialogue was proposed as a way to deal with contradictions between and within selves. Finally, some practical implications of this chapter were presented: the fostering of self-empathy, stimulating tolerance of shadow positions, and the influence of high-quality listening on the softening of the boundaries of positions so that the self becomes more open to bringing good and bad together on the moral middle ground.

CHAPTER 6

Multilevel Identity and the Moral Middle Ground
Toward a Human and Ecological Identity

Out beyond ideas of wrongdoing and rightdoing, there is a field. I'll meet you there.

Attributed to Rumi, Persian poet[1]

Nowadays, "identity" is a key term and a central focus in research and theory in the social sciences, and it has become a familiar term in many public debates and political controversies. In the past, identity was not such a controversial subject when societies were more stable and hierarchically organized. In that period, identity was to be assigned rather than selected and cultivated. Today, however, identity carries the full weight of developing a sense of who one is in situations that offer a multitude of possible routes in contexts of overwhelming and rapid change.[2]

In this chapter, I propose a multilevel identity model with four levels: individual, group, human, and ecological. In past decades, studies in psychology, including moral psychology, have placed a heavy emphasis on *individual* and *group* identities. I will argue that in our time of geopolitical tensions and pressing ecological problems, we need to acknowledge the pervasive influence of these identities but, at the same time, become aware of the necessity of *human* and *ecological* identities that are crucial for self and society as never before. However, I realize that these broader identities are, in themselves, not strong enough to provide an effective counterweight to the powerful individual and group identities that are predominant in our Western world. Therefore, I suggest that it makes sense to search for *coalitions* between the broader human and ecological identities and the more restricted individual and group identities. More specifically, I will explore the role that the moral middle ground can play in the construction of such coalitions. The basic idea is that, via a process of "transpositioning," the energy of the restricted identity levels

[1] Elephant Journal, www.elephantjournal.com/2016/12/the-rumi-poem-we-should-all-read/.
[2] Howard (2000).

223

(individual and group) can be transferred to the broader levels (human and ecological). If this is possible, and I believe it is, the effect will be that the human and ecological identities can get a boost by receiving energy from the individual and group levels. Finally, I will investigate what this means for the notion of *conscience*, conceived of as a multivocal dialogical self that is based on a more expanded identity definition that goes beyond the immediate social circles of one's attachment and empathy. This will lead to the formulation of some practical implications.

What Do We Mean by Identity?

The terms "self" and "identity" are often used interchangeably, although psychologists tend to prefer the notion of "self," while sociologists typically speak of "identity." However, what is the difference? And how can this difference be phrased in DST terms?

Here is an example. When I say: "Amsterdam is the capital of the Netherlands," I communicate a piece of information that people may or may not know. It's a bit of geographical information that has no personal meaning and does not convey any specific feelings. When I say: "I like Amsterdam very much!" I communicate something that has personal meaning and express an affective evaluation. When I proudly say: "I'm an Amsterdammer!" I let people know that I identify with this particular city and that it is part of my extended self. I belong to that city and the city belongs to me. Moreover, I want people to acknowledge me in this "I-dentity," including its personal and affective meaning. Therefore, identity is a "claim-concept": I want to position myself toward the world in this particular way and I want people to see and acknowledge me in this position. Moreover, identity is established and confirmed by the existence of differences with other individuals and groups: I'm different from them and they are different from me, so I know who I am and where I'm standing. It is also possible that an identity is attributed to us by the social group or society to which we belong. Beyond our personal choice, we can receive an identity as an immigrant, racist, "wokester,"[3] or any identity label that we feel as imposed on us but that does not always fit with our preferred self-definition. In those cases, the claim comes from our group or society.

Although self and identity are often used interchangeably, they are not identical. There are I-positions in the self that are significant in my life and

---

[3] Informal, often derogatory term for a woke person: someone holding left-wing views or attitudes, principally with regard to social justice.

play a central role in my self-reflections but that do not belong to my identity. I can position myself in my own life as an otherworldly dreamer, spiritual person, lover of classical music, marihuana smoker, visitor of museums, or enthusiastic hiker, but in these positions there is no identity claim as member of a social group. This is particularly true for "shadow" positions (e.g. I as envious, I as vengeful, I as inferior) that I experience as undesirable occupants of my own self but that are not a part of my identity as a social claim (for shadow positions, see Chapter 5).

Interestingly, some exceptional individuals claim an identity that their community defines as unacceptable and morally objectionable and that most people would experience as shadow positions in their own self. As we have seen in Chapter 2, the French novelist Jean Genet went so far as to pursue alternative forms of "sainthood" celebrating theft, betrayal, and homosexuality as "virtues" instead of vices. And Marquis de Sade worshipped crime as "the soul of lust," while at the same time he regarded God as evil and appreciated vileness as the source of human activity. In their reversal of good and bad, these authors elevated positions, usually depreciated as shadows, to the level of virtues defined as part of their antisocietal identities.

In short, I see identity as part of the broader concept of self. Identity refers to I-positions and we-positions with an identity claim, whereas the self encompasses I- and we-positions with *and* without such a claim. In agreement with the nuclear definition of the self as a dynamic multiplicity of I- and we-positions in the society of mind, identity is defined as a dynamic multiplicity of I-positions and we-positions that imply a social claim in both the society of mind and society at large. These definitions have the advantage that it becomes possible to transfer energy from individual and social (group) positions to the broader we-positions: we as humans and participants of our natural environment. As we will see in this chapter, the inclusion of broader identities offers a way to liberate the self from the loopholes of divisive identity politics.

Toward a Multilevel Conception of Identity

Some theoretical social scientists have delivered important contributions to the identity debate on which I would like to elaborate in my proposal of a multilevel identity conception. An influential multidimensional conception of the self was provided by social psychologist John Turner and colleagues,[4] the founders of Self-Categorization Theory. This theory

---

[4] Turner et al. (1987).

distinguishes three levels of self-categorization: (1) a subordinate level of *personal self-categorizations* based on differentiations between oneself as a unique individual and other individuals; (2) an intermediate level of *ingroup–outgroup categorizations* based on social similarities within a particular social group and differences between one's own group in distinction to other groups (e.g. American, female, black, student); and (3) a superordinate level of the self as a human being, referring to the common features one shares with other members of the human species in distinction to other forms of life. With these levels the authors define one's personal, social, and human identities on the basis of, respectively, interpersonal (within the group), intergroup (within the species), and interspecies (between one species and other species) differences.

Inspired by Self-Categorization Theory, I use the same levels as a starting point but add an ecological level as crucial for the survival and good functioning of living beings and nature as a whole. At that level, we do not contrast ourselves from other beings by setting us apart, but we are one species *among* other ones, we are *part* of them, even participants together *with* them at the larger ecological level. From a Dialogical Self Theory (DST) perspective, I reconceptualize the different categories as I-positions at the individual, social, human, and ecological levels. As we will see later in this chapter, this opens up the possibility to study not only the relative dominance of these positions, but also their dialogical relationships, as they can emerge both within and between individuals and groups. From a moral point of view, I add different kinds of responsibilities to the different identity levels: individual, social, collective, and ecological responsibilities.

There are four kinds of moral "response-ability" (see Table 6.1). Individual responsibility requires care and justice for yourself as an individual, including your relationships with significant others. Social responsibility refers to care and justice for the group(s) with whom you are associated. Collective responsibility appeals to care and justice for humanity as one great family. Ecological responsibility requires care and justice for our ecological environment, including other species and nature. In their combination, these forms of responsibility contribute to the development of a global and ecological awareness needed to prevent a situation in which individuals and groups establish and protect their own identities by closing off their boundaries from other individuals or from outgroups, a situation that entails the risk of increasing disidentification and even alienation from other individuals or groups. (Table 6.1 illustrates the basic structure of the rest of this chapter.)

Table 6.1 *Identity levels and their responsibilities.*[5]

I-position	Description	Responsibility
I as an individual	I position myself as an individual and as different from other people	Individual
I as a group member	I position myself as a group member and as different from other groups	Social
I as a human being	I position myself as a human being and include other individuals and social groups	Collective
I as part of nature	I position myself as part of nature that is common to all species	Ecological

Main Themes in Moral Psychology

In a meta-analysis of publications in the field of moral psychology, a group of social psychologists[6] performed an electronic literature search that yielded a total of 1,278 relevant research articles in this field published from 1940 through 2017. They performed a content and bibliometric analysis with the intention to classify research questions and relate them to empirical approaches to morality. They categorized these research questions into five different themes: moral reasoning, moral judgments, moral behavior, moral emotions, and moral self-views. Then, particularly relevant to this chapter, they classified these themes into four different levels of analysis:

- *Intrapersonal* level: referring to the ways in which people consider, think, and reason within themselves to determine what is morally right or wrong
- *Interpersonal* level: referring to the ways people relate to others, how they judge their moral behaviors, and how they respond in relation to others
- *Intragroup* level: referring to one's moral concerns in defining group norms, the tendency to conform to such norms, and the resulting inclusion versus exclusion from one's group
- *Intergroup* level: referring to the tendency of social groups to endorse specific moral guidelines as a way to define their distinct identity, including disagreements and conflicts between groups about the nature of important values or moral concerns

[5] Hermans (2022, p. 233).   [6] Ellemers et al. (2019).

Clearly, the mentioned levels in this analysis and, by implication, the great majority of the studies reviewed refer to individuals and social groups. The human level is not included as a separate one, and the ecological level is entirely lacking. The latter levels and their corresponding identities are of eminent importance in our time when we are facing the far-reaching implications of global problems such as pandemics, climate change, the divide between rich and poor, terrorism, genocide, and war. However, it is my belief that not only individual and group identities are crucial in moral studies, but also the development of our identities as part of the human family and as participants in an encompassing natural environment. In the following section, I will delve more deeply into these two levels: our human and ecological identities. And later on in this chapter I will relate those levels of identity to the individual and social levels.

Human Identity

The main argument for giving a central place to the human identity lies in the clear fact that we are living in an increasingly globalized and inter-dependent world society that wrestles, at the same time, with many separations, oppositions, and clashes between social groups. We are wit-nesses to ultranationalism, tribalism, and divisive forms of identity politics, the breakdown of communities, immigrants who are at risk of alienation from their culture of origin, and many people who are suffering from identity confusion.[7] As a result of the increasing globalization of the past centuries, people, products, information, technologies, finances, and even viruses are crossing national boundaries and are distributed across the globe as never before. Globalization cries out for the recognition of identities that transcend the boundaries of individuals and social groups. Two identities have the potential of contributing to transcending the walls of individual and group identities: the human identity, which gives us the feeling that we belong to one human family, and the ecological identity, which invites us, even pressures us, to become aware that we are part of nature, for which we have, as humans, a special responsibility. We participate in nature and have, at the same time, an environmental stewardship.

For the development of a human identity, in the sense of "we as belonging to one big human family," I see the research project started by Sam McFarland and colleagues[8] as highly relevant for establishing a productive relationship between self and society. After observing the fact

[7] Arnett (2002).   [8] McFarland et al. (2012).

that social psychological research is mainly focused on the group level, these researchers wondered whether humans can truly transcend this level and its associated prejudice and ethnocentrism via acknowledging the value of all humanity. In their review of the literature, they referred to a study[9] on individuals who rescued Jews during the Holocaust, and often did so at great personal risk. A common characteristic of these rescuers is that they shared the perspective "of belonging to one human family," which motivated them to transcend all distinctions of race, religion, and nationality. In another project, researchers[10] interviewed over 300 Holocaust rescuers and compared them to a matched group of nonrescuers. They marked the transcending quality of the rescuers as "extensivity," referring to their emotional empathy and sense of responsibility to other people regardless of their race or religion, a concept comparable to the breadth of one's moral circle as part of the extended domain of the dialogical self, as discussed in Chapter 3. It was this extensivity that, more than any other characteristic, distinguished rescuers from nonrescuers.

McFarland and colleagues[11] constructed a measurement instrument that they called the Identification With All Humanity (IWAH) Scale, consisting of three-response items such as:

- How much do you identify with (that is, feel a part of, feel love toward, have concern for) each of the following?
  (1) People in my community
  (2) Americans
  (3) All humans everywhere

Or, as another example:

- When they are in need, how much do you want to help each of the following?
  (1) People in my community
  (2) Americans
  (3) People all over the world

Application of this scale in a variety of contexts led to findings that showed the relevance of identification with humanity for wider levels of inclusiveness. For example, individuals who scored highly on this scale were more informed about global humanitarian issues, more concerned about global warming, and more prone to value the lives of outgroup members (people from Afghanistan in this study) as equal compared to the lives of ingroup

---

[9] Monroe (1996).   [10] Oliner and Oliner (1988).   [11] McFarland et al. (2013).

members (Americans). Furthermore, respondents who scored high on this IWAH Scale were concerned about humanitarian issues, supported universal human rights, and expressed agreement with sending troops to defend people in other parts of the world in cases of genocide or ethnic cleansing. Individuals scoring highly on this scale were willing to pledge larger contributions for international humanitarian relief. When the researchers compared members of a major humanitarian charity organization with a sample of people who did not belong to such a group, they found that the former scored substantially higher on the IWAH Scale than the latter.[12]

Despite these promising findings, we should notice that the human identity is at a more abstract level than the individual and group levels. The latter levels are more central in everyday life, are more prominent in the media, confirm one's self-esteem and group esteem, and are more prevalent in an era of individualism and a culture of narcissism. These differences confront us with a serious problem if we try to strengthen this identity, given the relative dominance of the more restricted forms of identity.

This problem became apparent when Italian researchers Chiara Imperato and Tiziana Mancini[13] analyzed the role of the dialogical self in online intercultural dialogues in order to understand how individuals position themselves and others at three levels of inclusiveness: individual, group, and human. With this purpose in mind, they programmed a private chatroom in which Italian participants had an online dialogue with a fictitious outgroup member, presented as a person from Senegal. Participants were divided in three different experimental conditions:

(1) *Personal condition:* "Kama/Ngalula really likes to chat online, especially to get to know the people he talks to in a 'deep' way … Kama/Ngalula is in fact a boy/girl who is very attentive to the needs and characteristics of the people he interacts with …"

(2) *Social (group) condition:* "Kama/Ngalula really enjoys chatting online, especially to meet other people who come from his/her own country …"

(3) *Human condition:* "Kama/Ngalula really enjoys chatting online, especially to get to know people regardless of their affiliations or

---

[12] From a societal perspective, the influential sociologist Émile Durkheim (1912) was concerned about the question of how societies can keep and protect their *integrity* and *coherence* in modernity, as in this new era traditional social and religious ties are much less strong than they were in earlier times. I consider the development of a human identity, in addition to individual and social identities, as a necessary element in the contemporary diversified and often fragmented global situation.

[13] Imperato and Mancini (2021).

diversity. Kama/Ngalula is in fact a boy/girl who is anxious to know the human side of people . . ."

What the researchers found is that the social level of inclusiveness was associated with ethnic/racial prejudice. Furthermore, the human level of inclusiveness was, in agreement with DST, associated with the inclusion of the other in the self.[14] Apparently, the participants felt close with their interlocutor when their human identity was emphasized. However, *unexpectedly*, the human level was also associated with prejudice toward the outgroup. On the basis of these results, the investigators drew a conclusion that is very relevant to understanding the workings of the human identity: When people interact online as human beings, *the differentiation processes necessary to defining one's own and the interlocutor's social identities are hindered*.[15] In other words, we have to take into account that, when the human identity is stimulated in isolation from the individual and group identities, the individual and group identities are less clearly defined, with the result that the participants emphasize these identities as a compensation. I think this result carries important implications for the dynamic relationship between the different identity levels that I will discuss more thoroughly later in this chapter. Let's first take a look at the status of human rights, as they are closely related to the human level of identity.

On the Threatened Universality of Human Rights

In the preceding sections of this chapter, two related findings deserve further examination. The first is McFarland and colleagues' finding of a positive relationship between concern about humanity (as measured by the IWAH Scale) and support for human rights. The second is Imperato and Mancini's finding that the endorsement of human identity as an isolated position might interfere with one's social identity. This leads to the questions: What is the status of human rights? And to what extent does ingroup–outgroup differentiation function as a threat to their acknowledgment. These questions are particularly pertinent in an era of increasing international tensions and divisive identity politics that are in need of a counterweight in the form of an awareness that we all belong to one human family.

---

[14] Measured with the Inclusion of Other in the Self Scale, developed by Aron et al. (1992).
[15] Imperato and Mancini (2021).

The Universal Declaration of Human Rights (UDHR)[16] was proclaimed by the United Nations (UN) General Assembly in Paris on December 10, 1948. It was regarded as a milestone step in the history of human rights and was intended as a common standard of achievement for all peoples and all nations. Translated into 500 languages, it set out, for the first time, which fundamental human rights had to be universally protected. The document was widely recognized as paving the way for the adoption of more than seventy human rights treaties, proposed as a permanent basis at global and regional levels.

Yet, more than seventy years later, human rights violations continue to occur.[17] In a review article[18] that describes a variety of threats to human rights, the ingroup–outgroup distinction receives a prominent place. For example, fear predicted hostility toward outgroup members and support for their deportation, even of those not associated with the 9/11 attacks in the US (e.g. Muslim Americans, Arabs, and immigrants).[19] Or perceived violations of the ingroups' human rights can be followed by retribution and retaliation, resulting in cycles of violence and mutual radicalization. Such cycles of violence – like in Africa between the Hutus and the Tutsis during the Rwandan genocide in 1994 – often involve the practice of dehumanization (see Chapter 3 for dehumanization as one of the "dead ends" in identity formation in the worldviews of Hitler and Putin and their followers).

When individuals glorify the idea that "our ingroup is good" (e.g. "The US is better than any other nation in all respects"), they have less strong claims on demanding justice and feel less guilty when they are faced with human rights violations by members of their own ingroup. People tend to justify torture and reduce their empathetic concern for the victims when their own ingroup members perform the torture. The reviewer of these studies, Kevin Carriere, concludes that "[n]ot only do we support our ingroup more, but we are willing to take steps to protect it at all costs."[20] Apparently, despite the laudable claims of the UN's UDHR, the ingroup–outgroup distinction is one of the main factors to play a role in violations of human rights. We have to acknowledge that this factor is strong enough to limit and even undermine the identity position of we as belonging to one big family. It seems evident that we need more than just to emphasize

---

[16] United Nations, Universal Declaration of Human Rights, www.un.org/en/about-us/universal-declaration-of-human-rights, retrieved August 4, 2022.
[17] Human Rights Watch (2022).   [18] Carriere (2019).   [19] Skitka et al. (2006).
[20] Carriere (2019, pp. 15–16).

the value of the human identity as an ideal in itself. Before taking up this topic, let's first consider the views of several thinkers in the field of theology who are very concerned about developing a human identity and its relationship with the moral value of *humanness*.

Increasing Concerns for a Human Identity and Humanness in Theology

In theological literature, we see there is much concern about the moral meaning of humanness that is, in my view, of direct relevance to the fostering of human identity and associated collective responsibility, understood as a sense of care and justice for *all* people. I will briefly bring up some of the work of two prominent theologians who have addressed this topic: Hans Küng and Karl Rahner.

In the chapter titled "What Is the True Religion? Toward an Ecumenical Criteriology," Hans Küng[21] starts his thesis by stating that no question in the history of the churches has evoked so many fierce disputes and bloody conflicts than this one: What is the truth? In all periods, all churches, and all religions, the blind zeal for the truth has led to ruthless destruction, murders, burnings, and injuries. In his reflection on a long history of bloody conflicts, Küng states that the Christian churches are increasingly involved in a moderation of earlier ferocious controversies. He observes that nowadays many Christians are becoming interested in the question of whether one can accept the truth of other religions without giving up the truth of one's own religion, and thereby one's own identity. A human ecumenical approach is Küng's main answer to the question.

Progress in the direction of *humanness* within the various religions is, in Küng's view, unmistakable. As examples, he refers to the elimination of the Inquisition's use of burnings and torture, the adjustment of penal laws in more progressive Islamic countries, and the elimination of human sacrifices and burning of widows in particular areas of India. Numerous conversations in the Far, Middle and Near East lead him to the awareness that in all the great religions there is a growing consciousness concerning the guarantee of human rights, world peace, the emancipation of women, the realization of social justice, and the immorality of war (for a recent counterexample, see Putin's invasion of Ukraine, supported by central figures of the Russian Orthodox Church, discussed in Chapter 3). These and other observations lead Küng to the following question: "Should it not

---

[21] Küng (1986).

be possible to formulate a general ethical *fundamental criterion* with an appeal to the *common humanity of all* which rests upon the *Humanum*, the *truly human*, concretely on human dignity and the *fundamental values* accorded to it?"[22] In his search for an answer to this question, he refers to different levels of humanness: "Human beings should accordingly realise their humanness in all their levels (including the level of feeding and instinct) and dimensions (including their relationships to society and nature) both as an individual and in society."[23] As a theologist, he adds that this humanness "would be flawed in its core if the dimension of the 'trans-human,' the unconditioned, the encompassing, the ultimate were denied or eliminated. Without this dimension humanness would be but a torso."[24] Whether one is a religious believer or not, for present purposes it is relevant to note that Küng observes, in Christianity and other religions, an increasing space for the moral value of humanity and humanness that transcends earlier divisive identities and their associated atrocities.

As a major change in the attitude of the Roman Catholic Church toward other religions, Küng refers to the Second Vatican Council (1964) that produced a declaration concerning non-Christian religions, which can be seen as a breach with its previous claims on universal religious truth. The church's new position culminated in this sentence: "The Catholic church rejects nothing of what is true and holy in these religions" (Art. 2).[25]

In a similar vein, another influential German catholic theologist, Karl Rahner, made a plea for developing a "world responsibility" by a "world church." He did so in his comment on the document *Gaudium et spes* (*Joy and Hope*), one of the four constitutions resulting from the Second Vatican Council in 1964:

> Church as a totality becomes conscious of its responsibility for the dawning history of humanity. Much of the Constitution may be conceived in a European way, as far as details go, but the Third World is truly present as part of the Church and as object of its responsibility. The sensitization of the European Church to its world responsibility may move ahead only with painstaking slowness. But this responsibility, our political theology, can no longer be excluded from the consciousness of a world Church.[26]

From a religious perspective, the quotations in this section emphasize the importance of moral responsibility, and in particular the connection between humanity and humanness, beyond the borders of one's own

---

[22] Ibid. (pp. 14–15, emphases in original).   [23] Ibid. (p. 15).   [24] Ibid.   [25] Ibid. (p. 7).
[26] Rahner (1979, p. 719).

religious doctrines and dogmas. This is in line with the notion of collective responsibility as associated with a human identity (Table 6.1).

Ecological Identity

I found the best "feeling" for the personal meaning of ecological identity in the work of social psychologist Susan Clayton.[27] She argues that the social aspects of identity are so obvious and, at the same time, so dominant in the ecological debate that psychologists often overlook the impacts of nonsocial and nonhuman entities in defining one's identity (she uses "identity" and "self" interchangeably). Yet, she observes, there are many people for whom significant aspects of their selves lie in connections with entities in the natural world – for example, with pets, trees, lakes, mountain formations, or with particular geographic locations, the latter often studied under the label of "place identity."[28] She emphasizes that this is not limited to those who call themselves "environmentalists" by virtue of a political position. Even many who consider themselves to be "antienvironmentalist" nevertheless demonstrate, through words or behavior, their love of some aspect of the natural world (e.g. flowers, the beauty of their gardens, the power of a tree).

In her further considerations, Clayton writes that she feels that parts of nature – certain trees, or storms, or mountains – have a personality of their own, and that she keeps mementos from the outdoors in her room, such as shells or rocks or feathers. In DST terms, such mementos refer to positions in her own self extended as it is to her natural environment. In a previous publication,[29] I have proposed not only that other people are considered as "other I-positions," but also that objects in the environments may have this quality. More specifically, it is possible not only to perceive other people as "other I-positions" in the extended self, but also to imagine nonhuman aspects or even objects in the environment as "living" I-positions that can "tell" their own stories. I argued, moreover, that the "subjectification" of objects in the world is not confined to the realm of spirituality, but can also be observed in the field of creativity and the arts. For example, a precious object received from a deceased family member may "tell" its own story, or an inspiring painting may convey a personal message to us.

In her own research, Clayton investigated the connection between environmental identity and morality. She presented students with three

---

[27] Clayton (2003).   [28] Proshansky et al. (1983).   [29] Hermans (2022).

different environmental conflict scenarios: one focused on a conflict between city governments and low-income city residents over abandoned lots; another one concerning the conflict about making national parks accessible to the public; and a third one about government regulation of private land development. Instead of resolving the conflict, the participants were asked to indicate how much weight they would give to a series of justice principles that could be considered in trying to arrive at a fair decision, such as equality, equity, fair process, rights, and responsibilities. After rating these scenarios, students filled out an Environment Identity (EID) Scale assessment that included statements like "I spend a lot of time in natural settings (woods, mountains, deserts, lakes, oceans)" or "I think of myself as a part of nature, not separate from it." She found that the EID Scale scores were positively related to the rated importance of two factors: "responsibility to other species" and "the rights of the environment."[30] This research suggests that an environmental identity serves as a part of individuals' self-definition and has significance as a determinant of how individuals position themselves with regard to environmental policies or conflicts over environmental resources.[31]

Considering the role of responsibility, Clayton remarks that it is easy to restrict ourselves to the connection with our own local or personal part of nature: to support a neighborhood park but not the preservation of national parks that we have never set a foot in; to support zoos but not protect the habitats of animals we never see or do not like; to plant a tree as compensation for making an international flight but condone the destruction of rainforests. We are all challenged, she adds, to learn to accept "responsibility without ownership"[32] – or, in DST terms, to expand our moral circle toward the extended domain of the self beyond our immediate local environment. This is the kind of responsibility that I had in mind when I associated ecological identity with ecological responsibility, as depicted in Table 6.1.

Over the decades, the natural environment has become a political issue that has placed controversial policies prominently on the public agenda. Environmental identity has brought people together in sharply demarcated social groups, resulting in political identities that are divisive rather than integrative. Environmental politics have become identity politics, and conflicts can escalate as people link their identity to particular political

---

[30] In a foreword to the book *Rattling the Cage: Toward Legal Rights for Animals* (Wise, 2000), the primatologist Jane Goodall writes "... this book can be seen as the animals' Magna Carta, Declaration of Independence, and Universal Declaration of Rights all in one" (p. ix).
[31] Clayton (2003).   [32] Ibid. (p. 61).

positions, with the risk of intergroup hostility.[33] This brings us to the question of how ecological identity is related to intergroup differences and, as we will see later in this chapter, how divisive identity politics can be reduced or avoided.

Ecological Identity and Ingroup–Outgroup Differences

In contrast to Clayton's proposal, environmental sociologists Tobin Walton and Robert Jones[34] criticize existing measures of environmental identity as being focused exclusively on identification with nature while failing to acknowledge that identities are also products of differentiation from others with a different perspective. They find this "surprising" because identity theorists, and social identity theorists in particular, have long acknowledged that identities are built up, at least in part, by drawing contrasts and distinctions between self and other and ingroups versus outgroups. Therefore, they believe it is important to understand the pervasive influence of this differentiation in defining and maintaining an environmental identity. In their view, it is necessary to take differentiation into account given its links to the intergroup dynamics and expressions of social power, prejudice, and discrimination that are often associated with conflicts over environmental management and policy.[35]

Elaborating on these considerations, Walton and Jones constructed an Ecological Identity Scale (EIS) with items that include not only identification with others who agree on matters regarding environmental care, but also with those who disagree with such issues. The questionnaire started with some general statements, for example:

I am someone who . . .

- – Is aware of and cares about my impact on the environment.
- – Is strongly connected to nature and the environment.

They then included a statement referring to identification with others who *agree* with them on the issue of environmental care:

I identify with people who . . .

- – Make significant changes in their lifestyle for environmental reasons.

They also included items referring to identification with *disagreeing others*, for example:

---

[33] Ibid. (p. 59).   [34] Walton and Jones (2018).   [35] Ibid. (p. 663).

I identify with people who . . .

- – Feel they have the right to consume as much as they want.
- – Doubt global warming is mostly caused by humans.[36]

Findings on the validation of the EIS led the investigators to conclude that the instrument offers a picture of self–environment relations that is substantially different from measures that don't recognize ingroup–outgroup differences. In their view, it taps into socially embedded meanings that place individuals within a web of socioecological relationships based not only on shared personal characteristics, but also on group memberships. They claim that their EIS is suitable for studying environmental identity in the broader context of social power and the intergroup dynamics characteristic of complex societies.

To summarize, we are faced here with two points of view on environmental identity that differ over an issue that I see as crucial to understanding the relationship between the different identity levels as depicted in Table 6.1. One view considers care for the environment as a matter of personal concern on the individual level (Clayton). The other one sees care for the environment as embedded in ingroup–outgroup differences (Walton and Jones). Because the concept of the moral middle ground is crucial to this book, the question arises: Can processes on the moral middle ground make a viable contribution to the strengthening of ecological identity in a way that it is *not solely dominated by ingroup–outgroup oppositions*?

The Moral Middle Ground between Economic and Ecological Identities

Justin Brown, cofounder and CEO of the education platform "Ideapod," starts his exposé by realizing that the potential future impact of climate change on the planet is "so immense that it's causing widespread traumatic stress amongst vast sectors of the global population."[37] This awareness brings him into a state of mind of what he calls "multiple personality," drawn as he feels into two contrasting positions, which he labels as "climate change activist" and "economic libertarian." In DST terms, these two I-positions are involved in frequent and intense dialogues with the goal of examining the values of both positions. This leads him to explore the existence of a common middle ground where the conflict between the two I-positions can, to some extent, be reconciled. I find both his

---

[36] For these and other items, see ibid. (p. 271).   [37] Brown (2021, n.p.).

reasoning and his contribution to the climate debate viable enough to
report them here in some detail.

On the one hand, Brown sees himself as an ardent climate change
activist who regards climate change as an incredibly serious problem, and
he thinks that actions are needed to reduce the impact of humans on the
environment. He adds that this problem is so urgent that we can't wait for
governments to solve the issue for us. Moreover, as long as big business is
focused on the increase of profits and the reduction of costs, they will
continue to pollute the environment. This will continue unless we create a
radical disruption in how we collectively organize ourselves and our modes
of production.

However, on the other hand, coexisting with his climate change activist
position is another position that he labels as the economic libertarian.
From the perspective of this position, Brown believes that humans are
incredibly adaptive and capable of creating solutions to the world's most
intricate problems. Although economic growth undoubtedly has negative
impacts on society, it also fuels often unforeseen technological innovations
and is a great harbinger of progress in human history. Let's have a look at
the nature of these viewpoints in some more detail.

The Climate Activist

In Brown's view, there is a seemingly irreconcilable conflict between the
mindsets of the climate activist and the economic libertarian concerning
the role of economic growth in our future. The activist is usually sympa-
thetic to the ideas of proponents of the degrowth movement, who argue
that if we want to meet the Intergovernmental Panel on Climate Change
(IPCC)[38] target of stabilizing global temperatures at no more than 1.5°C
of warming by 2050, our growth-based economic models have to be
changed. In opposition to the defenders of growth models, the degrowth
movement believes that humanity and our planet are being profoundly
harmed when many organizations continue to put profits over people and
production over the well-being of our natural world. In his considerations
on this issue, Brown refers to the work of Jason Hickel, an anthropologist
at the London School of Economics, known as one of the leading voices
for the degrowth movement and the author of the book *Less Is More: How
Degrowth Will Save the World*.[39] Hickel believes that degrowth is the only

---

[38] The IPCC is an intergovernmental body of the UN responsible for advancing knowledge on
human-induced climate change that was founded in 1988: see www.conservation.org.
[39] Hickel (2020).

real solution not only to reducing greenhouse gas emissions, but also to the evils of pollution, overfishing, deforestation, plastic destroying our oceans, and worldwide economic devastation. He argues that if we try to solve these problems on the basis of our current economic model, we are bound to fail.

Brown also refers to other leading scientists who echo similar warnings. Among them are ecology scientist William Ripple and others with a similar view, who anticipate that if we don't scale down our economies and growth aspirations, we run the risk of a full-on carbon apocalypse in the near future. Ripple and 11,000 other scientists warned in an open letter published in *BioScience* in 2020 that "[s]cientists have a moral obligation to clearly warn humanity of any catastrophic threat and to 'tell it like it is.' On the basis of this obligation ... we declare, with more than 11,000 scientist signatories from around the world, clearly and unequivocally that planet Earth is facing a climate emergency."[40] They observe that the climate crisis is accelerating faster than most scientists expected. "It is more severe than anticipated, threatening natural ecosystems and the fate of humanity."[41] Especially worrisome for them are irreversible climate tipping points in combination with nature's reinforcing feedbacks that could lead to a catastrophic "hothouse Earth," well beyond the control of humans, with chain reactions that could potentially make large areas of Earth uninhabitable.[42] In their view, one of the problems is that the climate crisis is closely linked to the excessive consumption and wealthy lifestyles of rich countries. Therefore, they recommend that we "need to drastically reduce the enormous amount of food waste around the world."[43]

Brown recognizes the validity of these warnings but expresses some doubt when he sees a key problem that isn't acknowledged sufficiently by the degrowth movement. We live in a global economy that has become so interconnected that consumerism in the First World gives a boost to the growth of the economies of the developing world. A large-scale reduction in consumerism in the rich economies could put restrictions on the emerging economies around the world. This was already demonstrated by the COVID-19 pandemic, which led to a reduction in consumption in rich countries. At the same time, this also contributed to poverty in the developing world as a consequence of the reduction of Western imports of goods. Therefore, Brown perceives a certain over-idealism in the position of thinkers such as Hickel and Ripple. However, despite his doubts, his

---

[40] Ripple et al. (2020, p. 8).   [41] Ibid. (p. 9).   [42] Ibid. (p. 9–10).   [43] Ibid. (p. 11).

inner climate activist can't simply deny the validity of their insights, and he realizes that we cannot continue on our current consumerist path. And, therefore, something has to change.

The Economic Libertarian

As part of Brown's inner dialogue, the economic libertarian believes that the benefits of market freedom and economic growth will eventually outweigh the devastating effects of climate change. When industries and technologies are allowed to continue unimpeded and when advancements such as renewable energy (think of green fuel technology) go together with letting the market correct itself based on a laissez-faire approach, humans will gain a better future. He quotes *Spiked*[44] columnist Tim Black, who promotes the challenging thesis that slowing down economic development is far more dangerous than global warming when "climate-change apparatchiks" get their way. Calling for limits to economic growth, Black believes, is a far bigger threat to public health than climate change. He writes that there is something grotesque about the tendency to frame climate change as a health emergency: "Almost all the advances in medicine, diet and general welfare that we enjoy today rest on economic, material development – in short, on growth. The energy powering our hospitals, the technology at work in water-sanitation plants, the agricultural revolution that fueled the expansion of food production – all this and so much more means that we now live longer, healthier lives than ever before."[45]

In support of his economic libertarian position, Brown further refers to the World Health Organization (WHO), which predicts that, if economic growth is to continue unabated, the global burden of disease is expected to go down by more than 30 percent between 2004 and 2030. Moreover, WHO cautions that turning away from economic growth and industrial progress could result in greater poverty, illness, and death around the world. Brown refers to economist Branko Milanovic, who notes that richer countries are generally better-off in almost all metrics, ranging from education, life expectancy, and child mortality to women's employment. On average, richer people are better educated, healthier, and happier.[46]

Therefore, economic libertarians regard slamming the brakes on economic growth as shortsighted and morally self-righteous because they ultimately harm humans more than they benefit them. The cure of throwing out our capitalist system could be even worse than the disease.[47]

---

[44] Spiked is a British Internet magazine that focuses on political, cultural, and societal issues.
[45] Black (2021).   [46] Milanovic (2021), cited by Brown (2021).   [47] Brown (2021).

In Search of a Moral Middle Ground

Weighing the pros and cons of the arguments of the two positions – the climate activist and the economic libertarian – Brown considers the possibility of a "common ground," where, in DST terms, the opponents take a third position that can be phrased as "we as passionate about the flourishing of human beings," although their ways of moving toward that end are very different. The economic libertarians expect that, when humans are unfettered to be creative, thriving and progress will be the results. The climate activists, on the other hand, think that for human progress it is essential to prevent overuse of natural resources and that we should empower those who are contributing to sustainability and ecological balance. These activists will certainly agree that economic growth is needed to increase human welfare and to reduce poverty, on the assumption that these economic activities are in harmony with the environment and the well-being of human society. In turn, the camp of the economic libertarians can sympathize with a balanced ecosystem and a safe planet in the future as long as sustainability contributes to driving the economy forward, increasing energy supply, providing jobs, and enhancing our prosperity. Indeed, economic growth will be hampered in a dehydrated and destroyed planet, and there is not much opportunity for achieving sustainability when economies are destroyed and technological progress is stunted.[48]

Therefore, Brown believes in the existence and potential of a common ground where the values of the two camps intersect. However, in order to give full credibility to this middle ground, we have to relinquish our tendency to judge the other side as exclusively "bad" or "wrong." Belonging to an ingroup and clinging to stereotypes about those on the opposite side may feel good, but such stereotypes are obstructions on our path to real solutions: "Climate change activists are not, by and large, looney-tunes humanity-hating extremists who want to shut down every business. They tend to be reasonable and compassionate people who simply want to help create a future where the planet won't burn."[49] Likewise, he notes, "Economic libertarians are not, by and large, money-worshipping fiends who torch forests for fun and think pollution is cool as long as it's profitable. They tend to be rational people who simply want to caution against moving too dramatically to scale down the advanced societies we've built."[50] In this way, Brown sketches the arguments and counterarguments of the two camps, denounces their good-versus-bad stereotypes, and searches for the existence of a middle ground where the two views can meet.

[48] Ibid.   [49] Ibid. (n.p.).   [50] Ibid. (n.p.).

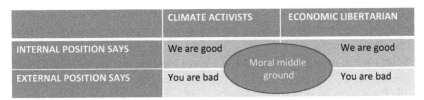

Figure 6.1   Positions "we are good" and "you are bad" and the moral middle ground that interconnects them.

Indeed, clinging to good-versus-bad forms of positioning, closely associated with ingroup-versus-outgroup distinctions, does not leave any space for the emergence of a moral middle ground. This middle ground can only be acknowledged when we assume that the opponent (*my* opponent) functions as an external position in the extended self. This creates the possibility of taking the role of the other, as sociologist George Herbert Mead[51] calls it, and in DST terms this is taking the position of the other and including it in one's considerations, self-reflection, and decision-making.

This brings us, again, to the crucial role of meta-positioning, which allows us to identify ourselves not only with our own internal positions, but also with those of other people, *including our opponents as significant, but negatively experienced, others-in-the-self.* The other is partly constructed on the basis of needs, assumptions, and anxieties that are associated with the internal positions in the self. The image of the opponent, as a construction in the external domain of the self, is strongly influenced by the emotions associated with the internal positions. The meta-position enables us to include not only the opponent as another in the self, but also our perception of the other as positioning us as opponents of them. The way we feel positioned by the other is then part of our extended self that we can confirm, reject, deny, or include in the dialogues with others and ourselves. If we bring the positioning of ourselves as good together with our perception of our opponent as seeing us as bad and if we reflect, from a meta-position, on our extended selves as good *and* bad (the two rows in Figure 6.1), then we have access to the moral middle ground. This extension can take place not only in our own self, but also in the self of the opponent.[52] If participants do so, a dialogical space unfolds that goes beyond any imprisoning stereotype or prejudice and also beyond a conception of the

---

[51] Mead (1934).
[52] Figure 6.1 is basically the same as Figure 3.7 in Chapter 3, where the same reasoning was used.

self as a purely individualized or group identity (see the practical implications at the end of this chapter that help to clarify the realizability of the model presented in Figure 6.1).

Because in my previous work[53] I have written on the possibilities of developing a "democratic self," I feel the need to refer, very briefly, to a link between the presented model in this chapter and the ideals of the French Revolution. The model, presented in Table 6.1, allows a linkage between the four identity levels and the democratic principles of liberty, equality, and brotherhood as celebrated by the French Revolution. Freedom is linked to the individual level (personal freedom) and the social level (emancipation of minority groups). Brotherhood is central to the human level, where we belong together as members of one human family. The ecological identity brings us together with nature, where we are equals as part of the Earth and its guardians at the same time.

The Moral Middle Ground as a Coalition of Identities

Looking back at the model presented in Table 6.1, we have distinguished four types of identity: individual, social (group), human, and ecological. Without any doubt, the first two levels (individual and group) are strongly emphasized in social scientific research and are primary sources of motivation in everyday life situations. Those levels instigate the greatest amount of energy, more than the other two identities (human and ecological) that are located at broader levels of inclusiveness. Even in times when the ecological identities of individuals and groups are increasingly regarded as a matter of survival of humans and other species, the individual and social identities are deeply engrained in our culture, with the result that, generally, people invest more energy in these identities than in the human and ecological ones. The consequence of this evaluation is that, as long as the different identities are functioning as competing forces, the individual and group identities arouse more energy than the human and ecological ones. Therefore, I think that describing identities as *separate* sources of energy or as competing forms of motivation is unproductive. A more fertile approach would be to search for the possibility of constructing *coalitions* among identities (see the examples later in this chapter). If this is possible, then the energies of the individual and/or group levels can be combined with the energies of the human and/or ecological levels, with the result that the latter levels can profit from the energies of the former ones. Such a

---

[53] Hermans (2020).

possibility is, from a theoretical point of view, in accordance with the concept of transpositioning (Chapter 1), which implies the transmission of the specific energy from one position to another one. This could have the significant practical advantage that people's individual and social ambitions, gains, and strivings are productively combined with human and ecological necessities. Along the lines of the popular adage "if you can't beat them, join them," I will sketch some examples of phenomena in which the moral middle ground can profit from coalitions between the more restricted identities and the broader ones.

The Moral Middle Ground between Individual and Human Positions

In an era of prominent individualism, the individual identity is strongly emphasized, as exemplified by personal goals, ambitions, aspirations, excellence, competition, and self-investment. These tendencies may be profitable for one's individual development (including a limited circle of significant others), but when isolated from the other positions they are involved in a process of "over-positioning" in the form of narcissism, as clearly phrased in psychologists Jean Twenge and Keith Campbell's book *The Narcissism Epidemic*:

> Understanding the narcissism epidemic is important because its long-term consequences are destructive to society. American culture's focus on self-admiration has caused a flight from reality to the land of grandiose fantasy. We have phony rich people (with interest-only mortgages and piles of debt), phony beauty (with plastic surgery and cosmetic procedures), phony athletes (with performance-enhancing drugs), phony celebrities (via reality TV and YouTube), phony genius students (with grade inflation), a phony national economy (with $11 trillion of government debt), phony feelings of being special among children (with parenting and education focused on self-esteem), and phony friends (with the social networking explosion). All this fantasy might feel good, but, unfortunately, reality always wins. The mortgage meltdown and the resulting financial crisis are just one demonstration of how inflated desires eventually crash to earth.[54]

The following questions then arise: If there is so much energy invested in individual identities, is it possible to establish any coalitions between these and the human identities? If so, what might be the function of the moral middle ground where such coalitions exist? And can this middle ground profit from the energies invested in the individual and group levels?

---

[54] Twenge and Campbell (2009, p. 4).

A telling example of the moral middle ground between the individual and the human levels was already discussed in Chapter 4: the case of Oskar Schindler. There, I showed that the very qualities that many of us would consider to be morally problematic – his hedonism, his avarice, and his ability to maintain convivial but actually instrumental relations with the SS – were precisely the qualities that put Schindler in a position to save many Jews from Hitler's "special treatment," an euphemism for mass murder by Nazi functionaries and the SS. Due to these qualities, he became an attractive person to various SS officers, who remained ignorant of Schindler's actual purposes.[55]

Schindler was on many occasions asked the question of why he helped Jews survive the Holocaust. To one of the survivors, Murray Pantirer, he gave this answer: "I was a Nazi, and I believed that the Germans were doing wrong ... when they started killing innocent people, it didn't mean anything to me that they were Jewish, to me they were just human beings, *Menschen*. I decided I am going to work against them and I am going to save as many as I can."[56] The individual and social identities that he exposed in his contact with the SS officers were combined with his human identity as a rescuer of war victims. These identities – morally problematic ones and a morally noble one – formed a coalition on the middle ground.

Another example of a coalition of individual and human identities is the existence of so-called moral exemplars, which were also discussed in Chapter 4. They were defined as "individuals who have achieved brilliance *with* wisdom, power *with* conscience, in their extraordinary commitments promoting benevolence, justice, or basic human welfare."[57] The existence of moral exemplars demonstrates that the usual dualistic rendition (self versus morality) does not apply to all people and fails to explain that there exist other identities or a combination of them that form powerful kinds of motivation. When we assume that the dualism between self-interest and the dictates of one's moral code is regarded as typical of most people, moral exemplars are an exception to this rule. They succeed at integrating their personal ambitions with their moral convictions, yielding a position of "enlightened self-interest," allowing their own interests to become aligned with the interests of others and a concern about basic human welfare.[58]

The Moral Middle Ground between Social and Human Positions

Productive coalitions can also be created on the moral middle ground between social (group) and human identities. An imaginative concept is

[55] Flanagan (1991).   [56] Merrill (2018, n.p.).
[57] Frimer et al. (2011, p. 149, emphases in the original).   [58] Ibid. (p. 150).

the notion of "moral power" coined by sociologists Jal Mehta and Christopher Winship.[59] They noticed that morality and power are often considered as opposites, with morality associated with altruism and a commitment to the common good, whereas social power is regarded as arising from self-interest. Their contention is that moral power, seemingly an oxymoron, is actually a common and influential factor in our social and political lives. They define it as "the degree to which an actor, by virtue of his or her perceived moral stature, is able to persuade others to adopt a particular belief or take a particular course of action."[60]

As an impressive example of the significant influence of social power on the interface of social identities and human rights, Mehta and Winship referred to a group of inner-city black ministers known as the Boston Ten Point Coalition,[61] who started to work together with the Boston Police Department in the 1990s in order to deal with the problems of youth violence and homicide.

At the height of their partnership, the police and ministers conducted "gang forums" as part of a program known as "Operation Cease-Fire." The purpose of the forums was to let perpetrators of violence and killings know that they needed to stop their "gang-banging" (gang violence), and that if they did they would receive help of various kinds. The authors quote a paraphrased summary of the message:

> You have a choice. Stop your gang-banging and we will help you – help you get back in school or get a job, help you deal with your family, your girlfriend; help you straighten out your life. Continue to gang-bang and we will work as hard as we can with the police to see that you are put in jail. Both for your own good, and the good of community. As long as you are gang-banging you are a danger to yourself and to others. What I ultimately want to avoid more than anything is presiding over your funeral.[62]

Mehta and Winship consider the Boston Ten Point Coalition story as interesting for two reasons. First, the cooperation with the ministers provided an "umbrella of legitimacy" for the police. Before starting an intervention, the police would confer with the ministers to ensure that what the police were planning was appropriate. People in the community knew that the ministers were well informed about what the police were doing to curb youth violence and trusted that, if the police activity was

---

[59] Mehta and Winship (2010).   [60] Ibid. (p. 4).

[61] The Boston Ten Point Coalition is an ecumenical group of Christian clergy and lay leaders working to mobilize the community around issues affecting black and Latino youth.

[62] Mehta and Winship (2010, p. 15).

illegitimate, the ministers would speak out loudly and publicly. Second, the cooperation delivered the ministers a significant degree of social power that gave a boost to their efforts to deactivate potential gang violence. Moreover, it helped them to negotiate favorable outcomes for youths who were charged with crimes.[63] The case shows a coalition between two groups: the ministers, who had access to moral authority; and the police, who had social and institutionalized power. Together, this cooperation had the potential of not only reducing criminality in the Boston area, but also, in a wider context, of contributing to the civil rights of the black population.

However, this creative coalition was not without controversy. As the ministers and the police knew very well, access to the media could enhance the moral power of the initiative. A critical role was played by *The Boston Globe*, who disseminated a narrative about the action, often called "The Boston Miracle." This referred to the claim that the cooperation between the Boston Police Department and the Ten Point ministers explained a decrease of 80 percent in Boston's homicide rate over the 1990s. The Ten Point ministers became aware of the importance of the media, made themselves available for interviews, became involved in publishing opinion pieces, and were not averse to embellishing their argument with pithy phrases.

Although the black ministers enjoyed considerable moral power within Boston's black community, many critics, particularly Boston's black politicians, were unhappy with their influence. The result was that the black ministers' behavior was constantly under scrutiny and criticized in newspaper articles. Sometimes it was claimed that the ministers' behavior was guided by self-interest and not sufficiently in line with the interests of Boston's black community. Mehta and Winship add that, if these claims had been persuasive, the influence of the initiative of the ministers and the police most certainly would have been undermined. The Ten Point ministers were under constant pressure to act in a way that was consistent with their image.[64] I mention this criticism to show that a concept like "moral power," as illustrated by the Boston Ten Point Coalition, is sensitive to controversy. In this respect, it is similar to other phenomena such as transgressive art, Machiavellianism, and grey hat hackers that are also controversial topics in social circles and cultures where people are used to thinking in terms of sharp separations between moral good and bad and to considering these as mutually exclusive. The middle ground is loaded with uncertainty, contradiction, and ambivalence, as it is located in a field of tension between positions evaluated as good and bad. Therefore, it is

[63] Ibid.   [64] Ibid.

problematic to give a quick and fixed answer to the question of what belongs on the middle ground or not, because this space resists any sharply differentiated "thumbs-up" or "thumbs-down" and goes beyond any simplifying "like" or "dislike," which are often used as "moral knives." This space is in need of dialogical deliberation of reasons for or against something (see Chapter 5).

The Moral Middle Ground between Social and Ecological Positions

Not only individual identities but also social identities can be elevated to such a degree that other identities become dominated or neglected. This is most apparent in expressions of what is usually called "identity politics." In a chapter on this theme, political scientist Amy Gutmann writes

> Identity groups occupy an uneasy place in democracy. Critics emphasize how much group identities constrain rather than liberate individuals. When people are identified as black or white, male or female, Irish or Arabic, Catholic or Jew, deaf or mute, they are stereotyped by race, gender, ethnicity, religion, and disability and denied a certain individuality that comes of their own distinctive character and freedom to affiliate as they see fit. When individuals themselves identify racially, ethnically, or religiously as a consequence of being identified with groups, they often develop hostilities toward other groups and a sense of superiority over them. Groups frequently vie against one another in uncompromising ways, sacrificing justice and even peace for vindicating their superiority as a group.[65]

As an example of a coalition of identities on the social (group) level and the ecological level, let's take a look at the case of Greenpeace, an organization that is concerned about ecological well-being. In their "Mission and Values" statement,[66] the organization presents itself as "an independent, nonprofit, global campaigning organization that uses non-violent, creative confrontation to expose global environmental problems and their causes." And they claim to be an organization that puts a premium on ecological responsibility (see also Table 6.1): "We champion environmentally responsible and socially just solutions, including scientific and technological innovation."[67] Let's review one of their actions, already described in Chapter 1.

On September 27, 2016, Greenpeace activists decided to prevent access for imports and exports from palm oil trader IOI[68] in the harbor of

---

[65] Gutmann (2003, p. 1).
[66] Greenpeace, Mission and Values, www.greenpeace.org/eastasia/mission-values/, retrieved August 10, 2022.
[67] Ibid. (n.p.). [68] IOI is a leading global palm oil player located in Malaysia.

Rotterdam in the Netherlands. This action was preceded by a report by Greenpeace mentioning that international palm oil companies like IOI were involved in forest destruction, peatland fires, and child labor. The Greenpeace ship *Esperanza* moored to the dock at the back of the refinery and prevented palm oil from being unloaded from incoming oil tankers. For sure, this blockage was illegal in the country where it happened and had economic and financial consequences for IOI and the traders involved in the business. Was this action good or bad from a moral perspective? It may be evaluated as good as far it was an action intended to protect forested areas and prevent child labor but as bad as an act of sabotage that prevented people from doing their work and honoring their commitments.

From a moral perspective, good and bad are not clearly opposed in this case, because good and bad have the potential of functioning as a coalition. Any conclusion about its moral nature would require discussion in terms of agreements and disagreements or fierce debates. But the moral judgment would not be clear from the outset. A different situation would have emerged if Greenpeace and IOI representatives had tried to find a solution to the problem via negotiations. In that case, the action would shift to the side of the moral good. However, suppose that Greenpeace had decided to sink the ship, resulting in casualties – then the action could have been categorized as morally bad.

The exploration of these possibilities, shifting to the realm of good *or* bad, is relevant from a theoretical point of view. It shows that the middle ground is not to be considered as a sharply demarcated area with fixed positions immovably located within its boundaries. It is an open space where I- and we-positions come in and form tension-loaded coalitions with other positions, with the possibility that, depending on changing circumstances and the intentions of the parties involved, they can become disconnected and move to the good or bad side of the moral spectrum.

An illustrative example is provided by another action by Greenpeace that was more morally problematic than the Rotterdam case. In 2014, environmentalists from the organization were accused of damaging ancient earth markings in Peru's coastal desert (Figure 6.2) by leaving footprints in the ground during a publicity stunt meant to send a message to the UN climate talk delegates in Lima.[69] A spokesman for Greenpeace said: "Without reservation Greenpeace apologizes to the people of Peru for the offence caused by our recent activity laying a message of hope at the site of the historic Nazca lines. We are deeply sorry for this." As part of

---

[69] Collyns (2014)

Figure 6.2   Example of the Nazca lines in Peru.
Source: DeAgostini/Getty Images.

their apology, they added: "Rather than relay an urgent message of hope and possibility to the leaders gathering at the Lima UN climate talks, we came across as careless and crass."[70] This happened after Peru's vice-minister for culture had accused Greenpeace of "extreme environmentalism" and ignoring what the Peruvian people "consider to be sacred,"[71] referring to the renowned Nazca lines, a group of geoglyphs made in the soil of the Nazca Desert in southern Peru created between 500 BCE and 500 CE, which have received the status of a UNESCO World Heritage site. When we take the accusation of "extreme environmentalism" and Greenpeace's apologies seriously, the action in Peru does not take place on the moral middle ground, and, as it shifts into the realm of bad, it is different from the Rotterdam example and not to be regarded as a coalition of good and bad.

The same dynamism also applies to individual identities. If individuals with healthy selfishness, described as a coalition of positions on the moral middle ground, were to move in the direction of pure selfishness, it would be morally problematic. On the other hand, if they were to become

---

[70] Ibid. (n.p.).   [71] Ibid.

altruistic, their actions would change toward the direction of moral good. These examples suggest that positions on the moral middle ground are not always neatly balanced, as one is often more dominant than the other, with the final result being that one of them disappears as part of the coalition.

In summary, in the previous sections, I presented some examples of coalitions at the interface of different identities on the moral middle ground: between individual and human positions (e.g. the case of Oskar Schindler), between social and human positions (e.g. the Boston Ten Pont Coalition), and between social and ecological positions (e.g. Greenpeace). With these examples, I wanted to demonstrate that the energy of one identity level can be transferred, via a process of transpositioning, to another identity level, with the result that the "weaker" identities (human and ecological) can profit from the energies of the more dominant ones (individual and group).

The Need for Dialogical Relationships between Positions as Parts of Coalitions

The theory presented in this book proposes the idea that there is not simply one identity position but a multiplicity of them, and that we are capable, contingent on situational changes, of moving from one position to another. These positions do not function in isolation from each other. They can meet and form coalitions, comparable with individuals in a society who meet and cooperate on a particular project. As sketched out in the preceding chapters, good and bad positions can meet on the moral middle ground and create coalitions that have the potential of adding vitality to self and society or of restoring this vitality if it is lost due to sharp good-versus-bad dualisms. However, the contribution of the different positions to such a coalition is, typically, not entirely equal and symmetrical, comparable with two individuals who meet and cooperate on a particular project but with one of them being relatively dominant. Moreover, just as in a real life, the contributions of the different "members" of a coalition are qualitatively different from one another, as each of them introduces their specific quality and experience. In this section, I will argue that coalitions of identity positions are in need of internal dialogue, particularly if there is some tension or conflict amongst them. This dialogical activity, in the form of internal deliberation, is then needed as a basis of action. In order to illustrate the role of dialogue associated with a coalition of positions, let's return to the example of the so-called Machiavellians that we already discussed in Chapter 4.

There, we saw how developmental psychologist Patricia Hawley[72] divided children in three distinctive groups: (1) *Prosocial controllers*, who put "getting along" over "getting ahead," are assessed as agreeable, socially skilled, conscientious and, as a result, enjoy a most favorable peer regard; (2) *coercive controllers*, who showed the opposite profile to that of the prosocial controllers, in that they are more concerned with getting ahead than getting along and, as a result, experience negative feedback from the social group; and (3) *bistrategic controllers*, who combine prosocial and coercive control. The latter group, so-called Machiavellians,[73] showed a combination of positive and negative characteristics, and, despite their aggression or even due to it, they were rated as socially central, liked by their peers, socially skilled, and well-adjusted. They appeared to be effective resource controllers who command a great deal of attention from the group and are admired by their peers.

Strikingly, Hawley found that teachers rated bistrategic controllers as socially acceptable to the same degree as prosocial controllers. She suspects that teachers may not be able to differentiate prosocial and bistrategic controllers in this age group because bistrategic children are skilled enough to hide their aggression from authority figures. Considering these factors, one can imagine that bistrategic controllers are, at least in some social situations, faced with a choice: "Shall I do this or not?" or "I want to do this, but maybe it is better to hide it." If the child is posing such questions to themselves, they are involved in some kind of internal deliberation before taking action. More generally, when one of the two components is experienced as morally bad or questionable in the eyes of a particular social group, some degree of self-reflection and internal dialogue before, during, or after the action is very likely.

Perhaps an even more convincing example of the close association between coalition and dialogue is the phenomenon described in Chapter 4 as "transgressive art" (see Figures 4.1 and 4.2). Recall Kieran Cashell, who observed that this art movement, by its shocking, disturbing nature and its tendency to subvert conventional beliefs, is regarded by many as "going too far" and as violating social norms. Yet, he observed that this art, due to its ethical relevance, has significantly expanded the horizon of artistic expression: "... shock is often required for the development of

[72] Hawley (2003).
[73] Niccolò Machiavelli (1469–1527) was an Italian Renaissance political philosopher whose most famous work, *The Prince* (*Il Principe*), brought him a reputation as an atheist and an immoral cynic; *Encyclopedia Britannica*, www.britannica.com/biography/Niccolo-Machiavelli, retrieved June 30, 2022.

an ethical perspective that is sensitive to the moral distinction between good and bad, right and wrong." And he added: "Such work shakes us, makes us think twice."[74]

The phrase "makes us think twice" suggest two successive ways of positioning oneself toward certain forms of transgressive art. The first response is: This is wrong! The second response is: Let's see: why is the artist doing that? Whereas the first position is more intuitive and emotional, the second one is more distant and invokes a broader range of responses. This process takes place on the level of meta-positioning: We take some distance, reconsider the initial emotional response, ask ourselves or others questions, and then move beyond our first impulse. At this meta-positional level, dialogue is stimulated, either with oneself or with others, and one enters a moral middle ground where nothing is good *or* bad and where a field of uncertainty opens itself up to posing deeper moral questions that transcend any immediate answer.

However, dialogue, understood as a generative interchange among positions, can have different forms. One distinction that I see as particularly useful for understanding processes on the moral middle ground is that between consonant and dissonant forms of dialogue. As I have explained in a previous publication,[75] consonant dialogue may start with participants holding differing perspectives, but the process moves toward agreement without giving an explicit place and time to the value of contradiction and disagreement. In the case of dissonant dialogue, however, contradictions, oppositions, or conflicts between the participants are central during the interchange and crucial for the emergence of not only commonality, but also innovation. Dissonant dialogue, more than consonant dialogue, requires an openness and willingness of the participants to change and develop their initial positions under the influence of the preceding interchange (see also Chapter 5). Both forms of dialogue take place in the self too. In consonant inner dialogue, one may agree with oneself after a phase of internal deliberation. In the case of dissonant inner dialogue, there is a strong field of tension between different positions, and more intense or longer dialogical processing is required before achieving consensus. We saw an example of dissonant internal dialogue in the thought process of Justin Brown earlier in this chapter. He described his mental state as a form of "multiple personality," like being drawn to two opposite sides, which he labeled as "climate change activist" and "economic libertarian." Although one can agree or disagree with the arguments for and against these two

[74] Cashell (2009, p. 15).   [75] Hermans (2018).

points of view, he was, via a tension-loaded dialogical interchange, searching for a common ground where the two positions could go beyond the all too familiar good versus bad stereotypes.

In this regard, we have witnessed in recent years, especially in 2022, many shocking events and developments in many parts of the world, such as war, populism, nationalism, animosity, political divisions, police brutality, and scapegoating. Let there be more disagreement and less animosity! Dialogue is inhibited not when participants stop agreeing, but when they stop disagreeing. Particularly in times where common values are lacking, dialogue becomes crucial for a society to survive.

In summary, the moral middle ground is a field of uncertainty because two contradicting positions (good versus bad) come together and require some kind of combination or reconciliation. Moreover, given the relative dominance of the two positions, this middle ground is open to a movement of one of the positions to the side of the good or the bad. In order to process these contradictions, including their relative dominance, dialogue is needed to arrive at a coalition that adds value and vitality to self and society. Given the strong tensions between the two positions, dissonant dialogue is needed to combine conflicting positions in a productive coalition.[76]

The Need for Dialogical Flexibility

Moving from one to another identity level in the self requires a certain degree of dialogical flexibility. In the case of the multilevel identity model proposed in this chapter, there is dialogical flexibility if the self is able and willing to move from one level of inclusiveness to other ones, in accordance with the requirements and opportunities of the specific situation. In contrast, restriction to and perseverance of one level only would lead to over-positioning, with the simultaneous neglect of the relevance and unique character of the other identity positions. Let me illustrate this with some examples. A narcissistic individual is fixed at the individual level and lacks the emotional empathy that enables them to stand in the shoes of other individuals or social groups and take their feelings and interests into account. Social groups striving for the protection of their social or political identities with the simultaneous neglection or rejection of the rights or dignity of outgroup members rely on the "glorification of differences" and perceive other groups via the clouded lenses of their own prejudices. Also,

[76] Hermans (2020).

the broader identity levels are sensitive to over-positioning. Seeing other individuals as human beings only, with the simultaneous neglect of their historical and cultural origins, may blind us to the fact that individuals derive self-esteem and pride from group membership and that they are subjected to innate tribalism as a deep-wired evolutionary response. When individuals are motivated by apocalyptic pessimism and, as a response, give absolute priority to ecological concerns, they are fixed at the ecological level and neglect the importance of the economic facilities and financial resources needed for environmental protection, health care, and job security.[77]

The development of a multilevel identity requires a degree of dialogical flexibility that enables the self to move from one level of inclusiveness to another in a way that prevents any over-positioning in the direction of a rigidly closed identity. Such a shift can be verbally represented in the form of dialogical "but sentences." At the interface of the social and human levels, an individual might say: "I'm concerned about the increasing number of refugees and asylum seekers that are coming to my country, but as a human being I'm concerned about the suffering of people who are threatened by political regimes." At the interface of the individual and ecological levels, a potential parent might say: "I would like to have children, but I have mixed feelings because we have reached an era of huge uncertainty caused by climate change and scarce resources in the future." Thus, internal dialogues are stimulated in an era of increased uncertainty, bringing people into a situation in which private or group aspirations are balanced against human and ecological concerns so that decision-making becomes more complex.

Level Confusion: Erroneous Problem Attributions

The model of multilevel identity may be helpful for understanding the phenomenon of "level confusion" that occurs when values attributed to one identity level become confused with values that actually belong to another level. This confusion can arise when the unique nature of a particular level is not recognized or insufficiently acknowledged. An extreme example can be found in Hitler's book *Mein Kampf* (see Chapter 3), where he went so far as to expect that individual citizens should sacrifice their lives in the service of the nation: "The greatness of the Aryan is not based on his intellectual powers, but rather on his willingness

[77] Ibid.

to devote all his faculties to the service of the community. Here the instinct for self-preservation has reached its noblest form; for the Aryan willingly subordinates his own ego to the common weal and when necessity calls he will even sacrifice his own life for the community."[78] Also, Putin, in his striving for the reparation of the original purity and unity of the Russian Empire, uses this ideal as a legitimation for blocking access to Facebook and major foreign media platforms and for enacting a law to punish anyone who would spread "false information" about the Ukraine invasion with up to fifteen years in prison (see Chapter 3). This can be seen as an assault on the uniqueness and value of the individual identity level, with the consequence that, in the case of dissidence, individuals are not allowed to speak from their own, original points of view.[79]

Level confusion also occurs in everyday situations. Influenced by stereotypes and prejudices, we may look at members of a certain identity group solely as members of that group and lose sight of the fact that they are also individuals with their own unique characteristics and preferences. For instance, when a white, Western European reads in the news about a crime committed by an immigrant or a person of color, they might not ascribe this crime just to this particular individual but spontaneously associate it with all members of the group. If the same crime was committed by a nonimmigrant or white person, then this person might perceive it simply as an act of the individual culprit without any association with a group or category. As a consequence of this level confusion, individuals of a particular group who have not committed the crime are brought into a position where they are forced to defend themselves against such generalizing accusations.

In his reflections about such level confusion, cultural anthropologist Toon van Meijl[80] observed that people with non-Western origins often complain that people from receiving countries classify them solely on the basis of their ethnicity or religion rather than as individuals. People prefer to be regarded not only as representatives of their own group, but also in terms of their identity as humans. Therefore, van Meijl advocates that people from receiving countries should make a shift from positioning others just as "foreigners" with exclusive group identities to positioning them as representatives of communal citizenship in a cross-border society. From the perspective of the self as a "mini-society of I-positions," he proposes that we acknowledge that an individual has more positions than

---

[78] Hitler (1939, p. 232). See also Chapter 3.
[79] For an extensive discussion of Putin's worldview, see Chapter 3.   [80] van Meijl (2020).

just being an immigrant or representative of a particular ethnicity, culture, religion, gender, or age. He recommends admitting that other individuals have positions in their repertoire that are familiar to our own lives, such as "I as a parent," "I as a neighbor," and "I as a professional." Giving such "linking positions" (between the individual and group levels) a more prominent place in communication facilitates meeting one another without getting stuck in "we versus they" separating forms of positioning. Instead of "locking up" immigrants in exclusive ethnic or religious identities, commonality, beyond stereotypes and prejudices, can be found by considering others in their multiplicity, not only as representatives of a particular social group, but also as individuals and as humans.

Level confusion can also be observed in the "global warming controversy," particularly in those situations where a problem that is actually located at the ecological and human identity levels is confused with the group level. The scientific literature has convincingly demonstrated that global surface temperatures have clearly increased in recent decades and that this trend is caused by human-induced emissions of greenhouse gases.[81] Yet, some representatives of industries focused on extracting fossil fuels and some politicians have tried to convince the public that climate change is not occurring, or, if it is, then it is not due to human influence. Some climate scientists have reported that government and oil industry representatives have put pressure on them to censor their work and even hide scientific data with directives to keep certain subjects away from public communications.[82] In spite of a high degree of scientific consensus, global warming has unfortunately become an issue of widespread political debate, often being split along political party lines. Shifting the climate problem from the ecological and human levels, where it belongs, to the (political) group level may motivate people to deny the serious nature of the problem and justify continuing with existing habits at the expense of the interests of future generations and people living in areas directly affected by such climate change. More than ever, the current global situation needs a more extended identity definition, one that exceeds the limited boundaries of the individual and the social group.[83]

Conscience

When we assume the validity of the claim that the current global situation requires a more extended identity definition, what then are the

---

[81] IPCC (2021, 2023).   [82] Vidal (2011).   [83] Hermans (2022).

consequences for our "conscience" and its role in our psychological makeup? Is it not naive to think that people are able to experience empathy and feel responsibility for people at the other end of the world?[84] And, related to the previous question: Can the moral middle ground have a place in one's conscience? This is what I will address in this section: the limitations of our conscience and its relationship with the moral middle ground.

As a starting point for this exploration, I refer to neuro-philosopher Patricia Churchland's book *Conscience: The Origins of Moral Intuition*,[85] in which she argues that the neural wiring for attachment and bonding, not only in humans but also in some animals, provides the motivational and emotional platform for sociality, social norms, and moral inhibitions. If mammals do not feel the powerful need to belong and do not care about the well-being of kith and kin, then their survival would have no security. Learning mechanisms, in which emotions play central roles, lead to building a complex brain model of the social world. Attachment to each other makes animals less apprehensive and more trusting, which leads to cooperation, grooming, food sharing, and mutual defense mechanisms. Bonding to others and hence caring for them is a profoundly significant feature of our nature as human animals.[86]

As a demonstration of the neurological basis of bonding and caring, Churchland gives the example of the difference between two kinds of small rodents: montane voles and prairie voles. After the male and female montane voles meet and mate, they go their separate ways. In contrast, when prairie voles meet and mate, they bond for life. Neuroscientific research led to the finding that the density of receptors in their brains' reward systems was much higher in the prairie voles than in the montane voles. It appears that oxytocin, a hormone produced in the hypothalamus, is an important component of feeling bonded, which, in turn, is a prerequisite for empathy.[87]

In an interview about her book, Churchland explains why she has a distaste for Kantians and representatives of utilitarianism.[88] She says:

---

[84] For the limitations of our empathy, see Bloom (2017). His plea for rational compassion fits with emotion–reason dialogue in DST (see earlier in this chapter).

[85] Churchland (2019). For a similar view on the evolutionary origins of morality, see Kurzban (2010).

[86] Churchland (2019). The evolutionary origin of morality is also emphasized by anthropologists who suggest that human moral preferences can be best understood as adaptations to the affordances of the fundamentally interdependent hunter–gatherer lifestyles of our hominin ancestors (Burkart et al., 2018).

[87] Samuel (2019), interview with Patricia Churchland.

[88] Utilitarianism is an ethical theory that holds that the most ethical choice is the one that will produce the greatest good for the greatest number.

"I think what's troubling about Kant and utilitarians is that they have this idea, which really is a romantic bit of nonsense, that if you could only articulate the one deepest rule of moral behavior, then you'd know what to do. It turns out that's not workable at all: There is no one deepest rule."[89] In her book, she is more explicit about this issue. She objects to Kant's view on moral obligation and quotes this sentence in his work: "The ground of obligation must be looked for, not in the nature of man nor in the circumstances in the world in which he is placed, but solely a priori in the concepts of pure reason." And she responds: "This statement makes Kant's point that our nature, along with our biological inclinations to care about others and to be social, should be set aside as irrelevant to morality, often even antithetical to it." In her view, "Morality does not and cannot emerge from pure logic alone. It cannot be disengaged from our deep desires to care for others and for those with whom our welfare and prosperity are entwined. It cannot be disengaged from our need to live social lives."[90]

Similarly, Churchland objects to the central principle of the utilitarians that prescribes that moral good is to produce the greatest happiness for the greatest number of people. She sees this as "totally unrealistic." If this principle were to be accepted, it would mean that "[t]here's no special consideration for your own children, family, friends. Biologically, that's just ridiculous. People can't live that way." In her view, one would "have a hard time arguing for the morality of abandoning your own two children in order to save 20 orphans ... I can't abandon my children for the sake of orphans on the other side of the planet whom I don't know, just because there's 20 of them and only two of mine. It's not psychologically feasible."[91] She agrees with psychologist Roy Baumeister, who notes: "The key point is that this empathic sensitivity seems to be selective. People may feel a great deal in some situations and towards some targets, but they seem to lack it utterly in others. And people are surprisingly flexible in their capacity to feel sensitive and empathic towards some and not others."[92] Therefore, Churchland concludes that most people have a limited capacity for empathy, and she goes so far as to argue: "We falter under empathy fatigue."[93]

Churchland's arguments often have a strong rhetorical content, and, when reading it, I realized that many people can feel a strong sense of empathy when they are confronted, via the media, with the suffering of

---

[89] Samuel (2019, n.p.).   [90] Churchland (2019, p. 130, electronic version).
[91] Samuel (2019, n.p.).
[92] Baumeister (1997), quoted by Churchland (2019, p. 84, electronic version).
[93] Churchland (2019, p. 84, electronic version).

people at the other side of the world. Many of them are willing to give donations to alleviate the misery of the victims. Yet, I can understand the essence of Churchland's point of view very well, as I have summarized it briefly here, because it offers powerful neuropsychological arguments and gives emotion a central place in her thesis. These arguments are largely neglected both in the Kantian moral principles that put a heavy weight on reason and in the rational assumptions of the utilitarians, who use a one-sided quantitative criterion (the greatest number) as the essence of their moral principle. This leads me to a question that is highly significant for my thesis that we need a more extended identity definition in the direction of the human and ecological realms, which lie beyond the immediate social circles of attachment and empathy. The question here is as follows: Is it possible to *expand* the circle of moral positions beyond one's ingroup while, at the same time, recognizing the urgent needs associated with the group identity level? In the field of the social psychology of morality, researchers have attempted to shed some light on this topic.

The Circle of Moral Regard

In a series of empirical studies, social psychologists Americus Reed and Karl Aquino[94] investigated the extent to which high self-importance of moral identity leads to a more extended conception of one's ingroup. They referred to their premise as the "circle of moral regard" hypothesis: "Rather than confining one's in-group to a narrow set of others (e.g., family, kin, fellow citizens), a person whose moral identity has high self-importance should include a larger set of social groups. In the extreme, this psychological boundary might include all of humanity."[95] Summarizing their findings, Reed and Aquino conclude that individuals with a strong internalized moral identity are more likely to favorably perceive the worthiness of relief efforts to outgroups. In one of their studies, they found a rigorous confirmation of the circle of moral regard hypothesis: A strong internalized moral identity was associated with actual donation behavior. When the participants of their study were forced to choose between giving more monetary support to either a deserving ingroup (New York Police and Fire Widows and Children's Benefit Fund) or a deserving outgroup (Afghani women and children), those who had a high internalized moral identity chose to extend support to the more socially distant outgroup. The investigators considered these results as confirming the circle of moral

[94] Reed and Aquino (2003).   [95] Ibid. (p. 1271).

regard hypothesis as transcending the boundaries of the American identity that usually is likely to motivate the contraction rather than the expansion of the circle of moral regard.

What I learned from this study is that the circle of moral regard is not the same for everybody and that people whose moral identity has high self-importance are able to widen their circle of moral regard beyond the usual ingroup–outgroup boundaries. The study of Reed and Aquino is (implicitly) based on the assumption that individuals have one moral identity. However, DST is based on the idea that the self works as a dynamic *multiplicity* of identities in the society of mind. What does this mean for extending one's moral circle beyond individual and social identities?

Extension of the Circle of Moral Regard

A definition of conscience from a DST perspective starts from the assumption that it is composed of a multiplicity of moral positions that are located at four identity levels: individual, social, human, and ecological. This definition encompasses not only individual positions (e.g. I as concerned about justice or I as a caring person), but also group positions (e.g. we as defending our rights), human positions (e.g. we all as one big family), and ecological positions (e.g. we as concerned about the well-being of animals). As we have seen earlier in this chapter, identity studies are strongly biased in the direction of individual and group identities. Not surprisingly, this is in accordance with the emphasis, particularly in Western cultures, on individualism and identity politics. As individuals, we tend to attribute our personal successes and material profits to our own efforts and initiatives, motivated by the ideology of a market-driven economy and its associated meritocracy that stimulate us to "invest in ourselves." As members of a social group or movement, we are driven by ingroup favoritism or as part of an organized structure that strives for emancipation on the basis of religion, ethnicity, race, sex, or gender. Cultural and political factors determine that both the individual and the social levels are associated with strong emotions that protect our self-esteem on the individual level and our group pride on the social level. As such, emotions are less pronounced on the human and ecological levels. These identities, although essential for the survival of nature, the Earth and humanity, lack the immediate urgency and emotional priority that are typical of the individual and group levels. So, the question arises as to whether it is possible for the human and ecological identities to derive energy from the individual and group levels. My answer would be that this is possible

Table 6.2 *Examples of coalitions between different identity positions.*

	Human	Ecological
Individual	Health care volunteer, philanthropist	Gardener, nature lover, minimalist
Social (group)	Amnesty International, Human Rights Watch	Environmental Defense Fund, Nature Friends International

because the different identities do not necessarily function in isolation of each other. When we understand the self as a dynamic multiplicity of *relatively autonomous* identity levels, this definition leaves space for identities to form coalitions that open channels along which energy can be transferred from the individual and group levels on the one hand to the human and ecological levels on the other. This process of transpositioning is something that occurs in reality. Table 6.2 gives some examples of I- and we-positions that represent some illustrative coalitions. These examples suggest that, for instance, the position of a philanthropist allows one to achieve personal excellence by publicly giving donations and by contributing to the human cause. Presenting yourself as a "minimalist" rewards you with a feeling of pride when you tell others that you prefer a materially simple lifestyle as a necessary and effective response to the ecological crisis. Being an active member or supporter of an organization like Amnesty International or any other organization or social group that aims to protect human rights enables one to derive group pride and dignity in combination with the feeling of satisfaction about doing something for vulnerable people in parts of the world where rights are violated. And being a member of an organization like Greenpeace or being an active supporter of such an organization or any other ecological organization provides one with the feeling that one is fighting *together* to take care of the environment.

What is the basic message behind these admittedly limited examples? It is a conception of conscience as something more than one's moral engagements as individuals or group members. It includes a moral involvement in taking care of humanity and being actively concerned about our broader environment, where we position ourselves not as "owners" but as engaged participants and caretakers. The definition and experience of our identities at extended levels of inclusiveness have the advantage that our conscience is extended beyond the limitations of our individual and social concerns. The coalitions of the various levels have the advantage that the energy of the more restricted identity levels can be invested in and combined with that of the broader ones. Organizing our self in this way has the potential of enlarging our circle of moral regard and gives it, moreover, an energy impetus from the emotionally powerful restricted levels. It also means that our moral concern, although limited by our neurological and evolutionary-based determinants (see Churchland's arguments earlier in this chapter), can be broadened not only toward vulnerable people in other parts of the world, but also to threatened animals, trees, plants, and nature in general.

The coalition of different identity levels may profit from a *coalition of emotion and reason*. Let's take the general definitions of these concepts provided by the Merriam-Webster dictionary. An emotion is a mental reaction (such as anger or fear) subjectively experienced as a strong feeling usually directed toward a specific object or person and typically accompanied by physiological and behavioral changes in the body. Reason is defined as the power of comprehending, inferring, or thinking, especially in orderly, rational ways. When we apply these descriptions to the identity levels, then we notice that many of our emotions are associated with our immediate individual needs, desires, and anxieties, whereas being part of our ingroup gives us pride, safety, belonging, and status. The broader levels are certainly not without emotions, and they can engage some people deeply, but compared with the restricted levels, they are, generally speaking, less intense, less easily aroused, and less immediately urgent. Therefore, the activation of the broader identities requires our reason,[96] which may provide us with *insights* into these "slower" developments that, in turn, may lead to disasters after longer periods of time (see also Chapter 3 for the four dead ends in identity construction that may finally end in wars) and the disappearance of forests, reductions in biodiversity, increasing draughts and floods, and other phenomena as a result of (human-made) climate change.

A classic problem in moral psychology is whether moral judgments are driven by intuition versus deliberate reasoning. Inspired by this problem, a group of social psychologists[97] explored the role of reappraisal, defined as an emotion regulation strategy that involves interpreting an emotion-eliciting situation in a way that diminishes the intensity of the emotion. They hypothesized that when particular situations evoke strong initial moral intuitions (e.g. "This is disgusting!"), reappraisal weakens the influence of these intuitions, leading to more deliberative moral judgments

[96] Hermans (2022).   [97] Feinberg et al. (2012).

(compare the relevance of the "second thought" in the case of evaluating transgressive art presented in Chapter 4). Reappraisal of an initial emotion by one's reasoning occurred when participants contemplated why they experienced a certain response and whether there was good reason to experience this particular emotion. The results of this research suggest that our reasoning processes have some potential to act as counter-positions that weaken an initial emotion. For the presented multilevel identity model, this means that emotion–reason dialogue has some potential to weaken the strength of emotional concerns on the individual and group levels so that more space can be created to become aware of the value of the human and ecological identity levels.

In summary, I propose the following definition of conscience in the context of DST: *Conscience emerges as a dynamic multiplicity of moral I- and we-positions involved in processes of internal and external dialogue aiming to create a balance of well-being between ourselves, our ingroups (e.g. family, friends, neighbors), others as participants of one human family, and our natural environment, all of which are perceived as valuable enough to receive our care and justice.*

Often, our conscience speaks with a soft voice rather than loudly, and therefore a distinction between foreground and background voices is meaningful in this context. Because the soft background voices can be contradictory to the louder foreground ones and, therefore, can be easily disregarded and tuned out, a well-developed meta-position and dialogical capability are required to let conscience function in its full multiplicity.

Jane Addams and Andrew Carnegie: Who of Them Is on the Moral Middle Ground?

I now arrive at a challenging undertaking: Is it possible to assign a place to someone on the moral middle ground in our description of conscience? To explore an answer to this question, I make a comparison between two famous philanthropists: Jane Addams and Andrew Carnegie. I select these figures because they share some similarities in their contributions to the welfare of society of their time, but, at the same time, they show some striking differences. I will argue that Addams is clearly and without any doubt located in the domain of moral good. Carnegie, however, is, in my view, located on the moral middle ground because his great achievements also have a remarkable shadow side.

From a conceptual point of view, the purpose behind my comparison of Addams and Carnegie is to introduce the concept the "promoter position,"[98] which plays a central organizing role in somebody's position repertoire. I will show that both persons were driven by the promoter position "I as a philanthropist," with Addams doing her work in the realm of the moral good, while Carnegie delivered his contributions on the moral middle ground. An additional reason to include them in this book is that, later in this chapter, in the section on "practical implications," I will propose that figures like Addams and Carnegie, and others in our everyday lives, can function as moral icons and as identification figures in the external domain of our selves.

Jane Addams: The Mother of Social Work

Jane Addams (1860–1935; Figure 6.3) was a prominent pacifist who, through her social reform work and voluminous writings, became one of the most famous American women of her time. Having no interest in marriage and discovering that most professions were closed to females, she ultimately developed a lifelong career based upon the establishment of voluntary associations. After visiting a social settlement[99] in London in which university men lived and worked among the poor, Addams decided to found a social settlement in the US. Together with her college friend Ellen Gates Starr, she started in 1889 the Hull-House social settlement in a crumbling mansion located in an immigrant community in Chicago. She believed that working and living with the poor would show her and her colleagues the path to understanding the best ways to combat poverty. In its first decade, Hull-House dramatically expanded to meet the needs of the surrounding community. The settlement offered a wide variety of educational classes and eventually included a gymnasium, a playground, a nursery, a music school, a cooperative boardinghouse, a theater, and an art gallery.[100]

After becoming the acknowledged leader of a movement that had organized 400 American settlements, she used her celebrity status to promote female suffrage and to campaign vigorously for Theodore Roosevelt's 1912 presidential campaign because his Progressive Party represented many of the reforms she advocated. When the US entered World War I (WWI), she protested, as a dedicated pacifist, against US

---

[98] Hermans and Hermans-Konopka (2010); Valsiner (2004).

[99] The settlement movement was a reformist social movement that started in the 1880s and peaked around the 1920s in England and the US. Its main goal was to bring the rich and the poor together in both physical proximity and social interconnection.

[100] Burlingame (2004).

Figure 6.3   Jane Addams writing.
Source: Bettmann/Getty Images.

interventionism. This resulted in her condemnation as unpatriotic in the eyes of the public. After WWI, she spent much time in Europe working for the Women's International League for Peace and Freedom. Eventually, she was awarded the Nobel Peace Prize (1931) and became an American icon. She died in 1935, three days after an operation revealed she had cancer.[101]

Undoubtedly, Jane Addams is generally celebrated as a classic philanthropist who put righteousness at the center of her cause, as already expressed in the first sentence of her book *Democracy and Social Ethics*: "It is well to remind ourselves, from time to time, that 'Ethics' is but another word for 'righteousness,' that for which many men and women of every generation have hungered and thirsted, and without which life

[101] Ibid.

becomes meaningless."[102] From a DST perspective, I as righteous and, more generally, I as a philanthropist can be conceived of as "promoter positions" taking central part in her self-organization. I use this concept here to demonstrate that "doing good" is not simply one of a (quantitative) multitude of moral positions that find their place side by side in the self, but rather it is a *central* position that functions as a motivational basis for the coordination and development of other, more specific I-positions. In the case of Jane Addams, we notice a multiplicity of moral positions, such as the charity provider, pacifist, democrat, suffragist, educator, politically engaged citizen, organizer, book author, and lecturer, as some of the most significant positions to which she devoted her unremitting efforts and attention. In some situations, one particular position would be activated, while another would be in other situations. However, looking at her moral behavior in this *quantitative* way would be limiting because this would be insufficient to understand the way in which her self was organized. Let's look at several features of a promoter position as organizing one's life in a *qualitative* way.

Analogous to leaders in society who promote the growth, development, or emancipation of others, promoter positions in the self also have some prominent characteristics[103]:

(1)   They *organize and give direction* to a diversity of more specialized I-positions that otherwise would go their own way and they serve as a "compass" for the self-system as a whole; in this way, they give direction in life and prevent the confusion that could occur if all specific I-positions were to follow their own trajectories.

(2)   They imply a considerable *openness* toward the future and have the potential to produce a diverse range of *new positions* that are relevant to the further development of the self.

(3)   They create *coherence* in a diversity of new and already existing positions that they bring together to form adaptive and productive *coalitions*; this coherence prevents the self from ending up in fragmentation or in a cacophony of voices.

(4)   They serve as "guards" of the *continuity* of the self, but, at the same time, they give room to an optimal degree of *discontinuity*; whereas continuity is guaranteed by their ability to link the past, present, and future of the self, a certain degree of discontinuity results from the introduction of new positions; the presence of a certain degree of

---

[102] Addams (1920, p. 1).   [103] Hermans and Hermans-Konopka (2010).

continuity gives the self a sufficient *hold* so that it is solid enough to open itself up to adopting new or unfamiliar positions.[104]

When applied to Jane Addams, her promoter position as a fighter for righteousness or as a philanthropist brought a range of moral and other specific positions together and organized them under a common theme that provided her with a clear direction in life. For many people, I-positions such I as a lecturer, I as a book author, or I as creating a new organization are not necessarily moral positions, but in Addams's case they were building blocks that were all brought under the umbrella of a long-term moral promoter position, serving as a permanent source of motivation that kept her going, in spite of her life-long health problems, until the end of her life. Jane Addams's actions were not typical of the moral middle ground. Her intentions and actions were clearly in the domain of moral good. However, can the same be said about another famous philanthropist, Andrew Carnegie?

Andrew Carnegie: The Gospel of Wealth

Andrew Carnegie (1835–1919; Figure 6.4), who lived in the same historical period as Jane Addams, was a Scottish-American industrialist who became a leading philanthropist in the US and in the British Empire.[105] He was instrumental in the expansion of the American steel industry in the late nineteenth century, and he became one of the richest Americans in history. At the age of thirty-three, he was already a multimillionaire in today's terms. Often called "the father of scientific philanthropy," he put forth three main arguments for the distribution of wealth.[106] First, he advised wealthy individuals not to spoil their heirs by leaving large amounts of money to them. In his view, it is much better that in the capitalistic system each individual makes their own career. Second, giving should be "wise giving" instead of becoming engaged in "indiscriminate charity." In his publication *The Gospel of Wealth*, he made this very clear: "Those who would administer wisely must, indeed, be wise, for one of the serious obstacles to the improvement of our race is indiscriminate charity. It were better for mankind that the millions of the rich were thrown into the sea than so spent as to encourage the slothful, the drunken, the unworthy."[107] His third argument was also in agreement with the ideal

---

[104] Hermans (2018).   [105] Nasaw (2007).   [106] Burlingame (2004).
[107] Carnegie (1906, p. 535).

Figure 6.4   Andrew Carnegie.
Source: Bettmann/Getty Images.

of the self-made man of capitalism: "In bestowing charity, the main consideration should be to help those who will help themselves."[108] These convictions led Carnegie to focus his donations on a vast number of public libraries, educational institutions, and other public organizations that would benefit those who chose to become involved in their own development. Although his ideals were very different from those of Jane Addams, he shared with her one basic insight that is still valid in our twenty-first century: "The problem of our age is the proper administration of wealth, so that the ties of brotherhood may still bind together the rich

[108] Ibid. (p. 536).

and poor in harmonious relationship."[109] In a note to himself, he wrote: "The man who dies thus rich dies disgraced."[110] Upon his death in 1919, writers in newspapers and magazines around the country characterized this event as the end of an era in American capitalism.[111] (Although we can observe that capitalism is still continuing and is expressed, often in unlimited ways, in the spending behavior of many rich people in our contemporary society.[112])

Was Carnegie Selfish?

The question can be posed as to whether Andrew Carnegie was selfish, and, if so, whether his behavior could be combined in a viable way with benevolence. In his search for Carnegie's moral status, American historian Richard Bushman[113] notes that, except for US president Abraham Lincoln and Benjamin Franklin, as the founding fathers of the US Declaration of Independence, no one is more firmly enshrined as a hero of the "American dream" than Andrew Carnegie. After his start as a penniless immigrant, he worked his way up from an employee in a cylinder factory and a telegraph office to the owner of the world's largest steel firm. This breathtaking ascent, due to the combination of hard work, skill, luck, and good-natured optimism, fits perfectly with the American dream that promises equal opportunity for all according to ability or achievement.

However, there are biographers, Bushman continues, who have objected to this interpretation and even reversed Carnegie's hero position, depicting him as a villain. Despised as a selfish businessman grabbing for wealth and power while cruelly "stepping on" his coworkers and competitors and callously neglecting the sufferings of his underpaid workers, a picture was sketched that was the obverse of the romantic image of the American dream. Bushman refers to John K. Winkler's book *The Incredible Carnegie*, which parodies Carnegie as perhaps the greediest little gentleman ever created: "As an infant in high chair he beat a loud tattoo upon the table enforcing a demand for two spoons wherewith to shovel double portions of porridge into his mouth."[114] Other critics, providing a more restrained picture, have characterized Carnegie's paramount

---

[109] Ibid. (p. 526).   [110] Wall (1992), quoted by Berlingame (2004, p. 60).
[111] Berlingame (2004).
[112] For an analysis of the influence of neoliberalism on the content and structure of the self, see Hermans (2020, pp. 185–192).
[113] Bushman (1965).   [114] Winkler (1931), quoted by Bushman (1965, p. 31).

motivation simply as "unqualified selfishness" or the "lust for gain," and they have also painted him as a villain subverting cherished American values.[115]

Carnegie was eager to belong to the higher ranks in society and used his extravagant wealth to reach that goal. Among his treasured possessions were thank-you notes from King Edward VII of the UK, who expressed his appreciation for Carnegie's gifts. Carnegie had said that he would be deeply grateful if these notes would be handed down to his descendants as something that would fill them with pride. His friend the writer Mark Twain was well aware of Carnegie's weakness for aristocratic recognition: "He thinks he is a scorner of kings and emperors and dukes, whereas he is like the rest of the human race: a slight attention from one of these can make him drunk for a week and keep his happy tongue wagging for seven years."[116] His wealth permitted Carnegie to play the role of the aristocrat himself. After his marriage in 1887, he lived half the year in a castle at Cluny in Scotland, and in 1898 he purchased the estate at Skibo on the North Sea, where he built a vast baronial castle with castellated stone towers.[117] But above all he wanted to prove himself the equal of anybody and wanted everyone to acknowledge this, which was a dominant motive in his business career. His priority was not the accumulation of money, which he seemed to dislike, even devaluating it as filthy lucre. At the end of his life, he related more with statesmen and nobles than with partners or competitors.[118]

As Bushman clearly indicates, Carnegie can be described as a person with strongly contrasting qualities. Some have portrayed him as a classic American hero, others as a selfish villain. Bushman is critical of both views: "Qualifying the extremes, which all of the authors do, does not eliminate the inaccuracies in either picture."[119] Carnegie's weaknesses do not remove indications of some deeper motivation. After selling his company in 1901, "he felt released from the compulsion to make money and steadily divested himself of the fortune he feared would corrupt his soul. By building libraries he realized in some measure his earlier ambition to educate the poor. He gave munificently to schools, hospitals, churches and to his own workers."[120]

The picture of Carnegie as it emerges from the preceding observations and quotations demonstrates how difficult it is to qualify someone as

---

[115] Bushman (1965).   [116] Ibid. (p. 35).   [117] Ibid.   [118] Ibid. (p. 36).
[119] Ibid. (p. 31).   [120] Ibid. (p. 33).

located on or moving onto the moral middle ground. We have a spontaneous tendency to classify a person or their actions as "good" or "bad,"
whereby we shift rapidly, almost mechanically, to one side or the other,
not "concentrating" enough to keep the contradictory features together
and consider them in their mutual dynamic relationship. When we look
more carefully at Carnegie's life, we discover a striking similarity with
Oskar Schindler's case (Chapter 4): He could do his beneficial work *not
despite, but due to his selfishness.* He was selfish enough to build up a huge
business imperium, but also generous enough to become dedicated to the
well-being of others. In other words, Carnegie's selfish position was not
simply juxtaposed to his giving position but was causally implicated with
it; that is, the one was needed to realize the other. He funded not only
many libraries, but also paid for thousands of church organs in the US and
around the world. His wealth helped to establish numerous colleges,
schools, nonprofit organizations, and associations. He became convinced
of the importance of a palace for peace and offered a large donation under
the condition that the Peace Palace (Figure 6.5), located in The Hague,
would not only house the Permanent Court of Arbitration, but also
function as a public legal library of the highest standard.

Figure 6.5   Meeting at the Peace Palace in The Hague.
Source: Jerry Lampen/ANP/AFP via Getty Images.

When we compare the lives of Andrew Carnegie and Jane Addams, there are many indications that one or more promoter positions were at work during their careers. While Addams worked in cooperation with the poor, Carnegie preferred the path of providing the means for the poor to help themselves. But, for sure, both were driven by promoter positions, each in their own way, as philanthropists devoted to the benefit of society and themselves.[121] As Carnegie's case demonstrates, not only specific positions but also promoter positions can have a place on the moral middle ground.

What's the main message here? Don't remove your ego. Instead, let it cooperate with another, better position so that its energy is not lost.

Practical Implications

The most basic practical implication of this chapter is that you do not have one identity, but a multiplicity of them. Accordingly, identity does not follow from the question of how you are *different* from others, but from the question of where and how are you *placing yourself* in the world, or, in other words, how you position yourself in relation to the world and yourself. A multilevel and more inclusive identity that transcends opposition and competition between individuals and between social groups provides space for concerns that are directly relevant to our relationship with humanity and our ecological environment.

Acceptance of the idea that identity is plural and more encompassing than purely group-based ways of positioning requires the acknowledgment that the different identities – individual, social, human, and ecological – each have their *unique qualities* and are not simply interchangeable with each other. The uniqueness of a particular identity is neglected or even denied if it is dominated by or put in the service of other identities. Therefore, I have extensively discussed, in Chapter 3, the worldviews of Hitler and Putin, who propagated a philosophy where individual identities are treated as subservient to the group (national) identity, culminating in the construction of enemy images. The uniqueness of the identities would also be denied, explicitly or implicitly, if persons were to define themselves as purely independent and autonomous individuals who put their personal interests above anything else, while simultaneously neglecting the

---

[121] For a comparable analysis of Carnegie's life, see McCarty (1988), who, like Bushman, deals not only with Carnegie's valuable contributions to society, but also with his selfish motivation.

responsibility they have as human beings and the potential value they can contribute to the protection of the natural environment.

Another practical implication is the relevance of *dialogical relationships* between different identities, resulting in decisions that are not instigated by one isolated identity only but by the productive contact between them. For example, as a citizen of this country (social identity), I feel uneasy about the increasing influx of refugees, but as a human being, I'm concerned about civil rights (human identity), and this makes me more tolerant. Or, as a consumer (individual identity), I wish to buy a certain product, but as someone who is concerned about my ecological footprint (ecological identity), I buy something else that is more sustainable. Instead of making decisions on the basis of one identity only, a multi-identity approach recommends stimulating dialogical relationships between identities in such a way that one identity acknowledges the wishes, goals, emotions, and values associated with the other identities. This implies that when one identity is activated in a particular situation, the other identities are put in the background, ready to be activated when the demands of the situation require them.

Creating relationships between identity levels profits particularly from *emotion–reason dialogue*. Why? As I argued in this chapter, the individual and social identities are associated with stronger emotions than the human and ecological identities. In this chapter, we have seen that our emotional empathy is primarily directed toward individuals who belong to our close circles and that, therefore, our circle of moral regard is typically limited to the here and now. In contrast, humans on the other side of our planet, even when they are in need of support, often fall outside this circle. The long-term climate challenges, although crucial to our survival and that of other species, do not have immediate emotional appeal, as they evolve over a longer time period and, generally, evoke less immediate emotions than dramatic events taking place in the individual and social arenas. Therefore, the identities on the human and ecological levels in particular need support from our reasoning capacities to help us to move beyond our immediate impulses and widen our circle of moral regard. For the presented multilevel identity model, this means that the emotion–reason dialogue has some power to weaken the strength of emotional concerns on the individual and group levels so that more space can be created for the awareness of the value of the human and ecological identity levels. This dialogue is all the more important because strong emotions have a tendency to find their justification in themselves. In DST terms, reason–emotion dialogue has the potential of opening up the otherwise closed boundaries of emotional positions in search for an exit in the direction of different emotions or alternative explanations.

A powerful way to strengthen the broader human and ecological levels is to place another person not in one but in *multiple categories*. For example, the human identity may be strengthened when the individual imagines that a person from a despised outgroup is, like us, the parent of a family or is, like us, an ardent lover of sports or cares about the flowers in their own garden. Recall the research[122] presented in Chapter 3 that compared the multiple categorization of a target (e.g. "Giuseppe is a black male young person. He was born in Italy, and his parents are immigrants") with the simple categorization in which the research participant was described on the basis of their skin color only (i.e. "Giuseppe is a black person"). It was found that in the multiple categorization condition participants endorsed human rights (e.g. equality, liberty, security) in favor of this particular person to a greater degree than in the simple categorization condition. Apparently, addressing people as representing a multiplicity of identities leads us to evaluate them as more human than when this multiplicity is not explicitly mentioned.

The empowerment of the broader identity levels can also be increased by identifying with *moral icons* and learning from their behavior and lifestyles. With this in mind, I have sketched out the lives of Jane Addams as an individual whose actions are clearly in the domain of the moral good and Andrew Carnegie as a more controversial philanthropist. We may learn from them that moral personalities do not simply have a (quantitative) multiplicity of moral I-positions in their repertoire, but that their positions are organized around a central (qualitative) promoter position that works as an integrating force in their self and serves as a moral compass that gives direction to a variety of specific positions underlying their behavior. I included Addams and Carnegie in this text with the intention to demonstrate the function of promoter positions in their selves. We notice here that individuals like them can be incorporated as promoter positions in the external domain of our own selves. By identifying with them and learning from them, they help us to find moral direction in our lives.

However, moral icons are not just found in historical documents, on TV, or in social media. They can be found in our own personal histories and everyday lives, such as an influential teacher who transmitted in their words or behavior a moral message that we remember for the rest of our

---

[122] Albarello and Rubini (2012).

lives, or a parent or grandparent who tells us stories about their own past or the past of their parents that impress us with their moral courage or ideals. We ourselves may develop promoter positions in our selves as dedicated volunteers supporting vulnerable immigrants, as activists for a sustainable future, or as being devoted members of a human welfare organization. The essential feature here is that we can intentionally and explicitly develop a promoter position that reaches beyond the individual and social levels while at the same time deriving energy from them.

Finally, the following question can be posed: Under what conditions is it morally justified to engage in an action on the moral middle ground? As suggested by the examples given in this book (Chapters 4, 5, and 6), such action has to be preceded by thorough self-exploration and dialogue with oneself and others while acknowledging not only the action itself, but also its intentions and goals and the individual, social, human, ecological, and historical context in which it occurs. A useful *rule of thumb* is to assess the relative dominance of the good or bad position within a good–bad coalition. If self-reflection and dialogue, with oneself or others, leads to the conclusion that the good position is *relatively* dominant over the bad one, the resulting judgment about a certain action, behavior, or person as belonging to the moral middle ground is a valid one.

Summary

After having presented a definition of identity, I proposed a multilevel conception of identity with individual, social, human, and ecological levels. After a brief exposé of the relative dominance of the individual and social levels, a more extensive description was provided of the human level (with attention given to human rights) and the ecological level (with a focus on the dispute between economic and ecological positions).

Then the moral middle ground was discussed as a coalition of identities. More specifically, the case of Oskar Schindler was reviewed (see also Chapter 4) as a coalition of individual and human identities. The Boston Ten Point Coalition was presented as a coalition of social and human identities, as well as the actions of Greenpeace (see also Chapter 1) as a coalition of social and ecological identities.

Emphasis was placed on the nature of the relationships between the different identity positions, with a focus on the value of dialogical flexibility and the usefulness of the distinction between consonant and dissonant dialogues. In contrast to the flexibility of positions, the risk of over-positioning was analyzed, indicating the one-sided exaggeration of one of the identities, and attention was devoted to the "level confusion" resulting from ignoring the unique quality of each identity.

An elaborate discussion of the concept of conscience was presented. From a neurological perspective, evidence shows that the natural inclination of bonding and caring puts limitations on our circle of moral regard. This led to a criticism of utilitarian and Kantian ethics as neglecting the nature-determined limitations of moral regard. Arguments were given to enlarge this circle by extending our identity to the human and ecological levels.

In order to elucidate the workings of promoter positions in relation to the moral middle ground, I compared the lives and work of two philanthropic icons, Jane Addams and Andrew Carnegie, the former being located outside the moral middle ground and the latter one as acting on this ground. In the case of Carnegie, I argued that his selfishness and moral engagement were not simply juxtaposed as two different sides of his personality. Rather, he could do his beneficial work not despite but *because of* his selfishness.

Finally, some practical implications of this chapter were presented: acknowledging that one has more than just one identity and that different identities each have their unique character; creating dialogical relationships between them, with special emphasis on the emotion–reason dialogue; placing people in multiple categories instead of one category only; identification with moral icons; and a rule of thumb for the inclusion of an action on the moral middle ground.

Glossary

Main Concepts of Dialogical Self Theory

Anti-position A position that places itself against another position as an act of opposition or antagonism.

Anti-promoter A position that functions as an obstacle to the development of a self, team, or organization.

Atmosphere The affective "climate" of the field in which positions are located.

Bandwidth The range of I- and we-positions allowed to enter the dialogical space.

Boundaries Borders (open, closed, soft, rigid, flexible) that link and separate positions.

Centralization Movements in the self that lead to order and structure in the position repertoire.

Challenge zone Space in the self where new positions emerge or existing positions are renewed and that is associated with feelings of uncertainty.

Coalition of positions Positions that cooperate and strengthen each other in achieving a particular goal or as a response to the demands of the situation.

Comfort zone Space in the self where one feels confident and at ease and that is associated with a sense of certainty and predictability.

Conscious position Position of which one is aware and from which one is able to reflect on self and situation.

Consonant dialogue Agreeing interchange with others or oneself.

Core position Central position on which the functioning of many other positions depends.

Counter-position A position that responds to another position from a different point of view.

279

Danger zone Space in the self that is loaded with anxiety and other negative emotions and that one typically wants to avoid.

Decentralization Movements in the self that destabilize the existing order in the position repertoire and create space for its innovation.

Depositioning The self is liberated from being localized in any specific I-position and becomes absorbed in an encompassing experience of connection with the wider environment.

Dialogical space An experiential space felt in oneself and between participants involved in a generative dialogue.

Dialogue Verbal or nonverbal interchange between localized positions.

Dissonant dialogue Disagreeable interchange with others or oneself.

Emotional position A way of positioning (such as "I'm angry at you"; "I accuse myself") toward another or oneself, subjectively experienced as strong feeling,
typically accompanied by physiological and behavioral changes in the body.

Energy The force that causes things to move.

External position A position in the external domain in the self, also indicated as the "other-in-the-self" who, in a positive or negative way, is experienced as "mine" (e.g. my parents, my teacher, my friend, my opponent, my enemy).

Generative dialogue A dialogical relationship among positions that leads to the emergence of new and common meanings.

Identity A position that claims recognition by other individuals, by a social group, or by society as a whole.

Implicit position A position that has not yet reached the level of awareness and has not yet received an explicit voice.

Internal position Position in the internal domain of the self (e.g. "I as a dedicated professional" or "I as a fighter who never gives up").

I-ness The extent to which a position is felt as close to oneself or as belonging to oneself.

I-position A position in which one places oneself toward other positions in the self or toward the positions of one's people or objects in the world. The I gives subjectivity and uniqueness to the position.

I-prison An I-position that has no exit and from which one cannot escape.

It-position An objectified position.

Linking position A position that connects different individuals, social groups, or identity levels.

Meta-position A superordinate position that allows a "helicopter view" of other positions and their patterning and offers a long-term and cross-situational perspective.

Monologue When the voice of one position doesn't give space to another position that doesn't receive the opportunity to express itself from its specific and unique point of view.

Nonconscious position A position that is working below the level of conscious awareness.

Outside position Persons, groups, or institutions in the outside world (located beyond the internal and external domains of the self).

Over-positioning Exaggerating a position to the degree that the balance in the self is lost due to the lack of limiting or correcting counter-positions.

Position The encompassing concept of I-positions and we-positions.

Positioning The process of receiving, finding, and taking one's place in a field of relationships.

Potential position An I-position that is possible to the self, but is not or not yet actually included in the position repertoire.

Promoter position A position that organizes other positions, gives direction to the self as a whole, and is able to generate new positions.

Reasoning position A position from where one argues, analyzes, considers, compares positives and negatives, and draws conclusions.

Recentralization After a phase of decentralization, centralization occurs again.

Repositioning Moving from one to another position that is different from the previous one and takes another direction.

Shadow position A disowned position that is rejected as unacceptable.

Society of mind Constellation of I-positions and we-positions analogous to positions in society at large.

Third position A position that combines and reconciles two different, opposite, or conflicting positions.

Transpositioning The strength or specific energy of a particular position is transferred to another position with a different experiential quality.

Vitality A sense of zest, enthusiasm, and strength.

We-ness The extent to which a position is felt as close to us or as belonging to us.

We-position Positioning ourselves as part of a group, humanity, or nature.

We-prison A we-position that has no exit and from which it is difficult to escape.

References

Addams, J. (1920). *Democracy and Social Ethics*. New York: Macmillan.

Albarello, F., & Rubini, M. (2012). Reducing dehumanisation outcomes towards Blacks: The role of multiple categorisation and of human identity. *European Journal of Social Psychology, 42*, 875–882.

Albrecht, K. (2010). The tyranny of two: Liberate yourself from the bonds of two-valued thinking. [Blog]. *Psychology Today*, August 18. Retrieved from www .psychologytoday.com/us/blog/brainsnacks/201008/the-tyranny-two

Alexander, J. C., & Smith, P. (eds.) (2005). *The Cambridge Companion to Durkheim*. Cambridge: Cambridge University Press.

Allport, G. (1954). *The Nature of Prejudice*. Reading, MA: Addison-Wesley.

Andersen, S. E., & Hovring, C. M. (2020). CSR stakeholder dialogue in disguise: Hypocrisy in story performances. *Journal of Business Research, 114*, 421–435.

Andrei, M. (2015). The world's first image of light as both a particle and a wave. *ZKE Science*, March 3.

Argo, J. J., & Shiv, B. (2012). Are white lies as innocuous as we think? *Journal of Consumer Research, 38*, 1093–1102.

Arnet, J. (2002). The psychology of globalization. *American Psychologist, 57*, 774–783.

Aron, A., Aron, E. N., & Smollan, D. (1992). Inclusion of other in the self scale and the structure of interpersonal closeness. *Journal of Personality and Social Psychology, 63*, 596–612.

Aron, A., Mashek, D., McLaughlin-Volpe, T., Wright, S., Lewandowski, G., & Aron, E. (2005). Including close others in the cognitive structure of the self. In M. Baldwin (ed.), *Interpersonal Cognition* (pp. 206–232). New York: Guilford Press.

Aronson, E. (1969). The theory of cognitive dissonance: A current perspective. *Advances in Experimental Social Psychology, 4*, 1–34.

Bachner-Melman, R., & Oakley, B. A. (2016). Giving "till it hurts": Eating disorders and pathological altruism. In Y. Latzer & D. Stein (eds.), *Bio-Psycho-Social Contributions to Understanding Eating Disorders* (pp. 91–103). New York: Springer.

Bakhtin, M. (1984). *Problems of Dostoevsky's Poetics* (C. Emerson, ed. and trans.). Minneapolis: University of Minnesota Press.

Bandura, A. (1990). Selective activation and disengagement of moral control. *Journal of Social Issues*, *46*, 27–46.

Barber, S. (2004). *Jean Genet*. London: Reaktion Books.

Batson, C. D., Kobrynowicz, D., Dinnerstein, J. L., Kampf, H. C., & Wilson, A. D. (1997). In a very different voice: Unmasking moral hypocrisy. *Journal of Personality and Social Psychology*, *72*, 1335–1348.

Batson, C. D., Lishner, D. A., Carpenter, A., Dulin, L., Harjusola-Webb, S., Stocks, E. L., Gale, S., Hassan, O., & Sampat, B. (2003). "… As you would have them do unto you": Does imagining yourself in the other's place stimulate moral action? *Personality and Social Psychology Bulletin*, *29*, 1190–1201.

Batson, C. D., Thompson, E. R., Seuferling, G., Whitney, H., & Strongman, J. A. (1999). Moral hypocrisy: Appearing moral to oneself without being so. *Journal of Personality and Social Psychology*, *77*, 525–537.

Baum, L. F. (1900). *The Wonderful Wizard of Oz*. Chicago, IL: Geo. M. Hill Co.

Baumeister, R. F. (1997). *Evil: Inside Human Violence and Cruelty*. New York: Holt.

Bella, T., & Westfall, S. (2022). Don't be "Putin's altar boy," Pope warns Russian Orthodox leader. *The Washington Post*, May 4.

Berry, J., & Berry, C. (1999). *Genocide in Rwanda: A Collective Memory*. Washington, DC: Howard University Press.

Bertau, M.-C., Goncalves, M. M., & Raggatt, P. T. F. (eds.) (2012). *Dialogic Formations: Investigations into the Origins and Development of the Dialogical Self*. Charlotte, NC: Information Age.

Bitter Winter (2022). A terrible sermon: Patriarch of Moscow blesses "metaphysical" war against the "world of gay prides." *Bitter Winter, a magazine on religious liberty and human rights*, March 7.

Black, T. (2021). Climate alarmism is the real threat to public health. *Spiked*, September 9.

Bloom, P. (2017). *Against Empathy: The Case for Rational Compassion*. London: The Bodley Head.

Boucher, H. C., Peng, K., Shi, J., & Wang, L. (2009). Culture and implicit self-esteem: Chinese are "good" and "bad" at the same time. *Journal of Cross-Cultural Psychology*, *40*, 24–45.

Brown, J. (2021). Multiple personalities and climate change: Resolving my inner conflict. *Ideapod*. Retrieved from https://ideapod.com/multiple-personalities-and-climate-change/, November.

Buber, M. (1965). *Between Man and Man*. New York: Norton.
  (1970). *I and Thou; A New Translation with a Prologue "I and You" and Notes by Walter Kaufmann*. Edinburgh: T. & T. Clark.

Burkart, J. M., Brügger, R. K., & van Schaik, C. P. (2018). Evolutionary origins of morality: Insights from non-human primates. *Frontiers in Sociology*, *3*, 1–12.

Burlingame, D. F. (ed.) (2004). *Philanthropy in America: A Comprehensive Historical Encyclopedia*. Santa Barbara, CA: ABC-CLIO.

Bushman, R. L. (1965). The romance of Andrew Carnegie. *Midcontinent American Studies Journal*, *6*, 30–40.

California Institute of Technology (2022). Proving that quantum entanglement is real: Researcher answers questions about his historical experiments. *Phys.org.*, September 20.

Callero, P. L. (2003). The sociology of the self. *Annual Review of Sociology, 29*, 115–133.

Cameron, C. D., Harris, L. T., & Payne, B. K. (2016). The emotional cost of humanity: Anticipated exhaustion motivates dehumanization of stigmatized targets. *Social Psychological and Personality Science, 7*, 105–112.

Capozza, D., Trifiletti, E., Vezzali, L., & Favara, I. (2013). Can intergroup contact improve humanity attributions? *International Journal of Psychology, 48*, 527–541.

Carnegie, A. (1906). The gospel of wealth. *The North American Review, 183*, 526–537.

Carriere, K. R. (2019). Threats to human rights: A general review. *Journal of Social and Political Psychology, 7*, 8–32.

Cashell, K. (2009). *Aftershock: The Ethics of Contemporary Transgressive Art.* London: I.B. Tauris.

Chen, F. (2018). Why the Aziz Ansari story and discussions of grey areas are central to the #MeToo movement: To develop more nuanced understandings of consent and prevent sexual assault, we need to discuss grey areas. *The Tech*, January 25.

Churchland, P. (2019). *Conscience: The Origins of Moral Intuition.* New York: Norton.

Clayton, S. (2003). Environmental identity: A conceptual and an operational definition. In S. Clayton & S. Opotow (eds.). *Identity and the Natural Environment: The Psychological Significance of Nature* (pp. 45–65). Cambridge, MA: MIT Press.

Coleman, P. T. (2021). The U.S. is suffering from toxic polarization. That's arguably a good thing. *Scientific American*, April 2.

Collyns, D. (2014). Greenpeace's "time for change" message next to the hummingbird geoglyph in Nazca. *The Guardian*, December 11.

Cooley, C. H. (1902). *Human Nature and the Social Order.* New York: Scribner's.

Damasio, A. R. (1994). *Descartes' Error: Emotion, Reason, and the Human Brain.* New York: Free Press.

Davies, B., & Harré, R. (1990). Positioning: The discursive production of selves. *Journal for the Theory of Social Behaviour, 20*, 43–63.

de Beauvoir, S. (1966). Introduction. In Marquis de Sade, *The 120 Days of Sodom and Other Writings.* Compiled and translated by A. Wainhouse & R. Seavor. New York: Grove Press.

de Bruijn, P. (2022). De WOII-films die Poetin's Rusland bezielen [The WWII films that inspire Putin's Russia]. *NRC*, May 4.

de Courtivron, I. (1993). The high priest of apostasy. *New York Times*, November 7.

de Valk, K. (2003). Max Weber en het ethisch dilemma [Max Weber and the ethical dilemma]. *Christen Democratische Verkenningen* (CDV), summer issue.

Dean, T. (2018). The greatest moral challenge of our time? It's how we think about morality itself. *The Conversation*, March 11.

Diener, E., & Wallbom, M. (1976). Effects of self-awareness on antinormative behavior. *Journal of Research in Personality, 10*, 107–111.

Domańska, M. (2022). Medvedev escalates anti-Ukrainian rhetoric. *Centre for Eastern Studies OSW*, April 5.

Du, S. (2017). Hackers: The good, the bad, and the in between. *English 102: Final Research Project*, March 23, https://sedonaengl.wordpress.com/2017/03/12/hackers-the-good-the-bad-and-the-in-between/

Dunne, J. (1996). Beyond sovereignty and deconstruction: The storied self. *Philosophy and Social Criticism, 21*, 137–157.

Durkheim, E. (1912). *Les formes élémentaires de la vie religieuse [The Elementary Forms of Religious Life]*. Paris: Presses Universitaires de France.

Duursma, M. (2022). Instrument van Poetin – of zijn souffleur? Profiel patriarch Kirill, leider van de Russisch-Orthodoxe Kerk [Instrument of Putin – or his blower? Profile Patriarch Kirill, leader of the Russian Orthodox Church]. *NRC*, May 6.

Dyrendal, A., Lewis, J. R., & Petersen, J. A. A. (2016). *The Invention of Satanism*. New York: Oxford University Press.

Ellemers, N., van der Toorn, J., Paunov, Y., & van Leeuwen, T. (2019). The psychology of morality: A review and analysis of empirical studies published from 1940 through 2017. *Personality and Social Psychology Review, 23*, 332–366.

Ezcurra, M. P. (2018). Beyond evil: Politics, ethics, and religion in León Ferrari's illustrated Nunca más. *Art Journal, 77*, 20–47.

Feinberg, M., Willer, R., Antonenko, O., & John, O. P. (2012). Liberating reason from the passions: Overriding intuitionist moral judgments through emotion reappraisal. *Psychological Science, 23*, 788–795.

Ferguson, N. (2022). Vlad the Invader: Putin is looking to rebuild Russia's empire. *The Spectator*, February 26.

Filipovic, J. (2018). The poorly reported Aziz Ansari exposé was a missed opportunity. *The Guardian*, January 16.

Flanagan, O. (1991). *Varieties of Moral Personality: Ethics and Psychological Realism*. Cambridge, MA: Harvard University Press.

Foster, M. D. (2015). *The Book of Yokai: Mysterious Creatures of Japanese Folklore*. Oakland: University of California Press.

Foucault, M. (2015). *Language, Madness, and Desire: On Literature*. Minneapolis: University of Minnesota Press.

Freud, S. (1958). The dynamics of transference. In J. Strachey (ed. & trans.), *The Standard Edition of the Complete Psychological Works of Sigmund Freud* (Vol. 12, pp. 97–108). London: Hogarth Press. Originally published in 1912.

Friedersdorf, C. (2018). How #MeToo can probe gray areas with less backlash. *The Atlantic*, January 18.

Frimer, J. A., Walker, L. J., Dunlop, W. L., Lee, B. H., & Riches, A. (2011). The integration of agency and communion in moral personality: Evidence of enlightened self-interest. *Journal of Personality and Social Psychology, 101*, 149–163.

Fromm, E. (1939). Selfishness and self-love. *Psychiatry, 2,* 507–523.

Gaertner, S. L., & Dovidio, J. F. (2000). *Reducing Intergroup Bias: The Common Ingroup Identity Model.* Philadelphia, PA: Psychology Press.

Garrett, K. N. (2016). The moralization of politics: Causes, consequences, and measurement of moral conviction. Dissertation, University of North Carolina at Chapel Hill.

Geertz, C. (1979). From the native's point of view: On the nature of anthropological understanding. In P. Rabinow & W. M. Sullivan (eds.), *Interpretive Social Science* (pp. 225–241). Berkeley: University of California Press.

Genet, J. (2004). *The Thief's Journal.* London: Olympia Press. Originally published by Gallimar in 1949.

(2020). *The Criminal Child: Selected Essays,* translated from French by C. Mandell & J. Zuckerman. New York: New York Review of Books, Inc. Originally published in 1949.

Gerlach, R. (2022). Het nachtleven is cultuur, geen horeca [Nightlife is culture not a catering industry]. *NRC,* 19 November.

Gerson, M. (2022). There's a reason Russian soldiers can't look their victims in the face. *Washington Post,* April 22.

Geurts, C. (2020). The Wisconsin Assembly reflects on the anniversary of *Roe v. Wade,* students should too. *The Badger Harald,* January 22.

Glaveanu, V. (2018). The possible as a field of inquiry. *Europe's Journal of Psychology, 14,* 519–530.

Goldhagen, D. (1996). *Hitler's Willing Executioners.* New York: Alfred Knopf.

Graham, J., Meindl, P., Koleva, S., Iyer, R., & Johnson, K. M. (2015). When values and behavior conflict: Moral pluralism and intrapersonal moral hypocrisy. *Social and Personality Psychology Compass, 9,* 158–170.

Gubanov, N. N., Gubanov, N. I., & Rokotyanskaya, L. (2018). Factors of black humor popularity. *Advances in Social Science, Education and Humanities Research, 283,* 379–383.

Güney, M., & Kayserili, M. S. (2020). A view history of European slavery on the Chris Ofili's artwork named The Holy Virgin Mary. Atatürk University. Available via Google Scholar.

Gutmann, A. (2003). *Identity in Democracy.* Princeton, NJ, and Oxford: Princeton University Press,

Haidt, J., & Graham, J. (2007). When morality opposes justice: Conservatives have moral intuitions that liberals may not recognize. *Social Justice Research, 20,* 98–116.

Ham, P. (2014). *Young Hitler.* Beverly Hills, CA: Endeavour Press.

Hardy, G. H. (1967). *A Mathematician's Apology.* Cambridge: Cambridge University Press.

Haslam, N., & Loughnan, S. (2014). Dehumanization and infrahumanization. *Annual Review of Psychology, 65,* 399–423.

Hawley, P. H. (2003). Prosocial and coercive configurations of resource control in early adolescence: A case for the well-adapted Machiavellian. *Merrill-Palmer Quarterly, 49,* 279–309.

(2014). The duality of human nature: Coercion and prosociality in youths' hierarchy ascension and social success. *Current Directions in Psychological Science, 23*, 433–438.

Herman, S. (2022). Is Putin the new Hitler? *VOA*, March 8.

Hermans, H. J. M. (2016). *Assessing and Stimulating a Dialogical Self in Groups, Teams, Cultures, and Organizations.* New York: Springer.

(2018). *Society in the Self: A Theory of Identity in Democracy.* New York: Oxford University Press.

(2020). *Inner Democracy: Empowering the Mind against a Polarizing Society.* New York: Oxford University Press.

(2022). *Liberation in the Face of Uncertainty: A New Development in Dialogical Self Theory.* Cambridge: Cambridge University Press.

Hermans, H. J. M., & Bartels, R. (2021). *Citizenship Education and the Personalization of Democracy.* London: Routledge.

Hermans, H. J. M., & Gieser, T. (eds.) (2012). *Handbook of Dialogical Self Theory.* Cambridge: Cambridge University Press.

Hermans, H. J. M., & Hermans-Jansen, E. (1995). *Self-Narratives: The Construction of Meaning in Psychotherapy.* New York: Guilford Press.

Hermans, H. J. M., & Hermans-Konopka, A. (2010). *Dialogical Self Theory: Positioning and Counter-Positioning in a Globalizing Society.* Cambridge: Cambridge University Press.

Hermans, H. J. M., & Kempen, H. J. G. (1993). *The Dialogical Self: Meaning as Movement.* San Diego, CA: Academic Press.

Hickel, J. (2020). *Less is More: How Degrowth Will Save the World.* London: Penguin Random House.

Hill, F., & Gaddy, C. G. (2013). *Mr. Putin: Operative in the Kremlin.* Washington, DC: Brookings Institution Press.

Hilton, R. H. (1958). The origins of Robin Hood. *Past & Present, 14*, 30–44.

Hitler, A. (1939). *Mein Kampf.* London: Hurst & Blackett. Originally published in German in 1925.

Horberg, E. J., Oveis, C., Keltner, D., & Cohen, A. B. (2009). Disgust and the moralization of purity. *Journal of Personality and Social Psychology, 97*, 963–976.

Howard, J. A. (2000). Social psychology of identities. *Annual Review of Sociology, 26*, 367–393.

Huffington Post (2022). Putin likens opponents to "gnats," evoking Stalin's dehumanizing language, March 19.

Human Rights Watch (2022). Why leaders of the world should do more to stand up for human rights and a fair world. Retrieved from www.hrw.org/sites/default/files/media_2022/02/World%20Report%202022%20ETR%20FINAL.pdf

Ignatieff, M. (2004). *The Lesser Evil: Political Ethics in an Age of Terror.* Princeton, NJ: Princeton University Press.

Imperato, C., & Mancini, T. (2021). Intergroup dialogues in the landscape of digital societies: How does the dialogical self affect intercultural relations in online contexts? *Societies, 11*, 84.

Introvigne, M. (2022). Putin officially embraces theories accusing the west of "Satanism." *Bitter Winter, a magazine of religious liberty and human rights*, October 3.

IPCC (2021). Climate change widespread, rapid, and intensifying. August 9. Retrieved from www.ipcc.ch/2021/08/09/ar6-wg1-20210809-pr

(2023). Synthesis Report of the IPCC Sixth Assessment Report (Ar6). Retrieved from www.ipcc.ch/report/sixth-assessment-report-cycle/

Itzchakov, G., Kluger, A. N., & Castro, D. R. (2017). I am aware of my inconsistencies but can tolerate them: The effect of high quality listening on speakers' attitude ambivalence. *Personality and Social Psychology Bulletin*, *43*, 105–120.

Jacobi, J. (1999). *Complex/Archetype/Symbol in the Psychology of C.G. Jung*. London: Routledge. Originally published in 1925.

James, W. (1890). *The Principles of Psychology* (vol. 1). London: Macmillan.

(1902/2002). *Varieties of Religious Experience: A Study in Human Nature*. London: Routledge.

Jansen, L. (2013). *Geheim: Het oorlogsverhaal van mijn vader* [*Secret: The War Story of My Father*]. Amsterdam: De Kring.

Jogalekar, A. (2022). In praise of contradiction. *The Curious Wavefunction: Musings on science, history, philosophy and literature*, September 5.

Johnson, M. (1993). *Moral Imagination: Implications of Cognitive Science for Ethics*. Chicago, IL: University of Chicago Press.

Jordan, J. V. (1984). Empathy and self boundaries. Work in Progress, no. 16. Wellesley, MA: Wellesley College. Retrieved from https://growthinconnection .org/wp-content/uploads/2021/03/1984EmpathyandSelfBoundaries.pdf

Jung, C. (1960). Good and evil in analytical psychology. *Journal of Analytical Psychology*, *5*, 91–99.

(1964). *Man and His Symbols*. New York: Anchor Press.

(1966). *Two Essays on Analytical Psychology. Collected Works. Vol. 7*. London: Routledge.

(2009). *The Red Book: Liber Novus*. Edited and introduced by S. Shamdasani. New York: Norton.

(2010). Answer to Job. In *The Collected Works of C. G. Jung* (vol. 11, Bollingen series XX), with a new foreword by S. Shamdasani. Originally published in 1958. Retrieved from https://cdnimpuls.com/politiko.al/uploads/2019/09/ C.-G.-Jung-Answer-to-Job-Princeton-University-Press-1952.pdf

Kamusella, T. (2022). Putin's Fascism. Research repository, University of St Andrews, UK. Retrieved from https://research-repository.st-andrews.ac.uk/bitstream/han dle/10023/25119/Kamusella_2022_Putins_fascism_Wachtyrz.eu.pdf

Kaufman, S. B., & Jauk, E. (2020). Healthy selfishness and pathological altruism: Measuring two paradoxical forms of selfishness. *Frontiers in Psychology*, *11*, 1006.

Kershaw, I. (2008). *Hitler, the Germans, and the Final Solution*. New Haven, CT: Yale University Press.

(2022). *Personality and Power*. London: Penguin Random House.

Kershner, I. (2022). Nazi tapes provide a chilling sequel to the Eichmann trial. *New York Times*, July 4.

Kohlberg, L. (1976). Moral stages and moralization: The cognitive-developmental approach. In T. Lickona (ed.), *Moral Development and Behavior: Theory, Research, and Social Issues* (pp. 31–53). New York: Holt, Rinehart & Winston.

Kohut, H. (1959). Introspection, empathy and psychoanalysis. *Journal of the American Psychoanalytic Association, 7*, 459–483.

Konopka, A., Hermans, H. J. M., & Goncalves, M. M. (eds.) (2019). *Handbook of Dialogical Self Theory and Psychotherapy: Bridging Psychotherapeutic and Cultural Traditions.* London: Routledge.

Koonz, C. (2003). *The Nazi Conscience.* Cambridge, MA: Harvard University Press.

Kundera, M. (1988). *The Art of the Novel* (L. Asher, trans.). London: Faber and Faber.

Küng, H. (1986). What is true religion? Toward an ecumenical criteriology. Lecture, presented at the Summer School at the University of Cape Town, February (L. Swidler, trans). http://harmonia.arts.cuhk.edu.hk/~twkwan/epi metheus/phi110b/Kueng-Hans-What-is-the-true-religion.pdf

Kurzban, R. (2010). *Why Everyone (Else) Is a Hypocrite: Evolution and the Modular Mind.* Princeton, NJ: Princeton University Press.

Lammers, J. (2011). Abstraction increases hypocrisy. *Journal of Experimental Social Psychology, 48*, 475–480.

LaVey, A. S. (1969). *The Satanic Bible.* Retrieved from www.cmszd.de/FTP/documents/Dark/The%20Satanic%20Bible%20-%20(Anton%20Lavey).pdf

Lehmann, O. V., & Valsiner, J. (eds.) (2017). *Deep Experiencing: Dialogues within the Self.* New York: Springer.

Leicester, J. (2022). War isn't funny but humor helps Ukrainians cope with trauma. *OkotoksTODAY*, June 14.

Lengelle, R. (2021a). Portrait of a scientist: In conversation with Hubert Hermans, founder of Dialogical Self Theory. *British Journal of Guidance & Counselling*, DOI: 10.1080/03069885.2021.1900779.

(2021b). *Writing the Self in Bereavement: A Story of Love, Spousal Loss, and Resilience.* London: Routledge.

Lepage, J.-D. (2009). *Hitler Youth, 1922–1945: An Illustrated History.* Jefferson, NC: McFarland & Company.

Lewis, M. D. (2002). The dialogical brain: Contributions of emotional neurobiology to understanding the dialogical self. *Theory and Psychology, 12*, 175–190.

Linville, P. W. (1985). Self-complexity and affective extremity: Don't put all of your eggs in one cognitive basket. *Social Cognition, 3*, 94–120.

Liu, G. & An, R. (2021). Applying a yin–yang perspective to the theory of paradox: A review of Chinese management. *Psychology Research and Behavior Management, 14*, 1591–1601.

Livingstone Smith, D. (2011). *Less than Human: Why We Demean, Enslave, and Exterminate Others.* New York: St. Martin's Press.

(2021). *Making Monsters: The Uncanny Power of Dehumanization.* Cambridge, MA: Harvard University Press.

Marquis de Sade (1785/1966). *The 120 Days of Sodom and Other Writings.* Compiled and translated by A. Wainhouse & R. Seavor, with introductions by S. de Beauvoir & P. Klossowski. New York: Grove Press.

(2018). *100 Erotic Illustrations: English Edition.* New York: Goliath Books.

Maslow, A. H. (1943/1996). Is human nature basically selfish? In E. Hoffman (ed.), *Future Visions: The Unpublished Papers of Abraham Maslow* (pp. 107–114). Thousand Oaks, CA: SAGE.

McCarty, R. (1988). Business and benevolence. *Business & Professional Ethics Journal, 7,* 63–83.

McFarland, S., Brown, D., & Webb, M. (2013). Identification with all humanity as a moral concept and psychological construct. *Current Directions in Psychological Science, 22,* 194–198.

McFarland, S., Webb, M., & Brown, D. (2012). All humanity is my ingroup: A measure and studies of identification with all humanity. *Journal of Personality and Social Psychology, 103,* 830–853.

McGraw, A. P., Warren, C., & Williams, L. E. (2014). The rise and fall of humor: Psychological distance modules humorous responses to tragedy. *Social Psychological and Personality Science, 5,* 566–572.

McIlhagga, S. (2022). History stokes Putin's dream of a "Greater Russia": Dating to imperial times, the notion has been invoked to incorporate Belarus and Ukraine. *New/Lines,* April 4.

Mead, G. H. (1934). *Mind, Self, and Society.* Chicago, IL: University of Chicago Press.

Mehta, J. & Winship, C. (2010). Moral power. In S. Hitlin & S. Vaisey (eds.), *Handbook of Sociology of Morality* (pp. 425–438). New York: Springer.

Meijers, F., & Hermans, H. J. M. (eds.) (2018). *The Dialogical Self Theory in Education: A Multicultural Perspective.* New York: Springer.

Merrill, A. (2018). Oskar Schindler's motivations, as told by Holocaust survivors. *US Holocaust Museum,* December 14.

Michel, C., Velasco, C., Gatti, E., & Spence, C. (2014). A taste of Kandinsky: Assessing the influence of the artistic visual presentation of food on the dining experience. *Flavour, 3,* 1–10.

Milanovic, B. (2021). Degrowth: Solving the impasse by magical thinking. *Global Policy,* February 23.

Mill, J.-S. (2015). *On Liberty, Utilitarianism and Other Essays,* 2nd edition. Edited by M. Philp and F. Rosen. New York: Oxford University Press.

Minsky, M. (1986). *The Society of Mind.* New York: Simon and Schuster.

Miron-Spektor, E., Emich, K. J., Argote, L., & Smith, W. K. (2022). Conceiving opposites together: Cultivating paradoxical frames and epistemic motivation fosters team creativity. *Organizational Behavior and Human Decision Processes, 171,* 104–153.

Mischel, W., & Mischel, H. N. (1976). A cognitive-social learning approach to socialization and self-regulation. In T. Likona (ed.), *Moral Development and Behavior: Theory, Research, and Social Issues* (pp. 84–107). New York: Holt, Rinehart & Winston.

Monereo, C. (ed.) (2022). *The Identity of Education Professionals: Positioning, Training, and Innovation*. Charlotte, NC: Information Age Publishing.

Monroe, K. (1996). *The Heart of Altruism: Perception of a Common Humanity*. Princeton, NJ: Princeton University Press.

Montaigne, M. de (2003). *Essays, Travel Journal, Letters*. Translated by D. M. Frame, with an Introduction by S. Hampshire. New York: Knopf.

Mulvey, L. (1975). Visual pleasure and narrative cinema. *Screen, 16*, 6–18.

Muskens, M. P. M. (1996). Armen mogen brood stelen [The poor are permitted to steal a bread]. *Trouw*, October 3.

Nasaw, D. (2007). *Andrew Carnegie*. London: Penguin Books.

Neimeyer, R. A. (2006). Narrating the dialogical self: Toward an expanded toolbox for the counselling psychologist. *Counselling Psychology Quarterly, 19*, 105–120.

Oliner, S., & Oliner, P. (1988). *The Altruistic Personality: Rescuers of Jews in Nazi Europe*. New York: Free Press.

Otto, B. K. (2001). *Fools Are Everywhere: The Court Jester Around the World*. Chicago, IL: University of Chicago Press.

Parth, K., Datz, F., Seidman, C., & Löffler-Stastka, H. (2017). Transference and countertransference: A review. *Bulletin of the Menninger Clinic, 81*, 167–211.

Pellizzoni, L. (2018). Responsibility and ultimate ends in the age of the unforeseeable: On the current relevance of Max Weber's political ethics. *Journal of Classical Sociology, 18*, 197–214.

Peterson, C., & Seligman, M. E. P. (2004). *Character Strengths and Virtues: A Handbook and Classification*. New York: Oxford University press.

Pettigrew, T. F., & Tropp, L. R. (2006). A meta-analytic test of intergroup contact theory. *Journal of Personality and Social Psychology, 90*, 751–783.

Phillips, J. (2005). *The Marquis de Sade: A Very Short Introduction*. New York: Oxford University Press.

(2022). Affective polarization: Over time, through the generations, and during the lifespan. *Political Behavior, 44*, 1483–1508.

Price Pierre, R. (2014). The minister who went to jail for financial-aid fraud. *The Atlantic*, December 10.

Proshansky, H. M., Fabian, A. K., & Kaminoff, R. (1983). Place-identity: Physical world socialization of the self. *Journal of Environmental Psychology, 3*, 57–83.

Putin, V. (2022). On the historical unity of Russians and Ukrainians. *Presidential Library*. Retrieved from www.prlib.ru/en/article-vladimir-putin-historical-unity-russians-and-ukrainians

Raggatt, P. T. F. (2012). Positioning in the dialogical self: Recent advances in theory construction. In H. J. M. Hermans & T. Gieser (eds.), *Handbook of Dialogical Self Theory* (pp. 29–45). Cambridge: Cambridge University Press.

Rahner, K. (1979). Towards a fundamental theological interpretation of Vatican II. Address delivered by Karl Rahner at an academic convocation in Cambridge, MA, April 8. Retrieved from https://journals.sagepub.com/doi/pdf/10.1177/004056397904000404?casa_token=IJZN_ZI3124AAAAA:FSjs1nf7_MVQhkN2TpX-

Rai, T. S., & Fiske, A. P. (2011). Moral psychology is relationship regulation: Moral motives for unity, hierarchy, equality, and proportionality. *Psychological Review, 118*, 57–75.

Reed, A., & Aquino, K. F. (2003). Moral identity and the expanding circle of moral regard toward out-groups. *Journal of Personality and Social Psychology, 84*, 1270–1286.

Rees, L. (2005). *Auschwitz: The Nazis and the "Final Solution".* London: BBC Books.

Reicher, S., & Haslam, A., & Rath, R. (2008). Making a virtue of evil: A five-step social identity model of the development of collective hate. *Social and Personality Psychology Compass, 2/3*, 1313–1344.

Riley, A. T. (2005). "Renegade Durkheimianism" and the transgressive left sacred. In J. C. Alexander & P. Smith (eds.), *The Cambridge Companion to Durkheim* (pp. 274–301). Cambridge: Cambridge University Press.

Ripple, W. J., Wolf, C., Newsome, T. M., Barnard, P., & Moomaw, W. R. (2020). World scientists' warning of a climate emergency. *BioScience, 70*, 8–12.

Roeser, S. & Alfano, V., & Nevejan, C. (2018). The role of art in emotional-moral reflection on risky and controversial technologies: The case of BNCI. *Ethic Theory Moral Practice, 21*, 275–289.

Roets, A., Kruglanski, A. W., Kossowska, M., Pierro, A., & Ying-yi Hong, Y. (2015). The motivated gatekeeper of our minds: New directions in need for closure theory and research. *Advances in Experimental Social Psychology, 52*, 221–283.

Rogers, C. R. (1951). *Client-Centered Therapy: Its Current Practice, Implications, and Theory.* Boston, MA: Houghton Mifflin.

Rosenberg, M. (1979). *Conceiving the Self.* New York: Basic Books.

Runciman, D. (2008). *Political Hypocrisy: The Mask of Power, from Hobbes to Orwell and Beyond.* Princeton, NJ: Princeton University Press.

Sakwa, R. (2004). *Putin: Russia's Choice.* London: Routledge.

Sampson, E. E. (1988). The debate on individualism: Indigenous psychologies of the individual and their role in personal and societal functioning. *American Psychologist, 43*, 15–22.

Samuel, S. (2019). How your brain invents morality. Neurophilosopher Patricia Churchland explains her theory of how we evolved a conscience. *Vox*, July 8.

Sartre, J.-P. (2012). *Saint Genet: Actor and Martyr.* Minneapolis: University of Minnesota Press.

Savat, S. (2022). WashU Expert: Putin is using "victim" narrative to justify Ukraine attack. *The Source*, February 24.

Schaper, F. (2015). *Het dictator virus: Slecht voorbeeld doet slecht volgen* [*The Dictator Virus: Bad Example Makes Bad Following*]. Schiedam: Scriptum.

Schellhammer, B. (2019). *Fremdheitsfähig werden: Zur Bedeutung von Selbstsorge für den Umgang mit Fremdem [Becoming Foreignness Capable: The Meaning of Self-Care for Dealing with Strangers]*. Freiburg/Munich: Verlag Karl Alber.

Schrödinger, E. (1935). Discussion of probability relations between separated systems. *Proceedings of the Cambridge Philosophical Society, 31,* 555–563.

Seikkula, J., & Trimble, D. (2005). Healing elements of therapeutic conversation: Dialogue as an embodiment of love. *Family Processes, 44,* 461–475.

Shrauger, J. S. & Schoeneman, T. J. (1979). Symbolic interactionist view of self-concept: Through the looking glass darkly. *Psychological Bulletin, 86,* 549–573.

Skitka, L. J., & Mullen, E. (2002). The dark side of moral conviction. *Analyses of Social Issues and Public Policy, 2,* 35–41.

Skitka, L. J., Bauman, C. W., Aramovich, N. P., & Morgan, G. S. (2006). Confrontational and preventative policy responses to terrorism: Anger wants a fight and fear wants "Them" to go away. *Basic and Applied Social Psychology, 28,* 375–384.

Snyder, T. (2018). Ivan Ilyin, Putin's philosopher of Russian fascism. *The New York Review*, April 5. Expanded version of Timothy Snyder's essay "God Is a Russian" in the April 5, 2018, issue of *The New York Review*.

Spencer-Rodgers, J., Williams, M. J., & Peng, K. (2010). Cultural differences in expectations of change and tolerance for contradiction: A decade of empirical research. *Personality and Social Psychology Review, 14,* 296–312.

Stein, M. (ed.) (1995). *Jung on Evil.* Retrieved from https://static1.squarespace.com/static/52cdf95ae4b0c18dd2d0316a/t/57775a0d197aead3b2866e07/1467439675032/Jung+on+evil+-+M+Stein.pdf

Stiles, W. B. (2019). Assimilation of problematic voices and the history of signs: How culture enters psychotherapy. In A. Konopka, H. J. M. Hermans, & M. M. Goncalves (eds.), *Handbook of Dialogical Self Theory and Psychotherapy: Bridging Psychotherapeutic and Cultural Traditions* (pp. 56–72). London: Routledge.

Struhl, K. J. (2020). What kind of an illusion is the illusion of self. *Comparative Philosophy, 11,* 113–139.

Suszek, H., Gabińska, A., & Kopera, M. (2023). Effects of priming different I-positions on motor behavior. *Journal of Constructivist Psychology*, DOI: 10.1080/10720537.2023.2194692.

Troianovski, A. (2022). Russia takes censorship to new extremes, stifling war coverage. *New York Times*, March 4.

Turner, J. C., Hogg, M. A., Oakes, P. J., Reicher, S. D., & Wetherell, M. S. (1987). *Rediscovering the Social Group: A Self-Categorization Theory.* Oxford: Blackwell.

Twenge, J. W., & Campbell, W. K. (2009). *The Narcissism Epidemic.* New York: Atria paperback. Simon and Schuster.

Valdesolo, P., & DeSteno, D. (2007). Moral hypocrisy: Social groups and the flexibility of virtue. *Psychological Science, 18,* 689–690.

Valsiner, J. (2004). The promoter sign: Developmental transformation within the structure of the dialogical self. Presented at *XVIII Biennial Meeting of the International Society for the Study of Behavioral Development*, Ghent, July 11–15.

van Geel, R., Houtmans, T., & Tenten, H. (2019). Introjective and anaclitic psychopathology in self-narratives: Idiographic assessment with Hermans' Self-Confrontation Method. *International Journal of Personality Psychology*, *5*, 36–63.

van Loon, R. (2017). *Creating Organizational Value through Dialogical Leadership: Boiling Rice in Still Water*. New York: Springer.

van Meijl, T. (2020). Dialog for de-radicalization in postcolonial Europe. *Journal of Constructivist Psychology*, *33*, 235–247.

van Oort, J. (2020). *Mani and Augustine: Collected Essays on Mani, Manichaeism and Augustine*. Leiden: Brill.

van Tongeren, P. J. M. (2006). Nietzsche and ethics. In K. A. Pearson (ed.), *A Companion to Nietzsche* (pp. 389–403). Oxford: Blackwell.

Vasil'eva, I. I. (1988). The importance of M. M. Bakhtin's idea of dialogue and dialogic relations for the psychology of communication. *Soviet Psychology*, *26*, 17–31.

Vidal, J. (2011). Climate sceptic Willie Soon received \$1 m from oil companies, papers show. *The Guardian*, June 27.

Wall, J. F. (ed.) (1992). *The Andrew Carnegie Reader*. Pittsburgh, PA: University of Pittsburgh Press.

Walton, T. N. & Jones, R. E. (2018). Ecological identity: The development and assessment of a measurement scale. *Environment and Behavior*, *50*, 657–689.

Weber, M. (1946). Politics as a vocation. In H. Gerth & C. M. Wright (eds.) *From Max Weber: Essays in Sociology* (pp. 77–128). New York: Oxford University Press.

White, E. (1993). *Genet: A Biography*. New York: Alfred A. Knopf.

White, S., & McAllister, I. (2008). The Putin phenomenon. *Journal of Communist Studies and Transition Politics*, *24*, 604–628.

Willinger, U., Hergovich, A., Schmoeger, M., Deckert, M., Stoettner, S., Bunda, I., et al. (2017). Cognitive and emotional demands of black humour processing: The role of intelligence, aggressiveness and mood. *Cognitive Processing*, *18*, 159–167.

Wilson, A. (2008). *Beautiful Shadow: A Life of Patricia Highsmith*. London: Bloomsbury Publishing.

Winkler, J. K. (1931). *Incredible Carnegie: The Life of Andrew Carnegie (1835–1919)*. New York: Vanguard Press.

Wise, S. M. (2000). *Rattling the Cage: Toward Legal Rights for Animals*. Philadelphia, PA: Da Capo Press.

Wood, E. A. (2011). Performing memory: Vladimir Putin and the celebration of World War II in Russia. *The Soviet and Post-Soviet Review*, *38*, 172–200.

Worley, C. (2016). North Carolina pastor. *Huffington Post*, February 2. Retrieved from www.huffpost.com/entry/north-carolina-pastor-gay-rant-starvation_n_1533463

Yang, C. (2021). On the conflict construction in Chris Ofili's paintings: Taking The Holy Virgin Mary as an example. *International Journal of Social Sciences in Universities*, *4*, 141–143.

Zhong, C.-B., & House, J. (2014). Dirt, pollution, and purity: A metaphorical perspective on morality. In M. Landau, M. D. Robinson, & B. P. Meier (eds.), *The Power of Metaphor: Examining Its Influence on Social Life* (pp. 109–131). Washington, DC: American Psychological Association.

Zigon, J. (2009). Morality and personal experience: The moral conceptions of a Muscovite man. *Ethos, Journal of the Society for Psychological Anthropology*, *37*, 78–101.

Zimbardo, P. (2007). *The Lucifer Effect: Understanding How Good People Turn Evil*. New York: Random House.

Index